CONTENTS

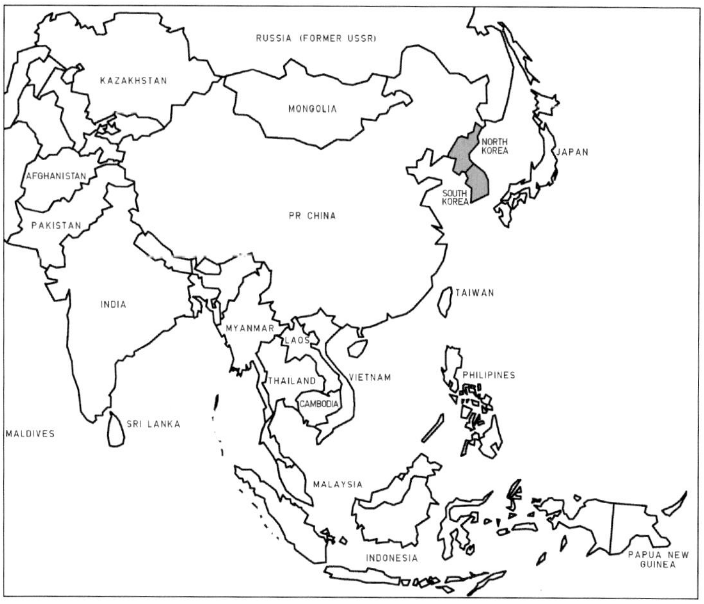

Helion & Company Limited
Unit 8 Amherst Business Centre
Budbrooke Road
Warwick
CV34 5WE
England
Tel. 01926 499 619
Fax 0121 711 4075
Email: info@helion.co.uk
Website: www.helion.co.uk
Twitter: @helionbooks
Visit our blog http://blog.helion.co.uk/

Published by Helion & Company 2019
Designed and typeset by Mach 3 Solutions Ltd (www.mach3solutions.co.uk)
Cover designed by Paul Hewitt, Battlefield Design (www.battlefield-design.co.uk)
Printed by Henry Ling Limited, Dorchester, Dorset

ISBN 978-1-912390-33-5

British Library Cataloguing-in-Publication Data.
A catalogue record for this book is available from the British Library.

For details of other military history titles published by Helion & Company Limited contact the above address, or visit our website: http://www.helion.co.uk.

We always welcome receiving book proposals from prospective authors.

Cover Images

The colourful and emotive background of this book's cover is from a KPAF Propaganda Poster contributed by Mr. André Wilderdijk; the excellent MiG-15 colour profile artwork is by Tom Cooper.

Note

Korean names have been Anglicized in many variations. For the purpose of consistency, all names in this book are as they appear in No Kum-Sok's book *A MiG-15 to Freedom: Memoir of the Wartime North Korean Defector Who First Delivered the Secret Fighter Jet to the Americans in 1953* – the only English-language book on the Korean air war written by a (former) North Korean.

Dedication

This book is dedicated to the three great American aviation historians who have researched and written so much about the aerial conflict of the Korean War: Larry Davis, the late Robert F. Dorr, and Warren Thompson. All Korean War historians and aviation enthusiasts owe a huge debt of gratitude to these three men for their diligent efforts to preserve the actions and sacrifices of the aviators who flew and fought in that otherwise 'forgotten war' – this work is my small payment towards that great debt.

Preface

North Korea remains the single most culturally closed, socially isolated, and information-denying nation in the world. Therefore, very little is known about the Korean People's Air Force (KPAF), its participation in the invasion of South Korea and the resulting Korean War, fought 1950-1953. However, with the availability of records from the former Union of Soviet Socialist Republics (the 'Soviet Union'), and the more recent research permitted in Chinese archives by Dr. Xiaoming Zhang, PhD, and with the release of daily intelligence summaries of the US Central Intelligence Agency (CIA) from the Korean War, it is time to close this gap in military aviation history.

In May 1950, only a month before Kim Il-Sung invaded South Korea, the Soviet Armed Forces General Staff authorized a total of 246 advisors, instructors, and 'educational' personnel to assist the Korean People's Army (KPA) and KPAF. Eleven of these individuals were placed in the KPA's General Headquarters (GHQ), while the rest were attached to KPA/KPAF divisions and regiments, including the air division and one of its aviation regiments. Although strictly forbidden by the Soviet General Staff from crossing the 38th Parallel, these men periodically provided detailed reports of North Korean operations – and assessments of the same – that are now stored in the Central Archives of the Ministry of Defense of the Russian Federation. Released to the US State Department in 1994, these reports have been translated and made available for further study through the Woodrow Wilson International Center for Scholars in Washington, D.C., and the Harry S. Truman Presidential Library in Independence, Missouri, providing an excellent basis for understanding and describing, and in some cases detailing, KPA/KPAF's Korean War operations and their results.

Furthermore, the similarly released (to the US State Department) records from the Archives of the President of the Russian Federation contain revealing message traffic between Soviet Premier Joseph Stalin, Chinese Chairman Mao Zedong and North Korea's Kim Il-Sung and thus provide insightful and sometimes detailed information regarding the three Communist nations' intentions, strategies and capabilities. Specifically, the reports by Stalin's personal envoy to Mao, General S. E. Zakharov, and his representatives to Kim, Generals Terentii F. Shtykov and Alexander N. Vasil'yev, describe the status, strength and operations of the KPAF in detail that otherwise would be completely lost to history.

Finally, the release of recently declassified CIA daily intelligence summaries, from June 1950 through December 1953, shed even more light on – and have opened yet another perspective on – the Communist coalition's units, operations, and other activities during the period covered in this book. In researching these formerly 'Top Secret' documents – which are largely compilations of the National Security Agency's (NSA), US Army's and United States Air Force's deciphered and translated Chinese and North Korean communications intercepts under Projects ACORN, SUEDE and CANOE – it is possible to not only confirm the information contained in the State Department (Russian) and Dr. Zhang's (Chinese) sources, but in many cases it is possible to 'fill in the gaps' regarding KPAF capabilities, strategy, and intentions.

Obviously, none of these are a truly adequate substitute to archival research in KPAF records in P'yongyang, or personal interviews with the few (and growing fewer every week) surviving KPAF leaders, pilots, aircrew and other members of this small, secretive air arm. However, until the Democratic People's Republic of Korea (DPRK) becomes a freer, more open society with a government willing to allow such research and interviews, there is no way to tell the story of the KPAF's participation in the Korean War than to 'piece it together' from the vast variety of external sources.

This book began as a short series of articles prepared for the quarterly aviation enthusiast publication *Small Air Forces Observer* (SAFO), managed and edited by Dr. James V. Sanders, PhD, of the Naval Postgraduate School in Monterrey, California. A true and wonderful friend, Jim Sanders was one of my most encouraging mentors as I had previously researched and written about 'under reported' military aviation subjects, which he published in SAFO.

At the time the SAFO series began I was working with another friend and mentor, Mr. Warren E. Thompson, one of the three great American aviation historians who studied and wrote extensively about the Korean War. We were writing a small monograph comparing the USAF F-86 Sabre with the MiG-15 in the Korean War. Warren is an expert on the F-86, having interviewed a host of Sabre pilots, and he covered their half of the story – I took the MiGs and the three nations flying them. To better understand just how it was that Soviet MiG-15 pilots came to be secretly fighting American F-86 pilots in what came to be called 'MiG Alley', I researched the KPAF's inception, early operations, and its quick initial demise. In doing so, I discovered several 'untapped veins' of information on the KPAF that had never been brought to publication before. Once these were accessed – with continual encouragement from both Jim and Warren – the SAFO KPAF series progressively expanded to 16 instalments, four years of articles covering the North Korean air force's participation in a three-year war.

About the time the series ended I was also working on another 'duel' book – this one pitting USAF F-15 Eagles versus MiG-23s and MiG-25s in Operation Desert Storm. My co-author on this project was Tom Cooper, a renowned aviation historian and prolific author specializing in Arab air forces and MiG (and other Soviet types) fighter operations world-wide. It was Tom's suggestion and encouragement that resulted in consolidating the 16-part SAFO series into this 12-chapter book for Helion & Company.

For their encouragement, mentoring, friendships, and cooperation, I thank first and foremost Jim Sanders, Warren Thompson, and Tom Cooper. Equally, I also thank Larry Davis and the late Robert F. Dorr who – like Warren – generously shared numerous photographs, participants' personal accounts, and source documents that enabled me to build a comprehensive impression of the American side to fighting the North Koreans.

Also I thank Mr. Stephen L. 'Cookie' Sewell, retired DIA analyst, for his translations of nearly a dozen Russian books and magazine articles on the Soviet participation in – and perspectives on – the Korean War. These publications had much to say about their North Korean comrades and the English-speaking world would be without this knowledge but for the persistent and tireless efforts of Cookie Sewell.

Additionally my appreciation also extends to Dr. Xiaoming Zhang, history professor at the USAF's Air War College, who has extensively researched Chinese archives and interviewed numerous Korean War veterans in writing his meticulously detailed *Red Wings Over the Yalu* (University of Texas A&M Press, 2000). This definitive (in English, anyway) study provides additional insights and details on KPAF operations in and from the Peoples Republic of China's perspective. Through several correspondence exchanges while developing the KPAF series for the SAFO, Dr. Zhang assisted me in understanding more comprehensively the nature of the organization and operations of the Communist coalition's air forces, both jointly and individually.

Finally, I thank a number of individuals – in addition to those named above – for their generous contributions of photographs to help illustrate this book. They include: Albert Grandolini, Detlef Billig, Jin Ho, Charles Euripides, Tim Callaway, Steve Zaloga, Nick Challoner, Chris Pinn, Andres Ramirez, and Zaur Eylanbekov (FoxbatFiles.com). Additionally, I thank Ms. Gina McNeely for her tireless efforts as photograph and document researcher at the US National Archive and Records Administration (NARA). Telling the story of the North Korean air force in the Korean War would have been much duller and far less interesting if it were not for the generous contributions of these individuals.

Lastly – but most significantly of all – I thank my dear wife, Annie, for her boundless patience, enthusiastic encouragement, enduring love and selfless support that she has shown throughout my writing projects, but especially during this one. Even though engaged in her crucial, individual battle with a life-threatening cancer, she was a constant inspiration of tenacity and determination to me, as well as to the scores of people who know her. My greatest and deepest thanks – and all my love – go to her.

Glossary and abbreviations

AAA	anti-aircraft artillery
AAD	Assault Aviation Division
AAR	Assault Aviation Regiment
AB	Air Base
AC&WS	Air Control & Warning Squadron
ADCOM	Advance Command and Liaison Group in Korea (US Army)
Adm	Admiral (commissioned military officer rank)
AF	Air Force (USAF)
AFU	Air Force Unit (ROKAF)
BS	Bombardment Squadron (USAF)
BW	Bombardment Wing (USAF)
CAB	Combined Air Brigade (PLAAF)
CAG	Carrier Air Group (USN)
CAP	combat air patrol
Cap	Captain (military officer commissioned rank)
CIA	Central Intelligence Agency (USA)
CAD	Combined Aviation Division
CinC	Commander-in-Chief
Col	Colonel (commissioned military officer rank)
COMINT	communications intelligence
CPVA	Chinese People's Volunteer Army
CPVAF	Chinese People's Volunteer Air Force
CWO	Chief Warrant Officer (non-commissioned military officer rank)
DPRK	Democratic People's Republic of Korea
ECM	electronic countermeasures
ELINT	electronic intelligence
EW	early warning
FAD	Fighter Aviation Division
FAR	Fighter Aviation Regiment
FAWS	Fighter All-Weather Squadron
FBS	Fighter Bomber Squadron
FBW	Fighter Bomber Wing
FEC	Far East Command (US Army)
FEAF	Far East Air Force (USAF)
FEMD	Far East Military District (USSR)
FIS	Fighter Interceptor Squadron (USAF)
FS	Fighter Squadron (USAF)
FW	Fighter Wing (USAF)

GCA	ground control approach
GCI	ground control intercept
GFAR	Guards Fighter Aviation Regiment (KPAF)
GHQ	General Headquarters
GvIAD	Gvardeyskiy Istrebitelniy Aviatsionniy Diviziya (Guards Fighter Aviation Division, V-VS)
GvIAP	Gvardeyskiy Istrebitelniy Aviatsionniy Polk (Guards Fighter Aviation Regiment, V-VS)
HDPRK	Hero of the Democratic People's Republic of Korea
HMS	Her/His Majesty's Ship (Royal Navy)
HQ	headquarters
HSU	Hero of the Soviet Union
IAD	Istrebilniy Aviatsionnyi Diviziya (Fighter Aviation Division, USSR)
IAP	Istrebilniy Aviatsionnyi Polk (Fighter Aviation Regiment, USSR)
IJAAF	Imperial Japanese Army Air Force
IJNAF	Imperial Japanese Navy Air Force
KAR	Korean Aviation Regiment
KIA	killed in action
KMT	Koumintang (Chinese Nationalist Party, later government of Taiwan/Formosa)
KPA	Korean People's Army
KPAF	Korean People's Air Force
KPAFAC	Korean People's Armed Forces Air Corps
Lt	Lieutenant (commissioned military officer rank)
Maj	Major (commissioned military officer rank)
MATS	Military Air Transport Service (USAF)
NAA	North American Aviation
NAS	Naval Air Squadron
NSA	National Security Agency (USA)
PAG	People's Army Group
PLA	People's Liberation Army (PRC)
PLAAF	People's Liberation Army Air Force (PRC)
PLANAF	People's Liberation Army Naval Air Force (PRC)
POW	prisoner or war
PPC	Peace Preservation Corps
PPI	P'yongyang Political Institute
PRC	People's Republic of China
RAAF	Royal Australian Air Force
ROK	Republic of Korea (South Korea)
ROKA	Republic of Korea Army
ROKAF	Republic of Korea Air Force
RS	Reconnaissance Squadron (USAF)
RW	Reconnaissance Wing (USAF)
SAAF	South African Air Force
SAFO	Small Air Forces Observer (magazine)
ShAP	Shturmovoy Aviatsionnyi Polk (Assault Aviation Regiment)
SIGINT	signals intelligence
SmAK	Smeshannyi Aviatsionnyi Korps (Combined Aviation Corps, V-VS)
SOTC	Security Officer Training Command
TADC	Tactical Air Direction Center (USAF)
TAR	Training Aviation Regiment
TCG	Tactical Control Group (USAF)
TCS	Tactical Control Squadron (USAF)
TCW	Troop Carrier Wing (USAF)
TRS	Tactical Reconnaissance Squadron (USAF)
TRW	Tactical Reconnaissance Wing (USAF)
UAA	United Air Army (KPAF & PLAAF)
UN	United Nations
UNC	United Nations Command
USA	United States of America
USMC	US Marine Corps
USN	US Navy
USS	United States Ship (USN)
USSR	Union of Soviet Socialist Republics (also 'Soviet Union')
VAdm	Vice Admiral (commissioned military officer rank)
V-MF/VMF	Voenno-Morskoj Flot (Military Maritime Fleet of the USSR)
V-VS/VVS	Voyenno-Vozdushnye Sily (Air Force of the USSR)

CHAPTER 1
HOW TO BUILD AN AIR FORCE

With the end of World War Two (WW2), most of the world's population breathed a huge sigh of relief that the great crusade to destroy the three tyrannical dictatorships – Hitler's Nazi Germany, Mussolini's Fascist Italy, and Tojo's militaristic Japan – had finally and successfully been concluded. In many countries the victory also heralded the end of colonialism – and occupation by the more powerful nations of the earth – spawning a new hope for the people longing for self-determination. As much as in any occupied European nation or any former imperial colony, these feelings and the associated hope for a new and better life soared high and strong amongst the Korean people.

Arbitrarily – and, to all intents and purposes, temporarily – in August 1945 the Korean Peninsula was divided at the 38th Parallel of Latitude by the United States (USA) and Soviet Union (USSR). The purpose of this division was to delineate the two 'occupied zones' that were intended to ensure a peaceful transition to the establishment of an indigenous Korean government that would rule the entire peninsula. In this setting, the Korean people began rebuilding their nation, and their culture, after 35 years of Japanese occupation. However, within each of the two 'spheres of influence' a number of potential political leaders arose, each vying for control over their respective region, with the occupying power determining the winner.

As their best hedge against an eventual Communist take-over, in the south the American government supported the ruthless US-educated strongman Dr. Syngman Rhee – 'a nineteenth century liberal with autocratic tendencies' – and the establishment of a form of democratic government. Placed under the auspices of the newly-formed United Nations (UN), in November 1947 – by a vote of 46 to 0 with the Eastern Bloc abstaining – the future of Korea was to be determined by free elections. Against Soviet objections and an eventual boycott, these were held on 10 May 1948, but only in the south, which established the National Assembly in Seoul that, in turn, elected Syngman Rhee as the president of the newly established Republic of Korea (ROK).[1]

In the north, the Soviets initially supported 62-year old Cho Man-Sik as Korea's designated leader. A well-respected educator who was an exceedingly popular dissident during the Japanese rule, Cho refused to embrace Communism or become Stalin's puppet. On the other hand the 33-year old Kim Il-Sung – an expatriate Korean who wound up in the USSR until his return to his own country after 25 years away – proved to be an accommodating Communist acolyte and an eager lieutenant to the Soviet occupying forces.[2]

As a Korean national who was also a captain in the Soviet army, Kim was given authority over an assortment of police and security organizations and quickly began to consolidate his power. First, he converted his personal paramilitary organization into the internal security force of the Communist Party. Originally named the 'Constabulary Discipline Corps', and later the 'Peace Preservation Corps' (PPC), this consisted of former anti-Japanese guerrillas, recently-released conscripted Korean soldiers, Japanese-raised colonial police, some 40,000 veterans of the Korean Volunteer Army who had served in Mao Zedong's Chinese Communist People's Liberation Army (PLA), and another 2,500 veterans from the Soviet Army. By mid-1946, the PPC totalled approximately 135,000 men.[3]

All that was needed was an air force.

First, get some people to organize one…

The genesis – and the basis for later growth – of the Korean People's Air Force (KPAF) was the formation of a 'civilian aviation advocacy organization' – actually a paramilitary 'flying club', patterned after those in the USSR. Called the 'Korean Aviation Society', this was organized by Lee Whal[4], a Korean pilot who had served in the Imperial Japanese Army Air Force (IJAAF) during the World War 2. Founded at the abandoned IJAAF airfield at Sinuiju, just across the Yalu River from Andong (also known as Antung at the time, now Dandong), in China, the 'Sinuiju Air Unit' was established in October 1945. This operated several reconditioned IJAAF aircraft – including a few Tachikawa Ki-9 (Army Type 95 Intermediate Trainer) 'Spruce' biplanes and even fewer Ki-55 (Army Type 99 Advanced Trainer) 'Ida' monoplanes – in a purely flying training role.

Calling upon the Soviet Union to materially support his military establishment, in September 1946 Kim Il-Sung began to reorganize the disparate elements of his PPC into a conventional military force. Already in May 1946, he had established the Security Officer Training Command (SOTC) as his headquarters (HQ) in P'yongyang. Concurrently, the Sinuiju Air Unit was transferred to the Heijo airfield, across the Taedong River from P'yongyang, to become the SOTC's Air Squadron.[5]

As the Communist regime grew under the protection of the Soviet occupying forces, the former civilian flying club was militarized, enlarged, and internally reorganized. On 20 August 1947, it was re-organized as the PPC's 'Air Force Branch'. Correspondingly, this date is ever since celebrated as the official birthday of the KPAF. Still only a flight training organization, by this time the unit began receiving a few Polikarpov Po-2 biplanes and Yakovlev UT-2 fixed-gear monoplanes from the USSR to replace the flying clubs' worn-out former-Japanese equipment.[6]

A month later, Kim Il-Sung renamed the PPC as the 'People's Army Group' (PAG). This comprised three infantry divisions, three mixed brigades, one security regiment, the SOTC Air Squadron, Central Hospital, the Central Security Officers School (later the KPA Military Academy), and a GHQ disguised as the 'P'yongyang Political Institute' (PPI). Kim Il-Sung appointed himself the 'Supreme Commander-in-Chief' with the rank of field marshal. On 8 February 1948, the People's Assembly of North Korea formally established the State Security Department, which assumed control of the PAG, renaming it the Korean People's Army, and appointed General Choi Yung-Kun (also Choe Yong-Gun) as the Minister of National Defence and the KPA's deputy commander.[7]

The re-organisation of 8 February 1947 also established 'Korean People's Armed Forces Air Corps' (KPAFAC) by combining of the Air Squadron (re-designated as the 25th Flight Wing), with the KPA's anti-aircraft artillery (AAA) units. Commanded by General Van Len, the air arm's new title indicated that it was directly subordinate to the State Security Department ('armed forces'), and had equal status to the army and the navy.[8]

The KPAFAC's aviation branch was commanded by Major-General Wang Yong.[9] Wang was a 37-year old graduate of the Soviet Air Academy at Monino who began his military career as one of the many Koreans fighting with Mao Zedong's Communist revolutionaries. When WW2 started, he was sent to the USSR to receive additional training as a bomber crewman and studied aviation engineering, growing to become an aircraft commander and later an instructor and staff member at China's Northeast Aviation School. He returned to Korea in October 1946, and was the natural choice to head the PPI's Aviation Section. A slightly-built and deceptively mild-mannered man, he soon developed a reputation as a stern leader.[10]

Wang was ably assisted by Colonel Lee Whal as his vice-commander. At six feet, Lee towered above most Koreans, and thus was an imposing figure; a 'dashing' 32-year old pilot sporting a handlebar moustache who had organized the 'Korean Aviation Society' at Sinuiju. One of the few experienced pilots in Korea – and one of a very few with any college education whatsoever – early in 1946 he volunteered his services to the Korean Communist leadership in P'yongyang to help establish an air force and train

Kim Il-Sung attending the second 'Korea Unification' conference in 1947. (NARA)

its first pilots. After 1953, a former Soviet instructor noted that Lee had 'enjoyed the enormous respect of the North Korean pilots'. Coming from a wealthy family, he generously donated classrooms, dormitories and a dining hall (well before they would have been confiscated by the Communists) to provide the nascent air arm with training facilities. Despite the fact that he had flown for the IJAAF during WW2, his generosity proved his patriotism and he was readily accepted by the North Korean leadership, and its army.[11]

Abandoned IJAAF Ki.51 'Sonia' Type 99 attack aircraft at Kimpo AB, October 1945. (US Army)

Soviet Po-2 training biplanes in formation flight. (USAF)

...then get some combat aircraft...

To build a modern, effective air force is a daunting undertaking – and was so even in the middle of the 20th Century when WW2-surplus aircraft abounded all around the globe – but that is exactly what Wang and Lee attempted to do. Once sufficient numbers of locally-trained pilots were qualified, in November 1948 the 25th Flight Wing became the 'Korean Aviation Regiment' (KAR) with two squadron-sized battalions. The 1st Battalion was to become the embryonic air arm's fighter training unit, based at P'yongyang's Heijo airfield, and the 2nd Battalion was stationed at the more extensive former IJAAF base at Yonpo and would become the KPAF's offensive ground attack (or 'assault') unit.[12]

While USAF Intelligence of the day reported the KPAF inventory to be a polyglot assortment of war-surplus Soviet aircraft including Lend-Lease Bell P-39/63s,[13] the only combat types initially received were the Yakovlev Yak-9 fighter and Ilyushin Il-10 assault aircraft. Following the signing of a USSR-DPRK military assistance agreement in spring 1949, the Soviets shipped to North Korea 165 military aircraft, the bulk of these being Yak-9s and Il-10s, far exceeding the numbers of pilots available to fly them.

Initial shipments of the Yak fighter included nine Yak-9V two-seater trainers; 12 old, original Yak-9s; and 42 new Yak-9Ps – totalling 63 examples. Most of these appear to have come from the *582nd Istrebitelniy Aviatsionniy Polk* (Fighter Aviation Regiment, IAP) of the *149th Istrebitelniy Aviatsionniy Diviziya* (Fighter Aviation Division, IAD) based at Uchastok, in Khabarovsk Krai (Province).

Numerically more prevalent were Ilyushin Il-10 '*Shturmovik*' ground attack aircraft. While all other air arms had abandoned dedicated two-seat attack aircraft for faster, more manoeuvrable single-seat fighter-bombers, the Soviet *Voyenno-Vozdushnye Sily* (V-VS, literally meaning 'Military-Air Forces', which included 'Frontal Aviation', the branch directly supporting army operations) persisted with the 'assault aircraft' concept for one more iteration, its faith based on the wartime success of the Il-2 against invading German panzers, troops and artillery. Although protected by considerable armour, for survival the Il-10 still required a permissive operating environment provided by friendly air superiority. During 1949, the USSR supplied 67 Il-10s, including 13 UIl-10 trainers, to the DPRK. Reportedly most of these were provided by the *537th Shturmovoy Aviatsionnyi Polk* – and were said to already be 'well used' when they replaced the unit's wartime Il-2s in late 1947. The rest were from the other assault regiments of the Soviet Far East Military District (FEMD), which were 'ordered to 'donate' a few Il-10s to the Koreans'.[14]

The initial consignments of these arrived during the summer of 1949, allowing the Soviet ambassador to P'yongyang, Colonel-General (Col-Gen) Terentii F. Shtykov, to report to the Soviet Council of Ministers that, as of 15 September 1949, the KAR had an operational strength of '24 combat fighters [Yak-9s], 24 combat ground attack aircraft [Il-10s], and 18 combat trainers [Yak-9Vs and UIl-10s], and eight trainers [Yak-11s]'.[15]

Three months later, the growing size of the KAR allowed Wang to expand it into an aviation division on the Soviet V-VS format. Initially designated the 1st Aviation Division, it was comprised of three regiments – one each fighter, ground attack, and training – each with three squadron-size battalions[16] and a statutory strength of 44 aircraft.[17] The original 1st Battalion became the Yak-9P-equipped fighter regiment while the 2nd Battalion became the Il-10 assault regiment. At this time a training regiment was formed with its 1st Battalion being the fighter training unit at Heijo airfield, its 2nd Battalion being the Il-10 training squadron at Yonpo, and the 3rd Battalion being the mechanics/technician and communications training organization, also based at Yonpo. Additionally two independent 'technical battalions' were organized to maintain the airbases and their supply functions; these were initially assigned to the air division HQ at Heijo.[18]

In January 1950 the wartime organization of the KPAF was finalized, with the division being re-designated the 55th Combined Aviation Division (CAD). The Yak-9P fighter regiment became the 56th Fighter Aviation Regiment (FAR) and the Il-10-equipped regiment became the 57th Assault Aviation Regiment (AAR). This final reorganization also established the 58th Training Aviation Regiment (TAR) which was equipped with two dozen Yak-18 primary trainers and eight of the far more powerful Yak-11 (the USSR's equivalent of the North American T-6 Texan) advanced trainers, all of which were provided by the Soviets in 1949. At the time of the invasion, the KPAF training establishment totalled 43 aircraft.[19]

The air arm's transport unit – which was designated a Mixed Aviation Regiment (number unknown) because it contained different types of aircraft – was equipped with a handful of Douglas C-47s and their Lisunov Li-2 clones, a few Yak-6 four-passenger light twin-engine liaison aircraft, and at least one former IJAAF Tachikawa Ki-54c (Army Type 1 Model C) 'Hickory' twin-engine, eight-passenger light transport. Initially, these totalled about a dozen aircraft, to which were added the some 13 Po-2s – forming a liaison squadron – once the new Yak-18s supplanted them in the 58th TAR.[20]

Captured KPAF Il-10 #44 Assault Aircraft as evaluated at Wright-Patterson AFB. (Robert F. Dorr Collection)

KPAF Yak-18 Primary Training Aircraft. (Detlef Billig Collection)

KPAF Yak-6 Light Transport Aircraft. (Detlef Billig Collection)

...then train some people to fly them

The expansion of the KPAF from a two-squadron regiment to a three-regiment division was enabled by the success – limited though it was – of Lee Whal's pilot training programme which, by 1950, was graduating 50-60 pilots each year. Lee began in mid-1946 by organizing additional flying clubs at four other North Korean airfields[21] where Soviet occupation units were still stationed. Locally-based Soviet pilots, along with the few Korean former-IJAAF aviators who were considered 'politically reliable', became the instructors at these locations, teaching North Korean students to fly Po-2s and UT-2s, with the first Yak-18s being received shortly thereafter.

The 'First Swallows' began graduating at the end of 1947 and obtained early operational experience flying C-47/Li-2s from P'yongyang to Vladivostok and Khabarovsk in the USSR and Harbin in northeastern China as co-pilots to Soviets delivering diplomatic mail and ferrying Communist personnel between the Occupation Zone and the two 'brother partner' nations.[22]

By early 1949, Wang's KAR had approximately 75 trained pilots, including instructor pilots (IPs) – more pilots than aircraft for them to fly – so Kim began negotiations with Stalin's representatives to obtain combat aircraft, flying and classroom instructors to teach them how to fly and employ them, and military advisors for forming and employing combat units. With the signing of the USSR-DPRK military assistance agreement, on 20 May 1949 some 60 KAR pilots were sent to two airbases in the Soviet FEMD to learn how to fly the Yak-9 and Il-10. The most experienced of these – ten KAR IPs – soon returned to Heijo and Yonpo, beginning 16 June, to join the 70 Soviet IPs assigned to provide operational and combat instruction on these types, and the building of KPAF fighter and assault units began.[23]

The biggest limitation of the KPAF expansion programme was the lack of suitable pilot candidates. Until the Soviets' 'liberation' of what became North Korea, the only indigenous pilots were those that had served in the IJAAF and these were outcast as 'enemies of the people' and 'were not asked' to join the fledgling air arm. Additionally most literate members of Korean society had fled south into the 'US Korean Zone of Occupation' to escape persecution and 'rehabilitation' under 'the true light of Korean Socialism,' leaving behind an 80 per cent illiterate peasant population. Consequently, during 1946-47 'specialist recruiters' of the Soviet Army (primarily those of Chinese, Korean and Mongolian extraction) canvassed the 'Soviet Korean Zone of Occupation' to select and solicit young literate Koreans for induction into the flying clubs and their successors, the military aviation schools.[24]

Called 'ricepaddy workhorses' by the Soviets, the Korean peasants were turned into infantrymen fairly readily, but teaching them to fly a modern, complex aircraft was an entirely different matter. Consequently Soviet teaching techniques were necessarily very structured and methodical – 'more suitable to Communist peasant soldiers' – and progress was commensurately 'slow but thorough,' impeded by an almost insurmountable language barrier and the Koreans' lack of education.[25]

Following graduation, the Soviet-taught Yak-9 and Il-10 pilots returned to Heijo and Yonpo for operational and combat training. This allowed Shtykov to report to the USSR Council of Ministers that, as of 15 September 1949, the KAR had 'a total of 26 pilots trained for flights on combat aircraft' and that these would be supplemented by another '50 [that] will be graduated in October to fly on combat aircraft.'[26] However, because of their limitations and the laborious nature of the Soviet training programmes, the final phase – producing combat-qualified aviators – was exceedingly slow and frustrating.

By May 1950 the KPAF had 120 trained pilots, with another 151 undergoing training. However, at this time only 32 pilots were qualified as 'combat ready'. These amounted to ten Yak-9P pilots, 22 Il-10 pilots and 17 'aviation technicians' (gunner/radio operators).[27] So while the KPAF had sufficient numbers of aviators to 'flesh-out' the 55th CAD's two combat regiments, there were only enough 'combat-qualified' aircrew to man one fighter and two assault squadrons.

KPAF Student Pilots with Glider. (Charles Eurpides Collection)

Soviet C-47/Li-2 Transport of the FEMD Manchurian Command. (Charles Euripides Collection)

...And build some places to base them

The third ingredient essential to creating an operational air force was the establishment of airbases with landing strips and the facilities necessary to maintain modern combat aircraft, as well as support organizations manned and trained to do so. From the Japanese, the North Koreans inherited a dozen airfields; three of them had paved runways and well-developed facilities. These were the IJAAF's large Heijo[28] airfield at P'yongyang (K-23 in the American airfield identification system), Sinuiju (K-30) on the south side of the Yalu River, and Yonpo (K-27; near the abandoned IJNAF depot at Wonsan/K-25), on Korea's east coast. The KPAF also used the sod-surfaced Mirim-ri airstrip five miles (eight km) east of Heijo (known to USAF Intelligence as P'yongyang-East or K-24) and the similarly unimproved Onjong-ni airfield (K-22) on the coast west of P'yongyang, as well as the three former 'flying club' fields in the north-eastern part of the country.[29]

The KPAF was fortunate to possess the rather extensive former Japanese facilities at Heijo which, in addition to its 4,080ft concrete runway and modern aircraft maintenance hangars, warehouses and workshops, also included a major army arsenal manufacturing small arms and munitions, including artillery shells and aircraft bombs. During WW2 the 'air section' of the arsenal overhauled IJAAF aircraft, assembled aircraft arriving in kit form, and manufactured replacement parts, including some engines. The facility was supported by the nearby Showa Aircraft Company factory located at Mirim airfield, which produced aircraft landing gear assemblies and other components. Quite naturally, the Heijo depot became the KPAF's primary aircraft overhaul, maintenance, and supply facility.[30]

There, using abandoned Japanese equipment, Soviet technicians taught the new North Korean maintenance personnel the skills required to overhaul and rebuild aircraft. For example, the memoirs of one Soviet mechanic describes how they restored a Nakajima Ki-43-II (Army Type 1 Fighter) 'Oscar' from the remains of two derelict airframes. Never airworthy but complete with KPAF markings, the Japanese fighter was made the 'gate guardian' at Heijo airfield.[31]

To operate the KPAF's three bases and perform flight line maintenance on the aircraft, the Training Regiment's 3rd Battalion was split to form two 'aviation technical battalions' providing the essential services at base level. Each battalion included engineer, finance, supply, and aircraft maintenance companies and together they numbered 2,541 officers and enlisted men. The 1st Technical Battalion was stationed at Heijo (and its satellite Onjong-ni) airfield in the west side of the country, and the 2nd Technical Battalion was split between Yonpo and Wonsan airfields on the east coast. At the individual airfield level, the company- and battalion-size supporting elements, known as 'air force units', were usually numbered in the 800-series.[32]

Heijo Airfield as seen from P'yongyang during WW2. (USAF)

Ready or not...

In preparation for the planned invasion of South Korea, mid-April 1950 the Soviets supplied 63 additional Yaks and *Shturmoviki*, replacing losses due to accidents and an Il-10 lost in a defection, and amassing a war reserve inventory of 16 Yak-9Ps and 26 Il-10s. According to the Soviet advisors stationed in the North Korea, to start the war, the KPAF possessed a total of 79 Yak-9s, 93 Il-10s, and 67 trainers, transports and liaison aircraft.[33]

By any measure, despite its frenetic preparation in late 1949 and early 1950 the KPAF was not a mature military organization and was not ready for combat, much less a full campaign. Although it possessed a large inventory of obsolete leftover WW2 equipment, with only 26.7 per cent of its pilots combat-ready, it could hardly (and, in the event, did not) sustain a major offensive operation. Yet, just as Hitler thrust the Luftwaffe into a world war before it was fully prepared, 'The Great Leader of the Korean People' judged that his air arm was more than adequate to deal with the puny South Korean 'air force', and was undeterred by the potential involvement of the United States and its powerful, recently independent US Air Force and the US Navy's carrier-based and US Marine Corps' land-based air groups.

Unfamiliar with air power, its role and its requirements, Kim Il-Sung embarked upon a plan of conquest that did not consider air power as any more than an ancillary arm and failed to allow his air arm to mature to the point where it would actually make a significant contribution in the impending invasion of South Korea.

Table 1: KPAF ORBAT, June 1950[34]

Unit	Sub-Unit	Base	Aircraft Type	Notes
Korean People's Armed Forces Air Corps Commander: General Van Len Aviation Corps (Korean People's Air Force) Commander: Major-General Wang Yong				
55th Combined Aviation Division, CO: Brigadier-General Lee Whal				
56th Fighter Aviation Regiment		Heijo		partially operational
	3 x Fighter Aviation Battalions	Heijo	42 Yak-9P, 2 Yak-11	only one battalion operational
57th Assault Aviation Regiment		Yonpo		partially operational
	3 x Assault Aviation Battalions	Yonpo	44 Il-10 (22 operational)	only two battalions operational
58th Training Aviation Regiment	1st Battalion	Heijo	21 Yak-9/ Yak-9V	fighter training
	2nd Battalion	Yonpo	23 Il-10/UIl-10	assault training
	3rd Battalion	Heijo	6 Yak-11s, 24 Yak-18	flying training
Mixed Aviation Regiment		Heijo		established in June 1950
	Transport Battalion	Heijo	12 Yak-6 and C-47/Li-2s	
	Liaison Battalion	Heijo	13 Po-2s	

How to Plan a War

British General Sir Anthony Farrar-Hockley, explained:

> Evidence suggests that [Kim] Il-Sung had proposed invasion to Stalin early in 1949 and discussed the matter with Mao Tse-tung [Zedong] Chairman of the Chinese Communist Party in October 1949; that Stalin consulted with Mao during his visit to Moscow on 16 December 1949 and approved the operation in February 1950.[35]

The evidence that Farrar-Hockley refers to is the diplomatic 'message traffic' between P'yongyang, Moscow and Beijing, beginning in September 1949 with Ambassador Shtykov's report to Stalin, relating Kim Il-Sung's first earnest request for Stalin's support in reunifying the Korean peninsula 'by an armed attack against the South Korean government'. Initially Stalin was unwilling to support the idea, saying 'this attack has not been prepared from either a military or political standpoint' and he feared it would not 'ensure the complete defeat of the southern army and the capture of South Korea'.[36]

However, according to documents in the Archive of the President of the Russian Federation, following US Secretary of State Dean Acheson's famous 'Speech on the Far East' at the National Press Club on 12 January 1950 – in which Acheson notably excluded South Korea from America's 'defensive perimeter' along the Pacific Rim – at the end of the month, Stalin directed Shtykov to inform Kim that he was now willing to consider discussing the possibility of 'aggressive actions against the army of Syngman Rhee', but that 'the undertak[ing] needs large preparation' and, 'The matter must be organized so that there would not be too great a risk'.[37]

A week later, Kim petitioned Stalin for assistance in 'forming three additional infantry divisions so that the total number of the army will be brought to ten divisions' by 'us[ing] in 1950 the credit the Soviet government had allocated for 1951… to buy in the Soviet Union arms for three infantry divisions'.[38] Stalin demurred until he could discuss the prospects of Kim's proposal with Mao Zedong and, according to senior Russian military historian General D. Volkogonov, 'After consulting with Mao, Stalin approved Kim's invasion plan on 9 February, 1950'. Kim Il-Sung received the news enthusiastically and asked Shtykov several times to communicate to Comrade Stalin his gratitude for his assistance.[39]

Kim Il-Sung Secures Stalin's Support for Invading South Korea

On 30 March 1950, Kim Il-Sung secretly travelled to Moscow. He met with Stalin to discuss 'the path and methods of unification of the south and the north of the country'. Kim happily received his patron's 'conditional green light for an attack against South Korea', but as an insurance policy against the failure of Kim's enterprise, Stalin directed Kim to coordinate the invasion plan with the Soviet Armed Forces General Staff and appointed Major-General (Maj-Gen) Hero of the Soviet Union Alexander N. Vasil'yev, Chief of War Experience Analysis on the Soviet Armed Forces General Staff, as Kim's principal military advisor.[40]

Vasil'yev was sent to P'yongyang with a staff of 173 officers and 35 NCOs (increased to a total of 246 men on the eve of the invasion) as military advisors to the KPA, assisting the North Koreans at every echelon of command, from the Ministry of National Defence and service chiefs,[41] down through infantry, tank and artillery regiments, to include training organizations and officer's and political schools. According to Russian sources based on the Central Archives of the Ministry of Defense of the Russian Federation (formerly the Archive of the Soviet Armed Forces General Staff), 'the[se] military advisors… with the aid of the Soviet General Staff, developed all of the KPA operational plans in case of war on the Korean peninsula'. Accordingly, in a report to Chief of the Soviet Armed Forces General Staff, General Matvei V. Zakharov, Shtykov reported that 'the concentrations of the People's Army in the region near the 38th Parallel… was [accomplished as] prescribed in the plan of the General Staff'.[42]

The planning for the invasion went into high gear in Moscow and P'yongyang, and the next month (13 May 1950) Kim visited Beijing 'to secure Mao Zedong's approval for the planned offensive'. While Stalin remained apprehensive, especially about the possibility of a strong military response by the USA, Mao was considerably less worried, concluding, 'the Americans will not enter a third world war for such a small territory'.[43]

Two weeks after his return, on 29 May, the final version of the Plan of the General Staff was briefed to Kim by the KPA's chief of staff (also Minister of National Defence and the KPA's field commander), Choi Yung-Kun, and Vasil'yev. At that meeting, Kim approved the deployment plan and Choi's 'choice of the main blow during the attack', and made the precipitous decision to launch the invasion of South Korea. Kim's decision was communicated to Stalin, by Shtykov, the next day, who gave the operation the go ahead. Accordingly, KPA troop deployments began two weeks later, on 12 June.[44]

KPAF Yak-9Ps at Heijo prepare for training sortie. (Detlef Billig Collection)

Kim Il-Sung's Plan for Invading South Korea

The KPA's invasion plan originally intended a two-phase operation, the first of which would be disguised as a 'defensive manoeuvre' countering an alleged ROK Army (ROKA) 'invasion' from the isolated Ongjin Peninsula. Immediately after the 'counter-attack' into the peninsula, a broader offensive would be launched with two main axis of attack.[45] In the west, three infantry divisions (1st, 3rd, and 4th), each spearheaded by a regiment of Soviet-supplied T-34/85 tanks from the 105th Tank Brigade, would attack across a relatively narrow (40 mile/64km) front from Kaesŏng to Ch'orwon, advancing along major roads converging on Uijongbu, which was 'the ancient invasion route leading straight south to Seoul.'

A fourth division (6th) would secure the indefensible Ongjin Peninsula and drive southwest to capture Kimpo airbase (now Gimpo International Airport) and the port of Inch'on. Meanwhile two infantry divisions (2nd and 12th) and a motorized infantry regiment (603rd) would attack through the central mountain range to take Ch'unch'on, an important road center on the Pukhan River and the gateway leading south into the central part of Korea, in the hope of descending behind the ROKA forces defending Seoul, thus cutting off their retreat. Additionally reinforced 'border brigades' would provide flank coverage by advancing down each coast.[46]

Kim Il-Sung expected victory – and reunification – to be achieved by 15 August, the fifth anniversary of the liberation of Korea from Japanese rule, when a parliament elected by both North and South Korea would 'establish a new government of a united Korea in Seoul'.[47]

The KPAF had three squadrons of combat aircraft to support Kim's invasion. One Il-10 unit at Yonpo was dedicated to providing air support for the forces pushing through the central highlands because the mountainous terrain precluded conventional artillery operations. The second Il-10 squadron, and the Yak-9Ps based at Heijo, would support the main advance towards Seoul.[48] To allow these units to keep up with the advancing troops and tanks, especially for the short-legged Yak-9P interceptors, the KPAF constructed four forward operating airstrips near the 38th Parallel. The most significant of these 'campaign fields' were at Sinmak and Pyonggang.[49]

Comparing Korean Air Forces

Even though the KPAF was not the awesome air force that USAF Intelligence suspected, it was far more powerful than its direct adversary. Beginning in May 1948, the nascent ROKA formed its first air unit using former IJAAF aircraft – mostly a handful of Ki-9 'Spruce' training biplanes. In mid-September 1949 the United States provided ten Piper L-4 Grasshoppers (the ubiquitous little 'Piper Cub'), allowing the ROK air force (ROKAF) to be established on 1 October that year. The South Korean government purchased ten Noorduyn-built Harvard IIB (virtually identical to the T-6D Texan and designated AT-16 by the US) trainers from Canada, and requested ten North American Aviation (NAA) F-51Ds from the USA, but Harry Truman's administration proved reluctant to provide the South Koreans with combat aircraft.[50]

Of the ten L-4s, one was written off in an accident and in May 1950 a second was used by a pilot to defect to the North. Of the ten Harvards ordered, only three had been delivered by the time the war began.[51] Consequently, in June 1950 the ROKAF primarily consisted of a training unit with eight L-4s and three Harvards. The service had 39 qualified pilots with another 18 in training. The former were either IPs or members of a liaison/observation unit flying five Stinson L-5 Sentinel light observation and liaison planes. Both units were based at Youi-do airfield (fancifully referred to as 'Seoul International Airport'), but frequently flew to the USAF's Kimpo airbase (AB), across the Han River, and periodically to five other airfields – all 'under construction' at this time – where military detachments were stationed.[52]

The most significant airfield in South Korea, Kimpo was a former IJAAF base that had a 7,000ft (2,300m) long, 150ft (50m) wide, hard-surfaced runway that could accommodate up to 120,000lb cargo aircraft, with a smaller auxiliary dirt strip. It had a large hangar and modern terminal that were used by the USAF Military Air Transport Service (MATS) for delivering US military aid to the ROKA/ROKAF. The 'airbase' was operated by Northwest Airlines on a US government contract and the USAF contingent was only a small MATS aerial port detachment, weather observers, and air traffic control party.

KPAF Il-10s prepare for training sortie. (Albert Grandolini Collection)

ROKAF Ki-9 'Spruce' biplane at Taegu AB. (Australian War Memorial)

ROKAF Harvard IIB #101 at Taegu AB. (USAF)

The US Far East Air Forces

What the 'Great Leader of the Korean People' failed to reckon on was the USAF's Far East Air Forces (FEAF)[53] of which the Japan-based Fifth Air Force (AF) was the command nearest Korea, being responsible for the air defence of Japan. Fifth AF consisted of three fighter-bomber and interceptor wings (8th and 49th Fighter-Bomber Wings and 35th Fighter-Interceptor Wing), all flying jet-powered Lockheed F-80C Shooting Stars, and two independent former night fighter units (68th and 339th Fighter-All Weather Squadrons) equipped with propeller-driven NAA F-82G Twin Mustangs. Additionally Fifth AF possessed a two-squadron wing of Douglas B-26 Invaders (3rd Bombardment Wing [Light]) and another of four-engine Douglas C-54 Skymaster transports (374th Troop Carrier Wing), plus a jet photo-reconnaissance squadron flying RF-80As (8th Tactical Reconnaissance Squadron [Photo-Jet]).

Altogether Fifth AF had 271 serviceable combat aircraft (219 F-80Cs, 26 F-82Gs, and 26 B-26s) available, plus 25 reconnaissance and 40 transport aircraft. The command could also call upon additional F-80C and F-82G units based on Okinawa and in the Philippines, as well as a B-29 bomber unit (19th Bombardment Wing [Medium]) from FEAF's war-winning Twentieth AF.[54]

The USAF's jet-powered might was impressive, but in the coming conflict the longer endurance and greater manoeuvrability of propeller-driven ground attack aircraft – primarily the seemingly obsolete F-51 Mustang – would prove advantageous supporting the troops embattled on the frontlines. Fortunately, as Fifth AF fighter units converted to the new jet-powered Shooting Star, most of the 47 retired Mustangs were parked 'in storage' (awaiting scrapping) at Itazuke and Johnson ABs, Japan, while ten others were used by the F-80 wings as 'target tows' to maintain the F-80 pilots' aerial gunnery proficiency. Since many of the USAF fighter pilots had only recently transitioned from the F-51, it would be fairly easy to build Mustang-equipped combat units for the soon-to-be much needed close air support role.[55]

One unit that did not require 'rebuilding' as a Mustang unit was the Royal Australian Air Force's (RAAF's) Number 77 Squadron. The last original member of the British Commonwealth Occupational Forces' Air Component, the RAAF fighter unit possessed 26 F-51Ds being flown by an equal number of 'fully trained but mainly inexperienced pilots' at Iwakuni AB. Slated for return to Australia at the end of the month, the squadron was an independent unit, not attached to FEAF, but available with the consent of the Australian government.[56]

Although less important at the outset of the conflict than FEAF's land-based air forces, the US Navy, augmented by British Commonwealth naval forces, would eventually provide approximately 40 percent of the UN air effort against the invaders. The peninsular nature of the theatre made Kim's invading forces, as well as his rear areas and supply routes, particularly vulnerable to attack from the flanks by carrier-based aviation.

Initially this consisted of the USS *Valley Forge* (CV-45), the only one of the navy's seven 36,000-ton Essex-class carriers that was stationed in the Far East. The centrepiece of Vice Admiral (VAdm) Arthur D. Struble's Seventh Fleet, the 'Happy Valley' would soon eventually be joined by others so that the fleet's Task Force 77 would normally have at least three attack carriers on station. Typically each of these embarked a carrier air group (CAG) that included one or two squadrons of jet fighters (Grumman F9F Panthers

USAF F-80C Shooting Star flying past Mount Fuji, Japan. (NMUSAF)

USAF F-82G Twin Mustang on ground at Itazuki AB, Japan. (NMUSAF)

USN F9F Panther aboard USS *Valley Forge*. (US Navy)

or McDonnell F2H Banshees), two squadrons of Vought F4U Corsairs and one attack squadron with the new, powerful Douglas AD Skyraider. These were supplemented by small detachments of specialized photo-reconnaissance, electronic counter-measures, airborne early warning, and search and rescue aircraft.

These would be augmented by a British or Australian 19,000-ton Colossus/Majestic-class light fleet carrier (the combat equivalent of the USN's *Independence*-class light carriers) normally embarking a squadron of propeller-driven fighters (Supermarine Seafire F Mk 47s or Hawker Sea Fury FB 11s) and another of patrol/reconnaissance/attack two-seaters (Fairey Fireflies)

North Korea's Neighbours' Air Forces

The story of the KPAF cannot be told without an understanding of the air arms of North Korea's two neighbours – the Soviet Union and the newly-formed People's Republic of China – and their participation in the Korean War.

Northwards from the USSR's short border with Korea was the great nation's Primorsky Krai (literally 'Maritime Province', informally known as the Primorye Region), a territory defended by the aviation units of the FEMD. Comparable in strength to the USA's FEAF, the air forces of the FEMD were commanded by Col-Gen Stepan A. Kravoskiy and consisted of three 'Air Armies' (the equivalent of FEAF's 'numbered air forces') – none of which had jet-powered aircraft.[57]

This deficiency was alleviated in August 1950 – after Kim Il-Sung started the Korean War – with the arrival of the 303rd IAD, which was transferred from the the *Moskovskiĭ Voennyĭ Okrug* (Moscow Military District) Air Force. Commanded by Colonel (Col) Georgiy A. Lobov, this elite unit – it had been the second to convert to the MiG-15 and half of its pilots were Great Patriotic War veterans, many of them aces and Heroes of the Soviet Union (HSU, the nation's highest award 'for heroic feats in service to the Soviet state') – was hastily transferred to the FEMD to counter the threat posed by the USAF's jet-equipped Fifth AF and was directed to 'focus on quickly retraining the units of the 54th Air Army on jets'.[58]

On the other (southwest) side of the Korean Peninsula, towards the end of WW2 the Soviets leased the old Imperial Russian naval base at Dalian (formerly Port Arthur) from Chang Kai-Shek's government. It was defended by the *83rd Smeshannyi Aviatsionnyi Korpus* (Combined Aviation Corps or SmAK) consisting of two fighter, two bomber, and one assault aviation divisions. Additionally, the *Voenno-Morskoj Flot SSSR* (Military Maritime Fleet of the USSR, or VMF) had a fighter and a torpedo bomber regiment stationed there.[59]

In March 1950, as a direct result of the Sino-Soviet Treaty of Friendship, Alliance and Mutual Assistance signed the month before, the V-VS began training Communist Chinese pilots, aircrew, and maintenance personnel in the Shanghai area. The 106th IAD headquarters staff arrived from the Moscow Military District Air Force to take command of a disparate assortment of Frontal Aviation units collected to train the embryonic People's Liberation Army Air Force (PLAAF) to fly Soviet military equipment. The units assigned were the *29th Gvardeyskiy Istrebitelniy Aviatsionniy Polk* (Guards Fighter Aviation Regiment, GvIAP) flying new, jet-powered MiG-15s, the 351st IAP equipped with Lavochkin La-11 propeller-driven fighters and the *829th Smeshannyi Aviatsionnyi Polk* (Mixed Aviation Regiment, SmAP) with Tupolev Tu-2 twin-engine light bombers and Ilyushin Il-10 assault aircraft.[60]

After initially providing air defence against Koumintang (KMT or 'Nationalist') air raids launched from Taiwan – and shooting down six KMT intruders – in July the Soviets began training pilots, aircrew and ground personnel of the PLAAF's new 4th Combined Air Brigade (CAB) on these types. When training was completed in October, the Soviets left the Chinese with 38 MiG-15 jets, 39 La-11 prop fighters, 39 Tu-2 bombers and 25 Il-10s, plus 14 Yak-11 trainers and ten Li-2 transports.[61] Leaving their equipment with the new PLAAF units, personnel of the 29th GvIAP and 351st IAP were transferred to Dalian where they received fresh batches of MiG-15s and La-11s and were assigned to the 83rd SmAK for the defence of the Liaodong Peninsula and the Soviet naval base there.[62]

The PLAAF's only other air force unit was the former 'Nanyuan Flying Group' (named after the airfield at which it was formed), an *ad hoc* unit established in July 1949 to defend Beijing from KMT bombing raids. Of the polyglot assortment of former KMT aircraft, only ten of the NAA P-51 Mustangs were said to be operational, so in August 1950 the unit received 30 Lavochkin La-9s from the Soviet Union and the unit was formally re-designated the '1st People's Squadron'.[63]

To provide pilots, aircrew and ground personnel for further – and rapid – expansion of the PLAAF, the USSR provided 180 Yak-11/-18 trainers to seven aviation schools and sent 878 instructors and ground personnel to train the 1,911 student pilots recruited to join the PLAAF. The first six-month course began in May 1950 and 88 graduates from three of these schools were intended to become the next wave of Chinese MiG-15 pilots, PLAAF planning directing the formation of three fighter regiments under the 3rd Fighter Air Brigade at Shenyang, beginning in October. To conduct this training, in July the Soviet Armed Forces General Staff dispatched the *151st Gvardeyskiy Istrebitelniy Aviatsionniy Diviziya* (Guards Fighter Aviation Division, or GvIAD), under Col Ivan V. Belov, with 124 MiG-15s – each of the division's regiments would train a PLAAF regiment and transfer the jet fighters to their students once the task was completed.[64]

324th IAD MiG-15 demonstration team in flight. (Tim Callaway Collection)

29th GvIAP training the PLAAF's first MiG-15 regiment. (Tim Callaway Collection)

Il-10 tail number 61, used by Lt Lee Kun-Soon to defect to South Korea, April 1950. (Jin Ho Collection)

Defection, Intelligence and Final Adjustments

North Korean operations security (OpSec) was generally very effective. It was not until 21 June that the ROK government had any inkling of the coming invasion. This is despite the 28 April defection of Lieutenant (Lt) Lee Kun-Soon who flew an Il-10 (#61) to Seoul's Youi-do airport. Lee was a 24-year old sergeant and member of the KPAF's original cadre of flight instructors who was considered 'the best pilot in his training division'. Because his flying and teaching skills were so highly regarded Lee was promoted to lieutenant and placed in charge of the first class of pilot-cadets, despite the fact he was a devout Catholic.[65]

Upon landing at Seoul, Lee was interrogated by ROKA officials, with USAF personnel observing. He seemed to know little of intelligence value, reporting – only guessing – that the KPAF's strength amounted to only 35 Yak fighters, 35 trainers, and five twin-engine aircraft. He evinced no knowledge of KPA or KPAF operations, plans, or intentions, giving no indication of the forthcoming invasion.[66]

But the defection worried Kim Il-Sung; he feared that the South Koreans had become aware of his invasion plan. Four days before launching it, Kim pressed Stalin for permission to launch a full-scale offensive without waiting for the fake ROKA 'invasion' to be played out to justify the attack. Relaying Kim's request, Shtykov reported to Stalin, 'Instead of a local operation at Ongjin Peninsula as a prelude to the general offensive, Kim Il-Sung suggests and overall attack on 25 June along the whole front line'. That same day Stalin gave his approval for the KPA to 'advance along the whole front line' but to 'be sure to make it look to the world as though South Korea were [*sic*] starting the war.'[67]

CHAPTER 2
INITIAL OFFENSIVE OPERATIONS

In the early hours (0440hrs local) of a quiet Sunday morning – June 25th 1950 – beneath a slate gray overcast, and persistent rain, some 86,000 North Korean soldiers surged across the 38th Parallel following a 30-minute barrage by 787 guns and mortars, ousting the forward elements of the ROKA out of their rudimentary frontier fortifications. Led by 120 T-34/85 tanks, three KPA divisions overwhelmed the hurriedly responding ROKA, capturing Kaesŏng by 0930hrs. The secondary thrust towards Ch'unch'on in the central highlands initially made little progress while, beginning at 0525hrs, approximately 20 junks and sampans – escorted by a half dozen motor gunboats and motor torpedo boats – landed two naval infantry battalions on the east coast near Kannin, south of Kangnung (now Gangneung), on the east coast about 15 miles (24km) south of the 38th Parallel.[68]

Beginning the Fatherland Liberation War

The morning's low clouds and light rain precluded early KPAF operations but by 1315hrs the cloud deck began to break up, allowing a few ground attack missions in support of the attacking troops and tanks. Russian sources report that 'they made precision strikes on strong points and enemy troop concentrations… There was a complete lack of any kind of [enemy] air defense. Under such conditions operations by ground attack aviation [meaning 57th AAR Il-10s] were highly effective.'[69]

Additionally, an armed reconnaissance patrol by two Yak-9Ps roamed as far south as Seoul. Spotting targets at Kimpo AB and Youi-do airport, at 1700hrs six Yak-9Ps showed up to destroy them. One pair wrecked Kimpo's control tower and set a fuel dump ablaze with their cannon fire as well as damaging a MATS C-54D Skymaster (grounded with an elevator damaged by a forklift while unloading the day before) on the ramp. The other four Yaks strafed the eight L-4s and two Harvards parked at Youi-do, damaging or destroying seven of them.[70] Two hours later Kimpo was attacked again, further damaging the MATS C-54D. With the Skymaster severely damaged, the flight crew collapsed the nose gear, opened the fuel petcocks, and set the aircraft on fire, completing its destruction.[71] The next morning a pair of Il-10s, covered by Yak-9P fighter escorts, bombed and strafed the railway station in Seoul, blowing up an ammunition stockpile and causing significant South Korean casualties.[72]

Based on reports that the KPA's T-34s had penetrated as far south as Uijongbu, 18 miles north of Seoul, US Ambassador John J. Muccio ordered all American civilians evacuated, using two 4,800-ton Norwegian fertilizer ships (MS *Reinholt* and *Norge*) in Inch'on harbor. Augmenting the merchantmen, FEAF provided transport aircraft, as well as fighters to fly defensive cover, for the air and sea evacuations. Seven C-54s, along with ten C-47s and four C-46s scraped together from various FEAF base flights and other ancillary units, began evacuating personnel from Kimpo and Suwon airfields (20 miles south of Seoul) that morning. For air cover, 28 F-82G Twin Mustangs (4th, 68th and 339th FAWSs) were gathered at Itazuke AB, Japan,[73] and began flying Combat Air Patrols (CAPs) in relays over Inch'on, Seoul, and the road connecting them.[74]

Simultaneously the KPAF deployed its operational fighter squadron – ten Yak-9Ps and a pair of Il-10s – forward to Sinmak airfield, to give their short-ranged interceptors a deeper reach into South Korean airspace and more combat time when engaged. The day's only encounter occurred early in the afternoon (1330hrs) when two Yaks flew an armed reconnaissance mission from Seoul southwards. Following the road to Inch'on at just beneath the gray overcast, they soon spotted a pair of large black USAF F-82G Twin Mustangs (68th FAWS) at 11 o'clock low, patrolling northwards (covering a convoy of evacuees) at 500 ft altitude 'loitering' at a leisurely, fuel-conserving 160-180 knots. Both sides turned towards one another with the more maneuverable Yaks tightening their turns and splitting to attack the two American fighters. The Twin Mustangs jettisoned their external fuel tanks, accelerated and broke left to defeat the attacks. The lead Yak 'started firing from too far out and his bullets lagged behind [the F-82] for the entire firing pass'. The wingman never achieved a firing position and both Yaks turned north to escape. However, one of the F-82s had its right aileron and pitot tube damaged by the jettisoned fuel tank and the pilot landed at Suwon airfield. The next day a C-54 arrived with replacement parts and a repair crew.[75]

Meanwhile, as some 682 people were being evacuated from Inch'on aboard the two Norwegian freighters, the ROKA stiffened briefly, attempting a counter-attack that delayed the North Koreans in a tough, day-long battle near Uijongbu. However, the South Koreans were spent and that morning (27 June) the KPA's 3rd and 4th Divisions broke through. Supporting the renewed offensive, the 57th AAR's Il-10s bombed the Anyang railway station and a railroad bridge, a 'military train' and 'military storage depots and other enemy targets along the road between Seoul and Suwon'. As the routed defenders streamed back towards the Han River, the two KPA divisions and their tank regiments drove onto the heights overlooking the capital. The ROK government abandoned the city, moving to Taejon.[76]

Ahead of the armored thrust flew two waves of KPAF fighters. Arriving midday, the first was a formation of five Yaks – a two-seat Yak-11 trainer, probably being used as a reconnaissance aircraft, escorted by four Yak-9Ps – headed for Seoul at 10,000ft. On CAP over the Seoul-Kimpo-Inch'on area were three formations of USAF Twin Mustangs. One flight of four (68th FAWS) orbited below a broken cloud deck at 4,000ft between Kimpo and Suwon, while another formation (339th FAWS) patrolled at 8,000ft and four more (4th FAWS) provided top cover, above a solid overcast, at 12,000ft.[77]

Once again the KPAF fighters initially had the advantage, jumping the lowest CAP. Led by the Yak-11, they managed to get some hits on one of the big Twin Mustangs' tails before the Americans turned the tables on them. The Yak attempted to escape by climbing into the clouds, but 1st Lieutenant (1st Lt) William G. Hudson's F-82 ran down the slower trainer. As Hudson's Radar Operator (RO), 1st Lt Carl Fraser described, 'Our first burst hit the rear of the fuselage and knocked some pieces off. The Yak pilot racked it over in a steep turn to the right and we gave him another burst along the right wing. This set the gas tank on fire and took the right flap and aileron off. By this time we were so close we almost collided with him. I could clearly see the pilot turn around and say something to the observer. Then he pulled the canopy back and climbed out on the wing. Once again he leaned in and said something to the observer. But he was either scared or wounded as he never attempted to jump. The Yak pilot pulled the rip-cord and the chute dragged him off the wing just before the ship rolled over and went in.'[78]

After having his Twin Mustang hit in the tail during the Yak-11's firing pass and pulling up into a stall to escape further damage, 1st Lt Charles B. Moran recovered and descended onto the tail of one of the escorting Yak-9Ps as it flew past, shooting it down. The mid-level CAP heard the radio calls from the low formation, spotted the engagement through breaks in the clouds below and Major (Maj) James W. Little's flight dived into the mêlée, claiming three more Korean fighters. Uncertain of the outcome due to the weather, two of these were credited as 'probables'.[79]

At 1300hrs nine KPAF Il-10s crossed Seoul swinging southwest from Yonpo airfield to disrupt the aerial evacuation from Kimpo AB. By this time the Twin Mustangs had been replaced on CAP by four F-80C Shooting Stars (35th FBS/8th FBW), split into two pairs orbiting between cloud layers (broken deck at 5,000ft and an overcast at 12,000ft) from Suwon north to the 38th Parallel. The lead element (pair) spotted the approaching raiders, cruising south at 7,000ft altitude, above the lower cloud deck, in a long, loose right echelon formation. Needing to ensure that the intruders were not British Fleet Air Arm (FAA) Fireflies from the just-arrived aircraft carrier HMS *Triumph*, 1st Lt Robert E. Wayne accelerated from their 250 knot 'loiter speed' and led his wingman in a wide sweeping turn to visually identify the targets.

As Wayne recounted later,

> 'As I approached the number six aircraft, I could see the rear gunner firing at me… I broke left and lined up behind the leading machine, firing a few rounds into it until it exploded! I then made a tight 360-degree turn to the left and lined up behind the number two. I fired a second burst for the same results! I made another 360-degree turn to the left and rolled out where the number three man should have been, but the remnants of the enemy formation had all disappeared into the clouds below. I looked around the area for a few minutes trying to find any of the remaining [Il-10s] but it proved to be a futile search. Being below 'bingo' [return-to-base or RTB] fuel, I gathered up my wingman and headed back to base.'[80]

As Wayne and his wingman headed home, the second element of Shooting Stars – flown by Captain (Capt) Raymond E. Schillereff and 1st Lt Robert H. Dewald – raced to join the fight, descending through the clouds *en route*. As Dewald later recalled,

> 'Right in front of me I spotted dark green piston-engined aircraft, flying along the riverbed… as to whether this was

a North Korean I wasn't aware. I identified the aircraft as a single-seat fighter, but from right behind the cockpit of this 'single-seater' came a burst of tracer fire – this was the aerial gunner, and he was shooting at me! I snapped off a long burst from all six machine guns at the cockpit of the enemy aircraft. But nothing seemed to have happened as the aircraft continued flying as before. The enemy made no attempt to maneuver out away from the attack. I made a second attack, [and] could see fire still coming from the enemy gunner. Nobody was going to bother me, so this time I poured a long burst into the enemy's engine. I hit it but the enemy aircraft continued to fly on, as if it had not been hit: no smoke, nor any damage to the enemy aircraft, could be observed. On my third pass I closed to point-blank range and opened fire as soon as possible. Again, I saw no damage, but as I pulled my fighter up next to him, I noticed that his nose was beginning to waver, and that oil began to cover all of his cockpit windows. Got him! Over the radio I heard my commander, 'You shot him down!'"[81]

Schillereff also found another *Shturmovik* scurrying for home 'at treetop height' and shot it down near the Han River. Russian

56th FAR conducts dedication ceremony before flying into battle. (Charles Euripides Collection)

KPAF Yak-9Ps taking off for a mission. (Albert Grandolini Collection)

F-82G S/N 46-357 with damaged tail section. (NMUSAF)

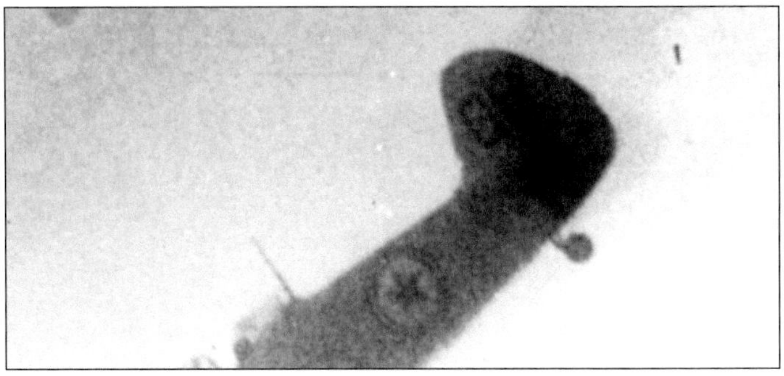

Yak-11 Shoot-down photo. (NMUSAF)

sources report that of the nine Il-10s sent to bomb Kimpo, four were shot down by intercepting American fighters and a fifth was so badly damaged 'it was unable to return to base'.[82]

The Rout of the ROKA

Seoul and Kimpo AB fell to the advancing North Korean forces on 28 June, the KPA taking the day to regroup before attempting to cross the Han River. FEAF transport operations were now centered on Suwon AB, bringing in 150 tons of ammunition for the beleaguered ROKA troops. Consequently it became the next target of KPAF air attacks.[83]

American defensive CAPs over Suwon proved insufficient and twice KPAF fighters evaded interception to strafe the airfield and do significant damage. The first was at 1330hrs when four Yak-9Ps caught a B-26B [13th BS(L)], C-54D (22nd TCS/374th TCW) and an F-82G (68th FAWS) on the ground,[84] severely damaging all three with their cannon fire. Five hours later six Yaks repeated the attack, one of them shooting up a C-54D (6th TCS/374th TCW) in the landing pattern and, according to the DPRK High Command report to the Soviet General Staff, 'put [it] to flight', the crew performing an emergency landing at Ashiya AB, Japan, where it was written off as damaged beyond repair (DBR).[85]

To help stem the seemingly relentless advance of the KPA, HQ FEAF deployed 18 (of its 22 serviceable) B-29 Superfortresses to Kadena AB, Okinawa and, on 28 June, the 19th Bombardment Wing (Medium) [19th BW(M)] launched its first mission of the Korean War, sending four big bombers to attack the Seoul railway station and marshalling yards and the bridges spanning the Han River. The DPRK High Command reported that these were intercepted by a flight of Yak-9Ps, led by Lt Lee Dong-Gyu, who 'repulsed an air attack by four American bombers on P'yongyang and shot down one of them'. However, at this time the American bombers were in fact specifically prohibited from flying north of Seoul; there are no reports by the B-29 crews about being attacked by North Korean aircraft, much less any damage done.[86]

Encouraged by the lack of effective air defense, the KPAF mounted six raids on Suwon the next day. In one case a formation of three Il-10s, escorted by six Yak-9 fighters, arrived between CAPs and made bombing attacks that wrecked the terminal building. However, two flights of F-80Cs were 'on station' when six more KPAF aircraft attempted do the same. One flight (80th FBS/8th FBW) shot down an Il-10 while the other (9th FBS/49th FBW) claimed one fighter (as a 'La-7').[87]

Truth be known, the Shooting Stars were not proving to be the best air defense fighter for the Americans – its Allison J33 turbojet engine's high fuel consumption limited their 'on station' time and its high speed frequently resulted in 'overshooting' their prop-driven targets. Two days earlier, FEAF had pulled ten F-51D Mustangs from 'target-towing' duties to provide to the now almost non-existent ROKAF (two surviving L-5s were shot down by KPA AAA fire during this period). During their 'ferry flight' to Taegu, eight of these were flown by 8th FBW pilots to help escort General Douglas MacArthur's C-54 on his flight to Suwon to confer with the ROKA HQ.[88]

USAF 22nd TCS C-54D S/N 42-72648 Burns at Suwon AB. (USAF)

Four Mustang pilots were flying their CAP over the educational facility (known as the Experimental Agriculture Building) where the conference was being held when they 'caught a flight of Il-10s preparing to attack Suwon', evidently escorted by at least two fighters. The faster Mustangs quickly intercepted them and, because they were 80mph slower, the KPAF assault aircraft could not get away and eventually three of them were shot down.[89] Two KPAF crewmen bailed out, one of whom was killed on the ground, the other was captured to become a prisoner of war (POW).[90]

KPAF's 'B-29 Nemesis', Lt Lee Dong-Gyu, who is said to have scored '5 kills over Seoul'. (Tom Cooper Collection)

During the day the Il-10s also struck Inch'on harbor – reporting to have sunk 11 small enemy ships – and bombed the Inch'on railway station while the Yak-9Ps, now with a small detachment forward deployed to the battered Kimpo AB, had their first real encounter with the Boeing B-29 Superfortress. The 19th BW(M) launched nine of the big bombers against Kimpo AB while two others were sent to bomb the railroad station at Seoul. When the Superfortresses 'walked their 500-pound bombs' across the airfield from 3,000ft, two Yak-9Ps scrambled, intercepting the four-engine bombers as they headed back to Kadena. None of the Superforts were hit by the interceptors' fire while one Yak was claimed shot down by B-29 gunners.[91]

KPA T-34s driving through Seoul. (Steven J. Zaloga Collection)

Destroyed F-82G S/N 46-364 at Suwon. (USAF)

Let the Bombings Begin

With KPAF airfield attack operations interrupting the resupply and evacuation airlift with alarming regularity – and with FEAF fighters, flying from Japan, unable to prevent their frequent successes – on his way to Suwon General MacArthur authorized FEAF to begin an immediate 'offensive counter-air' campaign to destroy the North Korean aircraft at their bases. He also sent an urgent message to Washington seeking approval for air attacks on enemy military facilities and lines of communication north of the 38th Parallel.[92]

At the end of the day – just as the sun was setting in the west and the KPAF was 'putting their planes to bed' at P'yongyang's Heijo airfield – 18 B-26 Invaders [3rd BW(L)] came roaring in at low altitude, dropping fragmentation bombs upon the ramp, hangars and revetments, and strafing the parked aircraft wherever they found them. Five Yak fighters scrambled out to the runway; but only two took off – the other three were straddled by fragmentation bombs and shredded by shrapnel. Climbing rapidly, the remaining pair attacked the right wing of the Invaders' formation and were driven off by defensive fire (one was claimed shot down by a B-26 gunner). The Americans got away without damage. Russian sources report 19 KPAF aircraft were destroyed in this, the very first American attack north of the 38th Parallel.[93]

The forward-deployed squadron of Yak-9Ps was unaffected by this devastating attack and when the KPA resumed its offensive, pushing across the Han River on 30 June, they flew a number of close air support (CAS) and protective air-cover missions. Along the river USAF F-80Cs manned CAPs over the defending ROKA units and a clash was inevitable. A pair of Yak-9Ps – flown by Lt Lee Dong-Gyu and his wingman Maj Tae Kuk-Sung – crossed the Han and reported spotting eight Shooting Stars and 'bounced' two of them at low altitude. The F-80s were flown by Lts John B. Thomas and Charles A. Wurster (36th FBS/8th FBW).

The two Americans fire-walled the throttles and accelerated out of range, wheeled around in a fast wide circle and came up behind the Yaks. Wurster reported that he 'got some damaging fire on one of them and the pilot bailed out near Suwon' and was credited with one victory. According to Russian sources, Lee Dong-Gyu, 'noticing that four F-80s were diving on his wingman, rushed to his assistance, downing one of the Shooting Stars… but his own Yak was damaged by an attack from behind by another F-80, which riddled his aircraft's fuel tank and forced him to bail out'. Wurster saw the second Yak closing on Thomas's tail and, 'I called for him to break hard, which he did. In a matter of seconds he had maneuvered his F-80 into a position to make a kill. We both watched as the second Yak pilot bailed out'. Lee Dong-Gyu survived the dogfight, and safely returned to his unit the next day. Tae Kuk-Sung flew back to base to report 'finishing off the attacking F-80'.[94]

In addition, DPRK High Command reported that the KPAF raided Suwon on several occasions, destroying 'two four-engine enemy aircraft and seven fighters'. Also an unnamed KPAF pilot was reported to have shot down a B-26 near Kaesŏng; there is no record of this encounter in any USAF histories.[95]

These air battles had no effect on the ground situation and that evening the Americans abandoned Suwon AB in a panic, one USAF officer leading some South Koreans back to the airfield to destroy the damaged aircraft left behind. The next defensive line centered on Ch'onan, but the badly beaten ROKA's ability to halt the KPA now depended upon the introduction of American combat troops. Once US President Harry Truman approved the American escalation, on 1 July six C-54 transports (374th TCW) began ferrying the first elements of the US Army's 24th Division – the HQ and the 21st Infantry Regiment's two battalions – to Pusan. One of the latter formed the basis of a 540-man combat team, called 'Task Force Smith', hastily sent forward to engage the KPA near Osan, twelve miles south of Suwon, while the rest

KPAF Il-10s peacetime parking line-up at Heijo AB, P'yongyang. (Albert Grandolini Collection)

USAF B-26 Light Bombers dropping bombs. (NARA)

KPAF Yak-9P squadron scramble. (Albert Grandolini Collection)

USN VF-51 F9F Panther in flight. (Warren Thompson Collection)

of the division arrived at Pusan by sea. In putting soldiers on the ground to face the advancing North Koreans the Americans made the single most significant investment – and the strongest possible political statement – in the defense of South Korea.[96]

The next day KPAF's Yonpo airfield was raided by ten B-29s. FEAF's initial photographic reconnaissance (on 28-29 June) showed some 65 KPAF aircraft (almost all Il-10s) based there, but within the next two days the 57th AAR deployed one squadron forward to Wonsan (former IJNAF) airfield and sent other detachments to Kimpo and the primitive 'campaign airstrip' at Pyonggang. When Superfortresses attacked, the crews counted only 16 aircraft on the field, but their 260-pound fragmentation bombs fell wide and apparently no damage was done.[97]

Simultaneously the US Navy's Task Force 77 (TF 77) arrived in the Yellow Sea, centred on the aircraft carriers USS *Valley Forge* (CV-45) and HMS *Triumph* (R16).[98] Aboard the *Valley Forge* was Carrier Air Group (CAG) 5 – two squadrons of F9F-3 Panther jets (VF-51 and -52) and three squadrons of propeller-driven F4U-4B Corsairs (VF-53 and -54) and AD-2 Skyraiders (VF-55) – while the *Triumph's* 13th CAG operated a dozen each Supermarine Seafire F Mk 47 fighters (NAS 800) and Fairey Firefly FR 1 reconnaissance and strike aircraft (NAS 827).[99]

Early on 3 July two KPAF airbases were hit by the naval strike fighters. From *Triumph* launched nine rocket-armed Fireflies escorted by a dozen Seafires, attacking the Haeju airfield, on the coast. No KPAF aircraft were seen but several buildings, including hangars, were hit. P'yongyang's Heijo airbase was attacked by a dozen Skyraiders and 16 Corsairs, with eight Panthers (VF-51) sweeping in ahead of the strike force.[100]

Three Yak-9Ps were caught scrambling to get airborne, two of them taking off towards each other! As Lieutenant (jg) Leonard Plog lined up for a strafing run, he spotted one of the Yaks beginning his take-off roll, stating later 'I lined up on the one that had just taken off and out of the corner of my eye, I saw another one coming straight at me and he evidently misjudged the speed of my aircraft because he missed. Ensign [Eldon] Brown saw a Yak coming in on another element of F9Fs, which consisted of the CAG [Carrier Air Group Commander Peter Lanham] and his wingman, Lt (jg) Bill Gortney. He closed on it quickly and blew him apart with his 20mm cannon. This allowed me to refocus on my Yak. I lined him up and fired a burst and a split second later, I saw his right wing disintegrate. We had killed two Yaks in a short period of time while our bombers worked over the field real good.'[101]

Two of the Yak-9Ps were flown by Majors Kim Hi-Kiung (also rendered Kim Hi-Gyung) and Tae Kuk-Sung, both future leaders in the KPAF fighter force. Unseen by the Americans, both managed to bail out of their disintegrating aircraft and returned safely to their unit, Kim claiming to have shot down (and was credited with) three Lockheed F-80C Shooting Stars. The third Yak was flown by Capt Ahn Sun-Duk who flew well away from the target area, and 'defended an important and strategic bridge [six miles north of] P'yongyang.'[102]

The Panthers' strafing set fire to a KPAF transport aircraft and destroyed two other aircraft on the ground at Heijo airfield. Then the F4Us and ADs arrived, bombing three hangars, the fuel depot, other facilities and a nearby railroad yard.[103]

Russian archive sources state that by 3 July the KPAF had lost 36 aircraft in combat operations. In addition to the 22 destroyed on the ground by USAF and USN attacks on P'yongyang, six Yaks of the 56th FAR had been lost in air-to-air combat and the 57th AAR lost eight Il-10s to USAF fighters. (USAF/USN official victory credits total seven fighters, some listed as 'La-7s', eight Il-10s, and one Yak-11.) In turn the KPAF fighters claimed to have destroyed the entire ROKAF air force (16 training and light observation aircraft) and 'nearly a dozen USAF transports'.[104]

CHAPTER 3
THE 56TH FIGHTER AVIATION REGIMENT IN ACTION

After 'spending a day or two searching [Seoul] for South Korean soldiers, police, and "nationalist traitors", most of which were shot at once', the KPA regrouped and began crossing the wide Han River. On 30 June the KPA's 3rd Division established a bridgehead east of the city, followed the next day by the 4th Division crossing to the south, attacking the ROKA 5th Division at Yongdungpo, the large industrial suburb that included the ROKAF's Youi-do airfield. Fighting without tank support, it took two days to subdue the defenders and capture the city. By 3 July, KPA tanks were also across the river, the 3rd and 4th Divisions were poised to continue their drive southwards, and the KPAF's 56th FAR deployed seven Yak-9P fighters to Kimpo AB to provide air support. Later joined by a detachment of four to six Il-10s, these were dispersed and camouflaged to try to prevent discovery and destruction by FEAF bombers.[105]

To aid the ROKA's defence, MacArthur's Far East Command established its Advance Command and Liaison Group in Korea (ADCOM), initially based at Suwon, but soon evacuated to Osan. Along with this advanced command echelon, the first American air units deployed onto Korean soil were from the US Army, the 24th Infantry Division's HQ and artillery aviation sections – a pair of fast, all-metal, retractable gear Ryan L-17B Navions, three Stinson L-5s and five Piper L-4s. Arriving 4 July, these provided battlefield observation, artillery spotting, and aerial courier/liaison service, deploying to Pyeongtaek airfield (K-6), about eight miles south of Osan. That same day, while adjusting mortar and 105mm howitzer fire supporting the American infantry, one of these was 'jumped' by three Yak-9Ps near Osan. The fast Yaks could not 'get a bead on' the slow but nimble observation aircraft, and proceeded on to Pyeongtaek to strafe the three light aircraft parked there.[106]

ADCOM's communications with MacArthur's GHQ in Japan were dependent on a commercial telephone relay station at Osan. Two days later, while the KPA's 107th Tank Regiment and 4th Division were destroying 'Task Force Smith', four Il-10s winged south, overflying the battle to bomb and strafe the Osan communications centre.[107]

The KPAF Moves South

Brushing aside the remnants of 'Task Force Smith', the invaders continued southwards and clashed with the next elements of the US 24th Division at Ch'onan. Attempting to bolster the crumbling defence, the USAF established a forward operating base (and Fifth AF's Advance HQ) at Taegu, about halfway between Taejon and Pusan. A 3,800ft (1,158m) clay-and-gravel airstrip, with only a few rudimentary former-IJAAF facilities, Taegu became home for what would become the ROKAF 1st Fighter Squadron with ten F-51Ds and were soon joined by a like number of Mustangs from an *ad hoc* USAF unit, 51st Fighter Squadron (Provisional).[108]

Taegu was also the staging base for the RAAF's 77 Squadron, flying its Mustangs from Iwakuni AB, Japan. Their first combat sorties were flown on 2 July – escorting medical evacuation (MedEvac) C-47s and the unproductive B-29 raid on Yonpo – the 'Aussies' soon turned to offensive missions, especially against KPA forces advancing down the east coast. On the sixth day of operations, the squadron's deputy commander, Squadron Leader (Sqn Ldr) Graham Strout failed to return from a rocket attack on a railway station near Samchok. His Mustang crashed a short distance north of the target, but was claimed by DPRK propaganda as one of the two victims of Yak fighters that day.[109]

The next day elements of the KPA's upgraded 105th Tank Division and its 4th Infantry Division ousted the US 21st Infantry Regiment from Ch'onan.[110] The Americans fell back and regrouped along a line from Chongju to Choch'iwon with the KPA hot on their heels. To keep pace with their ground forces' advance, Maj Gen Wang moved his operational HQ forward to Kimpo AB. Intent on making it his main operating base, he brought with him some 500 combat engineers, logisticians, clerks, and other support troops – as well as aircraft maintenance technicians – designating them the 877th Air Force Unit (AFU) commanded by Maj Kung Chan-So. To defend his new base, Wang was provided with the newly-formed 107th Security Regiment, commanded by Col Han Choi-Han, comprising about 1,500 partially-trained troops.[111]

As the KPA pushed deeper into South Korea, the 56th FAR reportedly deployed a flight of five Yak-9Ps to Suwon to continue flying CAS and air-cover missions. On 9 July DPRK propaganda claimed two unspecified American fighters were shot down by North Korean fighters. Next day four Il-10s bombed and strafed

Four ROKAF F-51D Mustangs in flight. (NMUSAF)

Yak-9P pilot climbing into his fighter aircraft. (Albert Grandolini Collection)

KPAF Yak-9P pilot Lee Moon-Soon. (Tom Cooper Collection)

RAAF F-51D Mustangs on Ramp at Iwakuni AB, Japan. (Warren Thompson Collection)

the US 19th Infantry Regiment at Chongju, supporting the 105th Tank Division 'attempting to penetrate the defences of the American 24th Infantry Division.'[112]

Two days later a pair of the far-ranging Yak-9Ps 'bounced' a US Army (USA) Ryan L-17B Navion while its USAF crew was performing airborne forward air control (FAC) for FEAF fighter-bombers. Another three Yaks attacked a flight of four F-80Cs strafing KPA troops near Chongju but failed to get any hits before the faster jets vacated the scene. The KPAF claimed no 'kills' on this date, but the following day (12 July), DPRK propaganda claimed that KPAF fighters engaged 20 American aircraft near Choch'iwon and shot down three – two B-26s and an unspecified fighter – without loss. The next day two Yaks, flown by Kim Gi-Ohk and Lee Moon-Soon, were reported to have 'attacked ten enemy aircraft near Pyeongtaek and downed three of them', although this may be a repeat of the previous assertion.[113]

In fact, on 12 July a formation of Shooting Stars strafing KPA's frontlines was 'jumped' by a pair of Yak-9Ps, but once again the faster jets got away undamaged. Not so lucky was an L-4 Grasshopper shot down by a pair of Yak-9Ps while directing artillery fire near Chongju, covering the withdrawal across the Kum River by the 21st and 34th Infantry Regiments; both army crewmen were seriously injured in the Piper's ensuing crash.[114]

According to Russian sources, by mid-July the 57th AAR was badly depleted, being reduced to 'about two dozen functional Il-10s remaining'. These were dispersed in groups of four to six aircraft to various 'campaign fields' and from 16-19 July conducted 'continual', though sporadic – desultory by Western standards – attacks supporting advancing KPA units 'on the approaches to Pusan'. Their biggest day was on 18 July when they reportedly attacked a column of 100 enemy vehicles and destroyed 60 per cent of them.[115]

Aerial Action Intensifies

More significant was the KPAF's destruction of the first American B-29 Superfortress in combat. On 12 July, FEAF's Superforts were dispatched to roam the KPA's 'lines of communications', dropping their 35 500-pound bombs individually on bridges, tunnel entrances, and road junctions – as well as on any observed troop concentrations, supply dumps, truck convoys, and even individual tanks. Two Yak-9Ps and a two-seat Yak-9V– probably scrambling from Kimpo AB – intercepted one of these B-29s [28th BS/19th BW(M)] near Seoul, Lt Lee Dong-Gyu shot out the number three engine with his cannon. Ablaze, the B-29 escaped out to sea where the crew bailed out: two members were captured by North Koreans, but the remaining 11 men were rescued by the British sloop, HMS *Alacrity*.[116]

One week later, three Yak-9Ps intercepted one of ten B-29s dispatched to bomb bridges spanning the Han River. Catching the bomber [30th BS/19th BW(M)] near Seoul, the Yaks riddled it, causing severe damage (over 100 shell holes) and wounding the pilot, Capt John W. Edenbo. According to one of the gunners, 'three Yak pilots came right up at us while we were on the bombing run. They were very quick-moving little prop-driven fighters, and they also seemed to be very well briefed. It was clear that they had some respect for our guns. They came in from behind, but dropped back out of range of our guns. We took hits in the bomb-bay, and... Capt. Edenbo dropped the bombs and dived into a cloud. By then we had been hit in several places by gunfire from the Yaks'. KPAF propaganda maintains that pilot Kim Gi-Ohk destroyed the B-29 by ramming.[117]

Recovering from the repeated UN air attacks by moving and massing only at night, the KPA resumed their assaults on 14 July, outflanking the 34th Infantry Regiment, destroying the supporting 63rd Field Artillery Battalion, and forcing the Americans from the Kum River line. The US 24th Infantry Division fell back to Taejon. Severely mauled, with many elements committed to battle piecemeal and, predictably, destroyed in detail, US 24th Infantry Division could not stop the two KPA divisions, led by 107th Tank Regiment, from swinging around their left flank, threatening to encircle them. FEAF called for a 'maximum effort' of CAS.

The fighters of the 56th FAR sporadically attempted to intervene. Their most successful mission was on 15 July, when two Yak-9Ps 'jumped' four B-26s [13th BS/3rd BW(L)] that were attacking a ground target. Kim Gi-Ohk damaged one so badly – shooting out one engine – it had to be force-landed at Taejon's small dirt airfield. Balancing the books, the USAF credited Capts Robert A. Coffin (39th FIS/35th FIW) and Francis B. Clark (36th FBS/8th FBW) with victories over Yak-9s on 15 and 17 July, respectively.[118]

Two days later, at 0720hrs six KPAF aircraft overflew the 21st Infantry Regiment with two of them (probably Il-10s from Kimpo) dropping four bombs on a railroad bridge northwest of Okch'on in an effort to cut off the Americans' retreat. Meanwhile two pairs of Yak-9Ps – led by Majors Kim Hi-Kiung and Tae Kuk-Sung – strafed the regiment's command post and then the airfield.[119]

As the North Korean fighters egressed northwards at 6,000ft a ground FAC informed a flight of four F-80Cs (36th FBS/8th FBW) about them. Capt Howard E. Odell and his wingman launched a pursuit, with Lts Robert D. McKee and Charles A. Wurster covering them from 2,000ft above and 1,000ft behind. Jettisoning their air-to-ground rockets and tip tanks, the Shooting Stars quickly caught the Yaks 20 miles northeast of Taejon. From 12,000ft, Second Lieutenant (2nd Lt) Elwood A. Kees spotted the four Yak-9Ps 6,000ft below them headed north. When attacked, one pair broke left and down, the other right and up and a confusing four-vs-four 'furball' ensued. The Shooting Stars split as well, Kees and McKee quickly destroying one from each pair. McKee later related:

'I used my gyro [stabilized gun]sight and closed in on the lead ship and started to fire at 15-20 degrees off, slightly above him at 1,000ft range. My hits were clustered around the engine, cockpit and left wingroot and he began trailing a white-gray smoke with a small fire on the bottom of the wing...'

Wurster reported the Yak pilot bailed out before his stricken fighter went into 'a steep smoking dive straight ahead... [and] crashed into a hillside'. He attacked a second Yak but was warded off by the last one and, when McKee engaged it in a tight turning fight, Wurster took over the attack on the other. Wurster later recounted that he 'got good hits on the enemy aircraft [and] saw coolant draining from the aircraft and knew it wasn't going to fly for long'.

Eventually, the last Yak-9P escaped; both Kim Hi-Kiung and Tae Kuk-Sung bailed out and survived the engagement. However, the slower, lighter Yaks could turn a tighter circle and one of them evidently damaged Odell's Shooting Star. Attempting a forced landing at Taejon, the F-80C crashed 'while on base leg [turning onto final approach a mile short of the runway] his aircraft suddenly went straight ahead into the ground', killing the pilot.[120]

Late that afternoon, the 56th FAR scored another success, attacking one of the few remaining US Army observation planes. The L-4 was at 2,000ft just north of Taejon, spotting for American artillery bombarding approaching KPA armour. The dauntless pilot evaded the first attack by diving to low altitude, but the Yak's marksmanship was better on the second pass, cannon fire shattering the little airplane's wing, dropping it to the ground behind KPA lines. Both crewmen were injured in the crash, but were rescued by a ROKA patrol.[121]

The next day, about eight miles (13km) north of Taejon, another pair of Yak-9Ps tried to 'bounce' a flight of Shooting Stars (35th FBS/8th FBW). The Americans spotted the attacking Yaks and quickly split. As one Yak followed another of the accelerating jets, Capt Robert L. Lee circled in behind him and opened fire: 'The Yak started to fall apart, turned over on its back and went straight in.'[122] Meanwhile the second KPAF fighter tried to flee to the east, but the other pair of American jets quickly closed in. The Yak pulled up to evade the first firing pass, but then, as 1st Lt David H. Goodenough recalled, 'I climbed underneath and poured several rounds into the Yak's underside. For a few seconds, he continued to climb, then burst into flames, and started to spin toward the ground. The pilot managed to bail out.'[123]

In six days the 56th FAR's only operational squadron was virtually wiped out. From that day on, KPAF fighters no longer attempted taking part in frontline combat. Nevertheless, and despite valiant efforts by American and Australian air forces, KPA troops and tanks finally overwhelmed the US 24th Infantry Division at Taejon. In the four-day battle, the Americans suffered 3,602 soldiers killed and wounded and another 2,962 captured, including the division commander, Maj Gen William F. Dean. During this period the 56th FAR claimed to have shot down 18 USAF fighters and 29 bombers. For this 'accomplishment' the unit was awarded the honorific of 'Guards of Taejon', becoming the only 'guards regiment' in the KPAF order of battle.[124]

Destroyed/crashed Yak-9P 'Black 3' wreckage. (NARA)

The Final Beat Down

While F-80Cs were wiping out the single operational squadron of the 56th FAR in dogfights, FEAF Bomber Command was aggressively targeting KPAF airfields, striking first on 15 July with three Superfortresses bombing Kimpo AB, effectively cratering the runway after which escorting F-80s strafed and reported destroying 'two or three of [the] widely dispersed aircraft'.[125]

In preparation for the amphibious landing of the US Army's 1st Cavalry Division (actually a normal infantry unit with a legacy designation) at Pohang, and while the *Valley Forge's* Corsairs and Skyraiders were readied for CAS missions, eight F9F Panthers were sent to neutralize the KPAF fighters remaining at P'yongyang. At Heijo they found two rows of single-engine propeller aircraft parked about 30 yards apart. AAA fire was minimal so the F9Fs made several strafing passes, their 20mm cannon destroying another 14 aircraft and damaging 13 more.[126]

Two days later, once the amphibious landing proved unopposed, seven F9F Panthers (VF-51) raided Yonpo airfield, while CAG-5 Corsairs and Skyraiders bombed and rocketed the Wonsan oil refinery destroying 12,000 tons of petroleum products. At Yonpo 15 KPAF aircraft were reported destroyed, along with another three at the nearby Sondok auxiliary field.[127]

The most dramatic USAF counter-air strike was flown on 19 July when seven Shooting Stars (8th FBW) were launched after a FEAF RF-80A [8th TRS(PJ)] discovered the small dirt airfield at Pyonggang, just north of the 38th Parallel. Parked along the western edge of the airstrip were some two dozen KPAF aircraft – most likely Il-10s – camouflaged with tree branches. The F-80s arrived mid-afternoon, making repeated strafing runs on the undefended airfield. Fourteen North Korean aircraft – along with one twin-engine aircraft fancifully reported as a 'bomber' (probably an Li-2 or Yak-6 transport) – burst into flames and were destroyed; another seven were hit but did not burn, and were listed as damaged.[128]

Evidently, the deployment to Pyonggang was the 57th AAR's final attempt by them to bring their Il-10s into the battle, having regrouped and moved forward to support the KPA's final offensive, which was intended to crush the Pusan Pocket and oust American and ROK forces from the Korean Peninsula. Losing 21 aircraft destroyed and damaged on an isolated, primitive 'campaign field' effectively eliminated the *Shturmoviki* from the contest, resulting in the 57th AAR's withdrawal from combat. Next day, 14 Superfortresses raided against P'yongyang's Heijo and Onjong-ni airfields. Two Yaks rose to defend their bases, but were able to inflict only minor damage on one B-29. The Boeings badly cratered the runway and dispersal areas, knocking out the KPAF's main base for some time.[129]

Despite the nearly complete absence of North Korean aerial activity by this time, their bases continued to be targeted by FEAF any time aircraft were observed. On 4 August, Fifth AF F-51Ds (67th FBS/18th FBW) raided Kimpo after a formation of B-29s [19th BW(M)] bombing Seoul's railway yards reported seeing enemy fighters taking off. The marauding Mustangs strafed and bombed, claiming nine aircraft destroyed and another nine damaged. Two days later, P'yongyang was raided by the same unit, its pilots reporting another nine destroyed, plus three more damaged at Kimpo when they attacked it on the way home.[130]

Almost completely depleted of serviceable fighters, the KPAF's 56th 'Guards Taejon' FAR made a few sporadic, desultory appearances in August and September, most notably when a fighter (reported as an 'La-5') attempted to attack a B-29 (307th BG) on 15 August but was driven off by two bursts from the bomber's tailguns. On 1 September, DPRK propaganda reported that a Yak-9P shot down a ROKAF L-4 and F-51D and one other UNC aircraft, near Taegu. The only correlation with this claim is one ROKAF L-5, 'downed by enemy aircraft', with the loss of 1Lts Cheon Bong-Sik and Sin Jeong-Hyeon. During the B-29 raid on Sinuiju eight days later DPRK propaganda asserted that 'North Korean pilots... shot down four enemy bombers'. US loss data reports one B-29 shot down by AAA and another badly damaged.[131]

Having lost their ability to operate in the battlefield environment, the surviving detachments of the 57th AAR began a sporadic series of attacks on UN warships off the west coast of Korea. On the 23 August, two Il-10s led by Lt Ahn Hon-Zun – evidently flying from Kimpo – attacked the 1,825-ton RN destroyer HMS *Comus* (D20), some 85 miles west of Kunsan, South Korea. Their pilots spotted the destroyer at 0700hrs on patrol, steaming northeast towards Inch'on, and manoeuvred to attack from astern at 100ft altitude. Ahn strafed with cannon fire and dropped four 50kg bombs along the port side, holing the boiler room at the waterline and killing one sailor, while wounding another. *Comus* came hard starboard and opened fire with its 40mm Bofors and 20mm Oerlikons, spoiling the wingman's attack, his four bombs splashing into the water off the bow. This attacker escaped into the clouds while Ahn made a strafing re-attack to cover their withdrawal.[132]

Furthermore, DPRK propaganda reported that two enemy ships had been sunk the same day. One was reportedly a South Korean (former-USN) minesweeper attacked by a pair of Il-10s while two other *Shturmoviki* allegedly 'sank an American torpedo boat between the islands of Muchang and Ka-do near the mouth of the Yalu'. Pilots Ri Ra-Sun and Yang Chae-Hung were credited with the 'fatal attacks'. There is no correlation of damage to – much less losses of – USN or ROKN vessels in the US Navy's detailed chronology of the Korean War.[133]

With his air force virtually destroyed by the combined might of UN air power, in the last week of August, Wang 'threw in the towel', withdrawing almost all of his surviving aircraft – reported by Russian sources to be only 20 Il-10s and a single Yak-9P – to the small primitive ex-IJAAF airfield near Yanji, China, approximately 20 miles beyond the northeast corner of North Korea. One history reports that 'at least 152 [KPAF] aircraft were destroyed on the ground between the beginning of the war and September 1950'. Additionally FEAF and USN pilots were credited with destroying

Destroyed Il-10s wreckage at Wonsan. (Tom Cooper Collection)

Destroyed Yak-9P wreckage at Kimpo. (Australian War Memorial)

HMS *Comus* in drydock Kure harbour, 1950. (Australian War Memorial)

KPAF Yak-9P pilot Hero of DPRK Kim Gi-Ohk. (Tom Cooper Collection)

24 KPAF aircraft in aerial combat (plus two 'kills' claimed by bomber gunners).[134] Most critical to the KPAF was the fact that only six fighter pilots and 17 assault pilots survived their initial combat experience.[135]

The End of the Beginning

While the KPAF's role in the initial success of the North Korean invasion was not militarily significant compared with the KPA's operations – and certainly could not be compared with the USAF's activities – it demonstrated a persistent presence and until late July it remained an important consideration in FEAF's combat operations. The 57th AAR flew 94 sorties from 25 June to the end of August. Nine assault aircraft were lost in aerial combat to USAF fighters and upwards of 60 destroyed by the UN air arms' devastating airfield attacks.[136]

From 25 June through August, the 56th 'Guards Taejon' FAR flew 222 sorties and was credited with destroying 60 UN aircraft – including 11 B-29s – of which 45 were claimed in air combats, and the rest in strafing attacks. On 17 July, Heroes of the DPRK honours were awarded to eleven KPA officers and soldiers and to KPAF pilot Kim Gi-Ohk. Kim was recognized with this prestigious award by becoming the leading North Korean 'ace' credited with ten 'kills' (of an eventual 17), his first five victories being claimed in three engagements during 11 and 12 July. Squadron mates Lee Dong-Gyu – nicknamed the 'B-29 Nemesis' – was credited with downing eight American aircraft, including five B-29s during 11-14 July, and Lee Moon-Soon was also recognized as an 'ace', credited with shooting down two F-80s, two B-29s, and a 'B-17' from 25 June through 12 July.[137]

Intact Il-10 #44 in destroyed hangar at Kimpo. (NARA)

CHAPTER 4
REBUILDING THE KPAF – WITH A LITTLE HELP FROM THEIR FRIENDS

Little Korea in Big China

At the small town of Yanji, in Jilin (formerly Kirin), the northeastern-most province of China, the KPAF began rebuilding. Yanji had historically been a refuge for the Koreans whenever their peninsula was threatened from the east. Most recently it had been settled by large numbers of Koreans escaping the Japanese in the early part of the Twentieth Century. Even though they resided in Communist China, the Koreans were allowed to retain their national identity and language and were permitted to establish a Korean-language university, newspapers, and radio station. Consequently, the town and its surrounding countryside was a predominantly Korean self-governing prefecture within the new Communist nation and was the natural location for the KPAF to rebuild 'in exile'.

Major General Wang Yong moved his HQ to the airfield approximately ten miles east of town, even though he personally remained at his forward HQ at Kimpo AB – and here (now) Brigadier General (Brig Gen) Lee Whal began rebuilding the 'totally demoralized' air force through re-starting the flight training programme. Yanji's airfield was a primitive, former IJAAF facility, featuring a wide dirt runway, no hangars, and only five or six brick buildings along the north edge of the field. Available aircraft included the remains of the KPAF's training establishment, some 30 Yak-11/-18s and 15 Po-2 biplanes. While the ancient Po-2s would soon be used to form the basis of a 'night bomber squadron', they were supplemented by six additional Yak-18s and 22 Yak-11s delivered from the USSR. Primary training, using the Yak-18s, resumed at Yanji's satellite field about 30 miles (48km) northwest, while the Yak-11s were transferred to the large airfield at Jilin (another 125 miles northwest) to provide advanced training.[138]

Rebuilding the KPAF

To rebuild the KPAF's fighter force, at the end of August 1950, 'several dozen Koreans' (estimated to be 48 newly-minted 18-19 year old pilot training graduates) were shipped to Khorol'sk airfield in Primorsky Krai. There they were met by 12-14 IPs recruited from the V-VS 'Armavir Military Aviation School of Pilots' in Krasnodar Krai (between the Black and Caspian Seas) who formed a fighter training squadron to teach the North Koreans using Yak-9V two-seaters and old, obsolete Yak-3s. The course began in September and was frequently visited by Brig Gen Lee. As one of the Soviet IPs – retired Col V. N. Sinkevich – later related,

> 'He came to check on the preparation of his subordinates. The weakest pilots were kicked out of the training squadron and sent to a training squadron that prepared pilots on the Po-2, and they learned to drop bombs from this airplane... We taught the Koreans not only piloting skills, but also their combat application. During the entire time of training, we never had a single breakdown or crash. As a result, by the beginning of 1951, after five months of training, we had fully prepared the entire group of Korean pilots and handed them over to the KPAAF [*sic*]. On this occasion, a large banquet was organized in the school, after which the Korean pilots were shipped off to [Yanji] China'.[139]

Meanwhile, the 56th GFAR's withdrawal from combat opened the North Korean skies to unrelenting bombing attacks of P'yongyang, other major cities, and its industrial areas. The situation became so grim that Kim Il-Sung desperately appealed to Moscow to provide defensive air cover. Initially, Stalin approved the request and on 21 September the 147th IAD's 84th IAP was alerted for movement from its base near Voroshilov (now Ussuriysk), Primorsky Krai, and was ordered to deploy 40 Yak-9Ps via Yanji and Andong to P'yongyang. However, these orders were soon changed and the 32nd IAD's 304th IAP (with 42 La-9s) from Spassk airfield was substituted, with a scheduled arrival date of 3 October.

Already *en route*, the 84th IAP's journey evidently ended at Yanji where it began providing training to KPAF's new pilots on the Yak-9Ps before transferring its equipment to the 56th GFAR. This allowed the North Koreans to re-establish their premier fighter unit with two 12-aircraft squadrons. Near the end of October, Stalin's military envoy to Mao Zedong, General Semyon E. Zakharov, informed his chief that the KPAF now had two dozen operational Yak-9Ps and 26 qualified pilots.[140]

Meanwhile, the 304th IAP's ground echelon – maintenance technicians, airbase personnel, radio technicians and four radar units, an AAA battalion (16 guns), fuel stocks and munitions for 15 missions – arrived at P'yongyang by train on 25 September. By this time, however, the UN advances across the 38th Parallel threatened the deployment and on 7 October they were, 'evacuated from the territory of Korea'.[141]

Arriving at Jilin, the 304th IAP brought with them 40 Lavochkin La-9s and a pair of La-9UTI two-seat, dual-control trainers. Since the KPAF had now exhausted the USSR's supply of Yak-9Ps in the Far East, the 304th was ordered to train the 'horseless' Korean fighter pilots on the new type. Because of the limited number of *spahrkas* (Russian slang for 'twins' [an abbreviation of *spahrennoye oopravleniye* – meaning 'dual-controls'] as they called the two-seat La-9UTIs) the class sizes were small: the first class consisting of eight KPAF students, three of whom were veteran Yak-9P pilots with combat experience.[142]

The Korean students were scheduled to receive 17 hours of instruction (two hours dual and 15 solo) and graduate on 10 October, followed by a second group scheduled to graduate 20 days later. However, the 304th IAP commander soon reported that the La-9, 'differs from the Yak-9 in that it is a much more technically complex machine during takeoff and landing [therefore, the training of KPAF students] has gone extremely slowly'. In fact, during the first week the North Koreans wrecked one La-9UTI and two single-seaters. Consequently, the training completion dates were extended to 25 October for the first group and 25 November for the second.[143]

These two classes provided the cadre to establish a 28-aircraft La-9 fighter regiment, designated the 58th FAR (this number having originally been used for the KPAF's flight training regiment). The new unit comprised two 10-aircraft squadrons, with eight aircraft (including the surviving La-9UTI two-seater) for training and reserve, and was initially based at Yanji. According to NSA's communications intelligence intercepts (COMINT; 'Project Acorn'), following operational activation in the winter of 1950-51, by March the next year the 58th FAR was deployed to Fengcheng, about 28 miles (45km) north-northwest of Andong, to provide 'back-up' for the 56th GFAR when it was deployed forward to Sinuiju.[144]

Much less is known about the reestablishment of the KPAF's assault aviation arm. Evidently the KPAF's 20 surviving Il-10s were only suited for training and, along with a few Yak-18s, were moved to Fengcheng, where training resumed, bringing the total combat-qualified Il-10 pilots up from 17 to 25 by the end of October. At that time, in his communication with Stalin, Zakharov reported that the KPAF had sufficient qualified pilots to re-establish an assault aviation regiment 'but up to now there are no planes for them'. This was accompanied by a formal request from Col A. Petrachev, the Soviet air force advisor to the KPAF, for '25 Il-10 planes'. During the next two months, 40 Il-10s – plus eight UIl-10s – were supplied to the KPAF, allowing the reestablishment the 57th AAR as a combat unit. Most of these came from the 537th ShAP, which in December 1950 flew 26 of its new Il-10s to Andong for delivery to the KPAF assault aviation unit. The resurrected 57th AAR formed the basis of the 11th Assault Aviation Division (11th AAD) which was established at Fengcheng with 33 operational *Shturmoviki* under Col Kim Tal-Hion.[145]

For the long-term expansion of the KPAF and its combat capabilities, in mid-November Kim requested the USSR to train 119 student pilots on jet fighters and twin-engine bombers, 120 bomber aviation technicians (navigators, bombardiers, radio operators and gunners), and 30 assault aircrew members (radio operator/gunners). Additionally, to relieve KPAF instructors for combat duty, he requested that the 170 student pilots recently inducted into the Korean training program, who would complete their academic training by the end of the year, be sent to the USSR for their flight training. Furthermore, he sought to have the 200-300 'Korean students [recently] sent to the USSR for education' be recruited as pilot candidates.[146]

North Korean and Chinese pilots inspect a Yak-11 at Yanji, PRC. (Tom Cooper)

KPAF pilot and a group of North Korean students in front of a Yak-18 trainer. (Charles Euripides Collection)

La-9 Training. (Albert Grandolini Collection)

This Il-10 (White 44) was captured nearly intact at P'yongyang Heijo airfield. (USAF via Larry Davis)

On 20 November Stalin responded, agreeing to train sufficient Korean pilots and aircrew to create two regiments of MiG-15s and another of Tu-2 bombers. The MiG-15 pilots would be trained 'at one of our jet divisions in Manchuria. After the preparation of the pilots, the appropriate number of MiG-15 aircraft will be delivered'. To establish the bomber regiment Stalin directed Kim to send 40 pilots and 120 aviation technician trainees to 'the Korean school we have [established] in the Far East Maritime Region. The materiel, Tu-2 aircraft for the bomber regiment, will also be given'. The bomber crewmembers were initially sent to Vozzhayevka airfield in the Amur Oblast, just north of Manuchuria, for specialized training in navigation, bombardment, radio operation, and aerial gunnery. Upon completion of their specialized courses, the crewmembers were sent to Khorol'sk for training on Tu-2s.[147]

Meanwhile, Back at Kimpo

While the rest of the KPAF withdrew to Yanji to reconstitute, a small contingent of *Shturmoviki* (two to four serviceable aircraft) remained at Kimpo AB. In the second week of September, Fifth AF launched a systematic campaign to eliminate any remaining vestiges of the KPAF's ability to threaten the dramatic amphibious counter-attack that MacArthur had planned. While FEAF bombers blasted Korean railways, bridges, tunnels and other choke-points to 'isolate the battlefield', UNC fighters ranged across the KPA rear areas, flying armed reconnaissance sweeps over all known North Korean airfields. On 11 September a formation of fighters destroyed one Yak-9P and a second, unidentified aircraft (probably another Yak) at Sinmak. Next day roving USAF fighters discovered four Yak-9Ps at Heijo airbase being camouflaged by their ground crews. Three were destroyed and the fourth damaged. However, the airfield attacks failed to eliminate the 57th AAR's small detachment at Kimpo.[148]

USS *Rochester*, the target of the Il-10 attacks. (US Navy)

On the morning of 15 September, the first of six battalions of the USMC's 1st and 5th Regiments came ashore at Wolmi-do Island, just off the port of Inch'on, with the rest, along with the 1st Korean Marine Corps (KMC) regiment, landing along the waterfront at Inch'on that afternoon. The naval bombardment, air strikes, and the 1st Marines destroyed the two 76.2mm artillery batteries of the KPA's 918th Coastal Artillery Regiment and drove the 2,000-man 226th Naval Infantry Regiment from their prepared defences, this unit's various disorganized elements retiring towards Kimpo AB with 25 per cent casualties.[149]

The next day the North Koreans began organizing a defence centred on holding the airfield against the approaching Marines. As the senior North Korean officer west of the Han River, the KPAF's Maj Gen Wang established the *ad hoc* 1st Air Force Division, consisting of Maj Kung's 877th AFU, Col Han's 107th Security Regiment, and the survivors of the 226th Naval Infantry Regiment – a force totalling some 3,000 men, but these were widely dispersed in small groups with little or no communication between them, or with Wang's HQ on the airfield.[150]

Early on 17 September, Wang launched his air force's second maritime strike mission using two of the Il-10s that remained operational at Kimpo. Just before dawn, the pair took off and, at 0555hrs, located the line of cruisers anchored in the channel off Wolmi-do Island, positioned to provide naval gunfire support for the Marines ashore. After flying from north to south down the line of anchored ships at 1,000ft, the leading Il-10 turned and made a shallow diving attack on the USS *Rochester* (CA 124), the flagship of 'Operation Chromite's' naval commander, VAdm Arthur D. Struble.

Two bombs were dropped, one of them glancing off the cruiser's aircraft handling crane on the stern, both exploding in the water. The second attacker also dropped two bombs, both falling wide. The two KPAF aircraft then turned and strafed HMS *Jamaica* with 23mm cannons and were greeted with anti-aircraft (AA) fire. One RN sailor was killed and another two wounded but the second attacker was shot down, the aircraft banking left and flashing across the bow to impact the water about 30 yards beyond the ship.[151]

Meanwhile, the advancing 5th US Marines and 1st KMC regiments approached Kimpo, investing the airfield on three sides. The situation was so dire that Han abandoned his 107th Security Regiment and fled across the river to Seoul. During the early morning hours of 18 September – from 0300hrs through dawn – Kung's 877th AFU launched four sporadic uncoordinated counter-attacks against the 5th Marines. Attacking piecemeal and without supporting artillery or heavy weapons, the futile charges were annihilated, with 395 KPAF troops – including Kung – being killed. Wang and his few surviving air force members evacuated across the Han River, leaving Kimpo AB to the US Marines who reported it secured at 1000hrs.[152]

On the airbase was discovered the remains of at least seven Il-10s and six Yak-9Ps.[153] Five of each were totally destroyed, but two Il-10s were relatively undamaged and repairable, and enough usable components were found to cobble together a flyable Yak-9P. These three 'trophies' were dismantled and shipped to the USA where they were rebuilt and repaired, and were examined and technically evaluated by the Cornell University's (formerly Curtiss Aircraft Corporation's) Aeronautics Laboratory, then sent to Wright-Patterson AFB, Ohio, for flying tests and operational exploitation.[154]

USMC troops inspecting one of five destroyed Il-10 at Kimpo AB. (USMC)

New Il-10s taxiing out for take-off. (Albert Grandolini Collection)

This fully intact Il-10 was found by US troops at P'yongyang's Heijo airfield. (USAF via Larry Davis)

'Guards Taejon' Return to Battle

Having withdrawn its fighters into China, the KPAF abdicated air supremacy over the entire Korean Peninsula to the UN air forces. Meanwhile, on the ground the stunning success of General MacArthur's 'Operation Chromite' suddenly and dramatically reversed the North Koreans' fortunes, the catastrophe being consummated with the 'breakout' from the Pusan Perimeter by the US Eighth Army. Together the two calamitous – for the North Koreans, anyway – operations resulted in the precipitous collapse of the KPA.[155]

When counter-attacking UN forces crossed the 38th Parallel into North Korea on 7 October – and showed no signs of halting until the DPRK was utterly destroyed – the leadership of the newly formed People's Republic of China (PRC) began organizing a massive military intervention, sending the 13th Army Group (initially twelve infantry and three artillery divisions) to their Northeast Military Region. Euphemistically called the 'Chinese People's Volunteer Army' (CPVA), its commanders were critically concerned about their total lack of air cover, especially in the face of the Americans' complete dominance of North Korean skies.[156]

The CPVA commanders were well aware that their own air force was wholly unprepared to participate in the series of offensives that were being planned to drive the UNC forces out of North Korea. At this time, the PLAAF consisted of only four air regiments totalling 141 Soviet-built fighters, bombers and assault aircraft based near Nanjing and, at Beijing, a regiment-size *ad hoc* unit of approximately 30 Lavochkin La-9 fighters about to begin conversion to MiG-9 jets.[157] All five of these units were undergoing further training with Soviet units in order to expand them into air divisions, so they were not available or even prepared for combat duties.[158]

Consequently, PRC's Chairman Mao Zedong appealed to Stalin for further assistance. By this time the USSR had two fighter divisions in China – the 50th IAD and 151st GvIAD – totalling 204 MiG-15s. Beginning in August the 50th IAD was stationed at Xiansilipu on the Liaodong Peninsula to guard against possible USN and RN/FAA air attacks against the Soviet naval base at Dalian. That same month the 151st GvIAD began arriving at two airfields near Shenyang to train the PLAAF's new 3rd and 4th Air Divisions (ADs) on the MiG-15, scheduled to start in late October.[159]

However, Stalin – having already changed his mind about providing air support for the crumbling KPA in North Korea – was afraid to directly confront the seemingly victorious Americans and agreed only to protect strategic Chinese assets – airfields, bridges, and crucial Sup'ung hydroelectric powerplant on the Yalu River – and the important railroad (RR) lines leading into North Korea. On 19 October – the same day that UNC forces entered P'yongyang – Mao Zedong ordered the CPVA, now heavily reinforced to 30 divisions, to cross the Yalu into North Korea and prepare for counter-offensive operations, with or without Soviet air support. At the last minute, Stalin consented and the Soviet General Staff ordered the 151st GvIAD to provide air cover 'for the troops of the PLA's 13th Army Group... [but do] not fly across the state border with the Korean People's Democratic Republic.'[160]

In fact, the only air cover available for CPVA and KPA forces south of the Yalu was the KPAF's reconstituted 56th GFAR. Near the end of October, the 'Guards Taejon' deployed to the ex-IJAAF airfield of Langtao, 12 miles (20km) west of Andong, near the mouth of the Yalu River. Andong was connected by two strategic road and railway bridges to Sinuiju, North Korea, where Kim Il-Sung had withdrawn his government. The massive 3,085ft (940m) long Andong-Sinuiju bridges were two of only six spanning the Yalu[161] and were critical for funnelling CPVA forces and their supplies into North Korea. To protect them, the old, former Japanese airfield at Sinuiju had been rebuilt into a modern airbase, complete with protected aircraft revetments.[162]

On 1 November, the 56th GFAR deployed 22 Yak-9Ps across the Yalu to Sinuiju airfield to resume combat operations. While the 151st GvIAD launched two four-ships of MiG-15s each from Anshan and Liaoyang airfields (28th and 72nd GvIAPs)[163] to cover the Andong-Sinuiju bridges, the KPAF launched two four-ships of Yak-9Ps from Sinuiju to attack American aircraft bombing and strafing CPVA and KPA units near Ansui.[164]

About 15 miles south of Sinuiju, near Yangsi, the two KPAF formations found USAF B-26s (730th BS[L]/452nd BW[L]), controlled by a T-6G 'Mosquito' FAC (6147th Tactical Air Control Squadron), and split to attack both. Fortunately a flight of F-51s (67th FBS/18th FBW) was around, strafing a convoy of oxcarts moving north.

Capt Alma Flake reported,

> 'During a low-altitude mission right below the Yalu, four Yaks in elements of two crossed the river on a southerly heading, just east of our position. Their movement was called out by [wingman 1st Lt Harold] Ausman. I ordered [him] to climb at maximum power and assume combat formation. Almost immediately the Yaks began a diving attack [on the B-26s]. As we came around behind the lead Yak, I fired a short burst and he broke to his left and down. I proceeded to engage, continuing a maximum right turn, and lost sight of him for just a moment. He was well below my position and, looking down, I picked him up again and manoeuvred to attack. It was evident that he had lost sight of me because he continued in a gentle climbing turn. This enabled me to gain a favourable firing position from behind and slightly inside his [turning] circle.
>
> 'At a slightly overtaking speed, and estimating a range of about 600ft, I pulled the trigger. Almost immediately the Yak began trailing smoke, and a few seconds later the pilot levelled the aircraft off and bailed out. The aircraft spiralled down and crashed. The pilot had a good "chute" and probably survived. The remaining three Yaks escaped back north of the river... diving [to just] above the ground and crossing the river before our element, in hot pursuit, could catch up.'[165]

Meanwhile, approaching the T-6G Texan, the other formation of Yak-9Ps spotted two other Mustangs strafing the convoy of oxcarts on a nearby road. Capt Robert D. Thresher later stated that while watching his wingman make his strafing attack,

> 'All of a sudden these big orange balls were snapping across my wing, and I yelled 'Flak'! Just as I got that out, a blur whizzed by me, and at that instant I realised that my problem wasn't ground fire, but a real fast Yak fighter! I immediately

initiated evasive action by making a hard left turn in the hope of hooking up with my wingman, but alas he was on the tail of another Yak. My bogie [unidentified aircraft] had disappeared, and I knew he was up there in the sun, but didn't know where. Suddenly, the 'Mosquito' pilot yelled, 'He's on your tail!' I turned my head in time to catch the winking flashes of the Yak's 12.7mm machine guns and his 20mm cannon. I went into a sharp turn and the blood drained out of my head, causing me to "grey out".

'In my panic, I knew the Yak could turn inside of me, but I held the stick over. Rolling out, I observed that the enemy pilot had gone across the top of my Mustang, and taking advantage of his speed, he had pulled [up] into a tight loop. Now he was above me and that put him in good position! I swung hard left to pass directly beneath him and keep him from coming out of the loop right on my tail! He was watching me, and he must have held his stick back too long, because he stalled out. He spun all the way down from 6,000ft.

'The Yak pilot recovered, and for a split second I thought I would tighten my turn and jump him while he was floundering out of his spin, but he snapped his fighter over and got his speed back in seconds – so much so that he started a steep climb... I knew he was unnerved because when he got to the top of [yet another] loop, his aircraft wobbled somewhat. I added throttle and waited him out. He fell unevenly this time, and I cut wide for a second. At the bottom of the loop he recovered and began his pull-up, but luckily my timing was good.

'I wrapped up my Mustang, and while still in my turn, I began firing. I saw my tracers converge and pour into his wing. Then a puff of blue smoke spouted from his wing. He wobbled slightly and fell out of his turn. Slowly, he rolled over and went into a long glide. The aircraft crashed into the ground with the pilot still in the cockpit.'[166]

In the meantime, back at Sinuiju, an RF-80A pilot (8th TRS[PJ]) reported '15 Yaks parked in revetments' and Fifth AF immediately dispatched an attack by a dozen Shooting Stars (51st FIW). Attacking the target was extremely challenging because the airfield's layout paralleled the Yalu, only a short distance from the river and the revetments faced north, forcing the Americans to attack from that direction. Forbidden to fly into PRC airspace, the Shooting Stars were squeezed between their target and the river and had to roll-in over the river exposing their bellies to Chinese AA guns lining the northern shore. Consequently one F-80C was lost, its pilot killed, and success was limited. Soviet sources report 'one Yak-9 was burned and three were put out of action, but it is possible to restore them'. Finding themselves still vulnerable to enemy airfield attacks, Koreans withdrew the 16 surviving fighters to Langtao, back inside the safety of 'the Manchurian sanctuary'.[167]

The next day the 'Guards Taejon' tried again, sending a four-ship formation against the Mustangs (12th and 67th FBS/18th FBW) bombing, strafing and rocketing Communist troops just south of Sinuiju. Once again Capt Alma Flake and 'Ace' Ausman were involved, Ausman spotting the four Yak-9Ps as one rolled in to attack 1st Lt James Glessner, leading the other pair of Mustangs. Flake recalled:

The following day, near the same area, we were again attacked by four Yak fighters. This time the combat lasted longer because it was pursued more vigorously by both sides. The pilot I fought was obviously highly trained and eager to engage. After we passed each other in a head-on pass, I pulled up almost vertically in order to gain altitude, while slowing my speed to quicken my turn. At my next sight of him he was above me and his nose was almost on me. Closing so fast, I figured he would probably be firing before I could get into a position to attack him. Rolling inverted, I headed straight down, with a most uneasy feeling that he was close behind me.

'I cannot recall the details of the various gyrations that ensued. Knowing that I could not turn with him, I felt my life depended on gaining the speed and altitude advantage. I used every ounce of power and speed of my Mustang to overcome his superior manoeuvrability. It ended in a series of vertical moves at 9,000-10,000ft before we headed straight back down again. He would hold the Yak in a vertical climb until it appeared to stop in mid-air, fall backwards and spin out. I would gain on him at the top of the climb, but just as I got in range, he would tumble back and you cannot hit a spinning target.

'After three or four of such manoeuvres I apparently got in some hits as he approached his peak again. He seemed to break out of his climb prematurely and head straight down. He pulled out very low over rolling hills and headed north. I was able to reach a good position behind him. As I fired, his right wing appeared to pull away at the root. The Yak rolled abruptly and crashed, spreading flames and debris over a large area.'[168]

Meanwhile, a second Yak-9P turned in behind Ausman. Glessner engaged him:

'I finally caught him near the ground. I climbed within 100 feet of his tail and let him have it. Debris was flying off of him. He peeled off and spun down a couple of times, then he took off for the border. I went after him again. Before I could get at him, he did a wingover and bailed out. I saw his aircraft crash.'[169]

These losses were 'balanced' by the DPRK propaganda broadcast on 5 November, claiming that (then) Maj Kim Tal-Hion led eight 'North Korean fighters' that reportedly attacked 20 American aircraft south of the Yalu and shot down five B-26s and a B-29 without loss. This seems to be a rather contrived announcement since Kim Tal-Hion commanded the 57th AAR at the time, making the 'North Korean fighters' Il-10 assault aircraft. Actually, three B-26s (730th BS[L]/452nd BW[L]) were reportedly attacked by four Yak-9Ps, which damaged two of the Invaders.[170]

Finally, on 6 November, six Yak-9Ps took off from Langtao and headed east, climbing for altitude to 'bounce' three F-51Ds (67th FBS/18th FBW) flying an armed reconnaissance east of Sinuiju. The American flight leader, Capt Howard I. Price, recalled:

'On this mission... Yaks came up at us from east of the Yalu River, my wingman, 1st Lt George Olsen, calling them out.

They were climbing up from our 'nine o'clock' position and there were six of them in no specific formation. I turned into them so I could identify them as enemy aircraft, and although I could not see any insignia I knew they were Yak-9s. I called out to the two members of my flight, "They're Yaks! Let's get them!"

'Lt Olsen and I dived on the closest Yak. He saw us and panicked, snap-rolling and diving away. I picked up on the one closest to him. He started to turn sharply left, away from the other aircraft, and also snap rolled. I followed him down for a few seconds, and while he was turning I clobbered him. Pieces flew off, his engine quit and the pilot bailed out. I didn't see where he landed, as I was busy swinging round trying to get onto the tail of another Yak. All I saw was [1st Lt Harry] Reynolds chasing a lone aircraft, which meant the others must have dived for the ground.

'The Yaks were much slower than our F-51s and as I joined up with Reynolds he told me over the radio that his guns had jammed. The Yak was trying to head north to get back across the Yalu to safety. I slid down and across as Reynolds pulled off. I fired each of my rockets, trying to save the [machine gun] ammo. Each rocket missed – one went over and one under the Yak's wings. I then lined up slightly below the enemy fighter and fired my .50-cals, hitting the Yak in the cockpit and engine. I fired three or four bursts, as I remembered the Yaks were supposed to be armoured. All of a sudden bluish flames started coming out of the engine. At the same time as the fighter nosed over, all of its guns started firing. The aeroplane was soon in an almost vertical dive, and I think one of my rounds must have killed the pilot for he made no effort to pull out. I watched him all the way down to where he hit the ground close to Sinuiju.'[171]

Having lost ten Yak-9Ps to USAF Mustangs in aerial combat and from F-80C strafing attacks – and with no American aircraft shot down in return – on 7 November the 56th GFAR was once again withdrawn from combat. It is believed that in one of these air battles ace Lee Dong-Gyu was shot down – reportedly in a dogfight on 14 November 1950. Because there were no encounters reported on that date, it is possible he was wounded or injured in one of the above actions and died on that date. Replacing him was Baek Gi-Rak, who was credited with five victories over Sinuiju and was awarded 'Hero of the DPRK' honours. In January fresh graduates from the Soviet fighter training programme at Khorol'sk, along with ten new Lavochkins, were used to rebuild the 'Guards Taejon' back to a strength of 20 Yak-9Ps and La-9s.[172]

Coupled with FEAF's and the US Navy's increased and effective bombing of the vital Andong-Sinuiju bridges, the withdrawal of the 56th GFAR prompted the Chinese to urge the Soviets to provide increased air cover for the Yalu River. Stalin's acquiescence on this point resulted in committing two more MiG-15 divisions (303rd and 324th IADs) to the Korean War, thus initiating the two-and-a-half year long aerial duel in what became known to history as 'MiG Alley'.[173]

Line up of Yak-9Ps, probably at Yanji. (Albert Grandolini Collection)

KPAF Yak-9P pilot Ah Bong-Joon, who claimed three kills over Chongju, between 1 and 5 November 1950. (Tom Cooper Collection)

The Andong-Sinuiju bridges under attack by US Navy aircraft. (US Navy)

The Rise of 'Bedcheck Charlie'

While the rest of the KPAF was being reorganized and Soviet training programmes established, one small unpretentious element of the North Korean air arm started taking the fight to the enemy. Having seen his air force prove itself ineffective in traditional, conventional ground attack operations, the commander of the transport and liaison 'Mixed Aviation Regiment', Pak Den-Sik, initiated a seemingly insignificant form of aerial guerrilla warfare, using slow, clumsy Po-2 trainers as night bombers.[174]

Patterning their operations after Soviet WW2 'night heckler' missions, Pak Den-Sik's 'liaison squadron' began flying nocturnal harassment sorties against UNC ground forces and airbases in October. Because of the lack of night flying training and low experience levels, the first few weeks of operations proved very costly. Russian archival records report that by 1 November the squadron lost five Po-2s in takeoff/landing accidents and four more failed to return from their night bombing or training missions. On that date the unit had six Po-2s and 14 pilots remaining and the KPAF formally requested another ten aircraft from the USSR to allow it to support the CPVA's planned 'Second Phase Offensive' (25 November to 9 December)[175] with night bombing attacks. However, according to Russian sources, only half this number were provided.[176]

Wrecked KPAF Spruce biplane 'night bomber'. (USAF)

KPAF Po-2 in Flight. (Tom Cooper Collection)

While these nocturnal operations had been going on for weeks, the first real success was on 19 November when, just before daybreak, a pair of single engine aircraft attacked the Fifth AF forward airfield at Sunch'ŏn and Eighth Army emplacements along the Ch'ongch'on River. Six days later, two squadrons of F-51D Mustangs (8th FBG's 35th and 36th FBSs) arrived at P'yongyang's Heijo airfield, deploying forward to provide more responsive CAS for the advancing UNC ground forces. They immediately became a prime target for the KPAF's nascent 'night bombers'.

At 0300hrs on 28 November, a Po-2LSh dropped a string of small 20kg (44lb) fragmentation bombs across the ramp of the 36th FBS, killing one American and damaging eleven of the unit's Mustangs. By this time the UNC forces were falling back steadily before the sudden and massive CPVA onslaught and the KPAF's night raiders hit the airfield twice more before the 8th FBG evacuated five days later; three of the damaged Mustangs had to be destroyed and abandoned in the retreat. Meanwhile, on 1 December, Po-2s raided P'yongyang's nearby Onjong-ni airfield (K-22) damaging a C-47 transport.[177]

Subsequently, the 1st Night Bomber Battalion (as it was now called) mainly used its Po-2s in support of the KPA's II Corps which was advancing through the central highlands against the ROK III Corps. During the first two weeks of January – as the CPVA recaptured Seoul and Kimpo AB – Pak Den-Sik's unit flew at least nine night missions against their South Korean brothers. While little material damage was done, the Po-2s preyed effectively upon the psyche of their enemy, causing much alarm among the retreating, already fearful troops.[178]

CHAPTER 5
RETURN TO BATTLE

With the withdrawal of the 56th 'Guards Taejon' FAR from combat for the second time, the only air cover remaining for the CPVA was the Soviet 151st GvIAD, flying MiG-15s from Anshan and Liaoyang. During the first three weeks of November the Soviet MiGs, flying with PLAAF markings, regularly patrolled high above the Yalu River, intercepting and destroying two USAF Superfortresses.[179] However, they did not fare so well in fighter-versus-fighter combat, losing three of their number to straight-wing USAF Shooting Stars and USN Panthers. By the time the massive CPVA (36 divisions comprising the Ninth and Thirteenth 'Group Armies') began their overwhelming 'Second Phase Offensive' against US, ROK, and other UN forces on 25 November, the 151st GvIAD was withdrawn from combat to be restructured and resume teaching the PLAAF's new 3rd and 4th ADs on the MiG-15.[180]

About this time the reconstruction of Langtao airfield at Andong was completed as a jet-capable airbase, the original ex-IJAAF aerodrome's two gravel runways being replaced by a

6,000ft (1,800m) concrete one for jet operations, along with a hard-surfaced perimeter taxiway and revetments. As the 151st GvIAD returned to training duties, the 50th IAD arrived from Dalian and, after having KPAF markings affixed to their newer, more advanced MiG-15bis, the division's 29th GvIAP deployed to Langtao on 3 December, joined by the 177th IAP later in the month. This was the unit that first met the newly-arrived American F-86 Sabres (4th FIW) in combat, losing three MiGs shot down and a fourth DBR while only downing one of their adversaries, thus setting the scoring trend for two and a half years' of dogfighting.[181]

Following the CPVA's successful recapture of P'yongyang on 4 December, Mao Zedong ordered the Chinese and North Korea armies to establish a joint HQ. PLA General Peng Dehuai was appointed overall commander and political commissar, with KPA General Kim Ung as his deputy. The next month Mao directed the PLAAF commander, General Liu Yalou, to form a joint air HQ along similar lines to oversee and coordinate combat operations, engineering, logistics, and political functions of the two air arms. Established at Langtao airfield on 15 March, General Liu Zhen – commander of the CPVA's nearly non-existent air force (CPVAAF) – was appointed as commander with KPAF commander Wang Yong as his deputy; however, for the next six months Wang kept his HQ at P'yongyang, making communication, coordination, and his role in the joint command problematic.[182]

Because Mao had ordered priority be given to directly supporting CVPA troops, a forward HQ was established at P'yongyang under General Chang Qiankun, the PLAAF deputy commander, to oversee a large scale airfield 'rehabilitation' programme and logistics build-up. In addition to restoring to operations eight original KPAF airfields – with the KPA's VI Corps providing soldiers as labourers – six new airfield sites were chosen in northern Korea.[183] On these, three CPVA infantry divisions, five engineer regiments, and 1,000 civilian labourers began work in March. The Soviets supplied 36,000 pieces of PSP (pierced steel planking) and the Chinese shipped in 30,000 tons of concrete and, after some two million man-days of effort, four airfields were operational by the end of May.[184]

Soviet mechanics preparing a MiG-15 for flight at Langtao airfield, Andong. (Tim Callaway Collection)

At the time the joint air HQ was established, the PLAAF had only one Tu-2, an Il-10, one La-11, and five MiG-15 regiments operational, totalling some 200 combat aircraft. These were in the process of being expanded into five air divisions and, although they were assigned to the command on 25 April, they remained in training and would not be ready for combat until autumn.[185] The KPAF's contribution was the 56th GFAR and 57th AAD stationed at Sinuiju, but Kim Il-Sung refused to grant the joint HQ any authority over his units and all plans for employing them had to be negotiated between Beijing and P'yongyang.[186]

Even worse, the Chinese-led joint air HQ was given no authority over the collocated Soviet fighter divisions. Anticipating Peng's massive 'Second Phase Offensive', on 15 November 1950 the Soviet Armed Forces General Staff directed Col-Gen Kravoskiy, commanding the air forces in the FEMD, to establish an independent fighter aviation corps, the *64th Istrebitelniy Aviatsionnyi Korpus* ('Independent Aviation Corps' or IAK), with two MiG-15 divisions. Initially these were the 50th IAD (64 MiG-15bis), deployed to Langtao, and the 151st GvIAD (now 123 MiG-15s – one had been lost on a test flight) headquartered at Shenyang. The former 151st GvIAD commander, (now) Lieutenant-General (Lt-Gen) Ivan V. Belov, was given command of the new fighter corps.

Belov's mission was to 'protect political, administrative and economic centres from air strikes and American aerial reconnaissance, as well as [protect] industrial objects, railroad junctions, bridges, force concentrations, the bridges over the Yalu River, and electrical power stations in the Andong area'. To do so, Soviet pilots were allowed to fly and engage enemy

Two 4th FIW F-86A Sabres take off at Suwon AB, ROK, in April 1951. (NMUSAF)

aircraft over northern Korea, but were prohibited from flying south of the 'P'yongyang-Wonsan line' or over the sea. This was intended to prevent the capture of any downed Soviet MiG pilots, thus insuring some measure of 'plausible deniability' for Stalin's regime.[187]

With the 50th IAD due to depart in February – after it had completed its year-long 'tour of duty' in China (which it began as the 106th IAD at Shanghai) – and the 151st GvIAD committed to training the new PLAAF MiG-15 units, Belov was sent two of the V-VS's best MiG-15 units for this new air defence mission. One was the Soviets' premier jet fighter unit, the 324th IAD, commanded by three-time HSU winner Col Ivan N. Kozhedub, the Allies' highest scoring WW2 ace with 62 victories. This two-regiment division travelled by train to Dongfeng airfield in Jilin Province (about 120 miles/193km northeast of Shenyang), arriving in mid-December. Quickly assembling their 65 early-model MiG-15s, they began three months of intensive combat training at Anshan (about 57 miles/92km southwest of Shenyang) in preparation for meeting the Americans over the Yalu.[188]

Arriving six weeks later was (now) Maj-Gen Georgiy A. Lobov's 303rd IAD, a crack three-regiment division transferred from the Primorsky Krai with 91 of the more advanced MiG-15bis. Alerted for movement on 23 January, the division travelled to Shenyang where its pilots also underwent three months of combat training. The 324th IAD moved to Andong's Langtao airfield during the first three days in April and the 303rd IAD deployed its first regiment to the nearby, newly completed Dadonggou airfield (called Tatung-kao – or more colloquially Miaogou/Myaogou or Manpo – by the Russians), on 8 May.[189]

Back into Battle Again

Meanwhile, in January 1951, the rebuilt 56th GFAR and 57th AAR deployed to Sinuiju to resume combat operations. Totalling some 38 La-9s, Yak-9Ps, and Il-10s (according to USAF Intelligence) the two regiments were reportedly grouped together as the 1st CAD,[190] commanded by Brig Gen Lee. As the KPAF's new main operating base, Sinuiju had undergone extensive repair and improvement with the construction of new fuel, supply, and ammunition dumps and was now defended by a 'bristling array of anti-aircraft artillery'.[191]

The 1st CAD was stationed at Sinuiju ostensibly to provide air support for the CPVA's 'Third Phase Offensive' (December 31 to January 14) that recaptured Seoul on 4 January and began pushing deep into South Korea. Although KPAF aircraft were not seen over the frontlines in daylight, the ground offensive initially enjoyed great success, forcing the UNC's Fifth AF to evacuate many of its units from their threatened bases, thereby allowing the KPAF a freedom of action that it had not experienced since the previous July.[192]

Taking advantage of its renewed freedom of action, in mid-January the 56th GFAR further deployed (or at least staged) its Yak-9Ps forward to Heijo airfield to defend North Korea's now 'liberated' capital. Two KPAF pilots, 'Hero Ong' and 'Hero Kim' (most likely Kim Gi-Ohk), were featured daily by the DPRK radio propaganda commentators who saluted their bravery and audacity in taking their Yaks into the air 'to chase American aircraft away from P'yongyang'. Indeed, on 15 January one of them attacked a flight of B-26 Invaders (452nd BW[L]), but failed to score any hits.[193]

Once Peng's 'Third Phase Offensive' spent itself, Lieutenant General (Lt Gen) Matthew B. Ridgeway, commanding US Eighth Army, launched 'Operation Thunderbolt' – the first in a series of limited counter-offensives designed to regain lost territory, liberate Seoul again, and push the 'front lines' back to approximate the 38th Parallel. On 23 January, two days prior to initiating the operation, Fifth AF launched massive strikes against Sinuiju and Heijo in order to establish air superiority over northern Korea.[194]

At Sinuiju, two squadrons of F-84Es (27th FEG's 522nd and 524th FESs) attacked aircraft and hangars with rockets, fragmentation bombs, and strafing while the third (523rd FES) flew 'high cover'. The Soviet 29th GvIAP countered by launching 20 MiG-15s from Langtao. The MiGs intercepted the raiders after the first eight Thunderjets attacked and a large dogfight ensued. One MiG-15bis was shot down (pilot KIA) and another damaged (of three claimed destroyed) while no F-84Es were lost (of six claimed). However, the timely interception prevented any KPAF losses on the airfield.[195]

At P'yongyang's Heijo airfield 46 F-80Cs (49th FBG) attacked the 116 AA guns (53 large calibre guns and 63 lighter automatic weapons) while 21 B-29s (19th and 307th BGs) bombed the target, reportedly placing 90 per cent of their ordnance 'squarely on P'yongyang Main airfield'. While damage to KPAF aircraft and facilities was unknown, no USAF aircraft were lost on this raid either.[196]

On 25 January, the US I and IX Corps began slowly pushing the CPVA forces back northwards beneath a smothering umbrella of fighter-bombers ranging as far north as P'yongyang. However, the strikes had failed to eliminate the KPAF fighters. On the second day of the counter-offensive, one Yak-9P attempted to interfere with USAF F-84s Thunderjets (27th FEG/523rd FES) bombing a railway bridge approximately 20 miles (32km) from P'yongyang. 1st Lt Jacob 'Jake' Kratt, Jr., recalled:

> 'The defences around the bridge were light and the weather was not a factor. It was during my bomb run that someone called out a prop-driven aircraft on the deck, heading for the bridge and firing his guns [at an F-84E just pulling out of his bombing pass]. I had just released my last bomb when I made a quick visual sweep in all directions and, much to my amazement, I saw this intruder about 500 ft [150m] in front of my windscreen going from my right to left. I immediately applied full power to assist in executing a maximum-G turn to the left… [Ahead of me] two F-84s overshot due to excessive speed, so I reduced power and extended the speed brakes to bleed off speed. I already had my gunsight pipper trained on the target, and I fired a long burst. The Yak immediately started burning, rolled inverted and dove into the ground…'[197]

Ten days later, in much the same way, a Yak-9P attempted to interfere with USAF Mustangs (18th FBG/67th FBS) strafing ground targets near P'yongyang. Leading a flight of three attacking two trains and a truck convoy northwest of P'yongyang, Maj Arnold 'Moon' Mullins later related, 'I was pulling up from a strafing pass when I spotted a Yak directly above me. I [pulled up further and] let loose with a few bursts from my .50 calibre machine guns and scored direct hits in the cockpit and fuselage. The pilot must have been [hit] because he made a sloppy turn and just kept going. When he crashed it looked [like] two napalm bombs were exploding.'[198]

Three 27th FEW F-84E Thunderjets in flight. (NMUSAF)

A week afterwards, Peng launched his 'Fourth Phase Offensive' (11-18 February) but, in the face of fierce air attacks, it made little progress against UNC forces and was soon cancelled. Afterwards, resurgent UN forces resumed their counterattacks, liberating Seoul a second time on 14 March. Finally, when the serpentine frontlines approximated the 38th Parallel, the UNC – now commanded by Ridgeway – initiated a holding strategy intending to lead to a cease-fire along the pre-war 'border'.[199]

To regain all territory lost in Ridgeway's counter-attacks, Peng planned his 'Fifth Phase Offensive' to begin on 22 April, spending five weeks stockpiling supplies before launching his attacks. To support this offensive the KPAF included its newly-operational 58th FAR and its new, longer-ranged La-9s. Initially, the new unit was ordered to deploy forward to Awak, an unimproved (sod) airfield near North Korea's west coast, southwest of P'yongyang. However, mounting concerns that Ridgeway was planning an Inch'on-like amphibious counter-attack behind Communist lines at Wonsan Bay changed that.[200]

Intensified action by UNC naval forces and USN carrier-based attack aircraft had frustrated the small Korean People's Navy's (KPN) efforts to lay minefields in Wonsan harbour, with three of five 'motorships' carrying mines from Chongjin to Wonsan being damaged by carrier air attacks and naval gunfire, resulting in the a call for KPAF air support. Consequently, the 58th FAR's destination was changed to Iwon, an unimproved (dirt) airfield northeast of Hungnam, with the unit ordered to arrive 'by 27 March'.[201]

The deployment appears to have gone completely unnoticed by USAF and USN reconnaissance. Based on the size and condition of Iwon's primitive airfield, it is doubtful if more than one squadron – or a portion of one – executed the deployment, and the La-9s were not observed on the ground or airborne in the Hungnam-Wonsan area. But, fly they did, as evidenced by the 28 May attack on a USAF B-26 Invader in the Wonsan area. According to archived CIA reports, the deployment evidently ended in July when 'a group of LA-9s [*sic*] has been deployed to Sinuiju'.[202]

Lavochkin La-9 in the PLAAF Museum at Datangshan, PRC. (Photo by Nick Challoner)

VMF-312 F4U-4 Corsairs aboard USS Bataan (CVL-29). (US Navy)

Meanwhile, to make-up for the transfer of the 58th FAR from Awak to Iwon, the 56th GFAR was tasked with flying fighter sweeps along the west coast. On one of these – two days before Peng launched his offensive, four Yak-9Ps were sent on a patrol near Chinnamp'o harbour and Hojong-do island at 5,000 feet. Flying in a loose right echelon formation, they sighted one of a pair of USMC F4U-4 Corsairs (VMF-312 'Checkerboards') flying an armed reconnaissance mission from the USS *Bataan* (CVL-29). Focusing on the Corsair leader, Capt Philip C. DeLong, an 11-victory WW2 ace 3,000ft below, the North Koreans began a wide pursuit curve to intercept. DeLong's wingman, 1st Lt Harold Daigh, spotted the Yaks, but he initially mistook them for Mustangs, allowing them to close on DeLong and get some initial, but inconsequential, hits.[203]

'As soon as I was fired on,' DeLong later recounted, 'I executed a quick split-S to pick up airspeed... Although two of the Yaks attacked me again from astern [after pulling out of the dive], I was able to turn the tables. While I was in a defensive turn, one of them crossed in front of me from right to left'. DeLong opened fire and the Yak flew right through the streams of 20mm shells, went into a steep dive, streaming smoke, and hit the ground.'[204]

However, the KPAF pilots failed to see Daigh, who immediately pulled in behind the second pair of Yaks and, after following them through a 360 degree turn, pulled up underneath the trailing wingman. Daigh's long, accurate burst caught the Yak-9P in the tail, wing root, and rear fuselage. The Korean was just beginning a defensive break when the right wing broke off and the aircraft hit the ground with a big explosion.[205]

As Daigh chased the remaining Yak towards the east, the other survivor dived after him. DeLong told Daigh to break left (he did) and the Yak followed, DeLong damaging it with hits in the cockpit and wing root. As this fighter turned away, DeLong

'came up on the lead Yak, the one Daigh had been trailing [and] I opened fire and the rounds converged on the forward part of its fuselage. The aircraft started smoking, turned south, did a split-S and then recovered to the west. I followed it through this manoeuvre and continued scoring hits every time I fired. He was trailing thick black smoke, and pieces were falling away. At that point the pilot ceased his evasive tactics... jettisoned his canopy [and] then bailed out, and his aircraft went straight in.'[206]

Preparing for the 'Sixth Phase Offensive'

Peng's 'Fifth Phase Offensive' proved to be a disaster, having been defeated – according to his personal report to Mao on 21 February – by UN air attacks ravaging his logistics system. Only 60-70 per cent of the needed supplies – food, water, clothing, ammunition, and other equipment – reached the frontline troops. Therefore, he demanded that the Communist air forces achieve a measure of air superiority over the Chinese supply lines before his planned 'sixth phase offensive' – the final all-out attempt to push UNC forces off the Korean Peninsula – could be launched.[207]

Part of the reason for the overwhelming UN air supremacy was the neutralization of the KPAF airbase at Sinuiju. On 9 May – during the middle of Peng's offensive – the Fifth AF and 1st Marine Air Wing (MAW) launched one of the largest airfield attacks yet – 312 aircraft participating – on Sinuiju. While F-86s, F-84s, and F9Fs fended off the 18 (out of 50 launched) MiG-15s that challenged the raid, F-80Cs from all three wings (8th, 49th, and 51st) provided flak suppression while F-51s (18th FBG) and F4Us (1st MAW) used bombs, rockets, and napalm against the KPAF airbase's facilities and aircraft. The raiders claimed to have destroyed 'all the Red aircraft on the field', 106 buildings, a very large fuel dump, and 26 ammunition and supply dumps. One F-84E was damaged in the raid; no American aircraft were lost.[208]

Additionally, by mid-June the FEAF Bomber Command had located almost all of the new airfields under construction in central North Korea and, since the Soviet MiG-15s at Andong lacked the range to protect them, a massive American bombing campaign obliterated all but one. This limited Communist air forces to the two newly-arrived Soviet MiG-15 divisions (303rd and 324th IADs) at Andong, supplemented by the KPAF 1st CAD at Sinuiju and the small 1st Night Bomber Battalion at Sariwon – a well-camouflaged grass airstrip 35 miles (56km) south of P'yongyang.[209]

To support Peng's 'Sixth Phase Offensive', Pak Den-Sik's squadron of Po-2LSh biplanes sought to diminish the UNC's two major operational advantages – mobility and air superiority – by targeting American 'motor pools' and airfields. USAF airbase parking areas – as well as air force and army motor pools – were well lit at night to guard against infiltrators sabotaging aircraft and vehicles, but the many large floodlights also made them very visible targets for night raiders. Dubbed 'Bedcheck Charlies' (or 'Chinese alarm clocks') by the Americans, a pair of the doughty little Po-2s took off from Sariwon in the early hours of 14 June and attacked Suwon AB – one's bombs barely missing a squad of construction engineers repairing the runway – and the Eighth Army motor transport park at Inch'on.[210]

On the following night (15/16 June) Kimpo AB was reportedly strafed by a Beriev MBE-2bis pusher-type biplane flying boat, nearly hitting a jeepload of military policemen. Russian archive sources discount – in fact, scoff at American accounts of – the use of this flying boat type in the night attack role. The only other USAF report of the use of this rare aircraft type in the Korean conflict was on 6 May when 'a US aircraft observed a seaplane, with engines running 100 yards from the shore near Haeju [a KPAF coastal airfield]. There were six 20-foot boats close to the aircraft. This is the first sighting of a... light flying boat in the course of the Korean fighting [and] suggests that in view of recent enemy air activity at Onjong-ni airfield [another KPAF coastal airfield] this aircraft may have been delivering critically needed materiel or personnel to the area'.[211]

Since this is the only occasion that this type was reported as used for nocturnal raids, it is doubtful if this aircraft was actually part of the 1st Night Bomber Battalion: more likely its crew was taking advantage of their occasional nighttime supply/personnel delivery 'runs' to the bay offshore Haeju to participate in Pak Den-Sik's night operations against USAF air bases in preparation for the Soviets' launching their supporting air superiority campaign.

Two days later, Belov initiated a week-long (17-24 June) series of maximum effort launches with his two MiG-15 divisions, attempting to achieve aerial superiority as far south as the Ch'ongch'on River, thus providing effective air cover for Peng's long supply lines. To help gain an initial advantage for Belov's 'air superiority offensive', scheduled to begin at dawn on 17 June, two Po-2LShs once again raided Suwon AB, attacking at 0130hrs that morning, hoping to destroy some F-86s on the ground.

Destroyed 4th FIW F-86A Sabre S/N 49-1334 at Suwon. (Warren Thompson Collection)

The pair was led by La Woon-Yung, his wingman bombing the 802nd Engineer Aviation Battalion's motor pool while he scored a direct hit with two 20kg (44lb) fragmentation bombs on the 335th FIS parking ramp. One F-86A Sabre (S/N 49-1334) erupted into flames. The maintenance personnel – some of whom were wounded (along with one pilot) – frantically pushed other, damaged, jets away from the conflagration, saving them, but four more F-86s had been seriously damaged and another four less so. As La Woon-Yung later stated, 'I saw with my own eyes that many of the enemy aircraft had been destroyed by my bombing.'[212]

The 'Sixth Phase Offensive'

Under the cover of the high altitude air superiority contest spawned by Belov's 'offensive', to assist KPA forces attempting to re-capture Sinmi-do Island Lee's 1st CAD flew its most ambitious mission yet. The island is located just off the northwest coast, about 75 miles/120km southeast of Sinuiju, and was a base for ROK special forces and guerrilla insurgents raiding coastal areas south of the Yalu. On 20 June – half way through the Belov's air offensive – Lee's unit launched eight Il-10s escorted by six Yak-9Ps with 18 Soviet MiG-15s (324th IAD's 176th GvIAP) flying high cover.[213]

En route to the target, however, the *Shturmoviki* had the misfortune of being spotted by a flight of F-51D Mustangs on an armed reconnaissance mission along the roads south of Sinuiju. Leading the formation was 18th FBG commander, Lieutenant Colonel (Lt Col) Ralph H. Saltsman, Jr., who immediately called out the targets to his wingmen, pulled off the 'road recce', and chased down the slower Il-10s, shooting down one of them. One of his wingmen, Capt John J. Coleman (18th FBG/39th FIS), reportedly destroyed another and two other pilots (18th FBG/12th FBS) claimed two more Il-10s shot down.[214]

A second flight of Mustangs intercepted the Koreans just as the escorting Yak-9Ps attempted to join the fight. 1st Lt James B. Harrison (18th FBG/67th FBS) later recalled,

> 'We were about 15 minutes into destroying some targets when word reached us that there were six 'bogies' below us, and our flight lead told us to go down and identify the aircraft. As we approached the enemy [Yak-9P] aircraft they saw us coming and turned in towards us. As my flight leader made a firing pass on one of the aircraft, his wingman turned right into me and I was able to get onto his tail. I fired several bursts and the Yak-9 caught fire. The pilot immediately rolled over and bailed out. My only comment was that the pilot was evidently straight out of flight school, with no training in combat situations.'[215]

At this point the Soviet MiGs dived to the rescue, one of them blowing the left wing off Coleman's F-51D with his 23mm/37mm cannon fire. Trapped by G-forces, Coleman could not get out of the corkscrewing aircraft and died in the crash. Immediately the rest of the Mustangs scattered for survival as 4th FIW Sabres finally engaged, damaging two MiGs and wounding one pilot. In the confusion of the swirling jet combat, the raid was aborted.[216]

Il-10s being prepared for a mission. (Albert Grandolini Collection)

KPAF Il-10 being shot down by 18th FBG F-51D on 17 June 1951. (NMUSAF)

Although the week-long challenge to the Sabres' superiority in MiG Alley was serious, it was ultimately unsuccessful, the Soviets reported losing seven MiG-15s destroyed and four pilots killed – while the 4th FIW lost four Sabres and three pilots KIA.[217] The ambitious Communist air operations did little to diminish the UNC's air supremacy over North Korea – the repulsed raid on Sinmi-do being dramatic evidence to that effect. Consequently, General Peng cancelled his planned 'Sixth Phase Offensive' and – with cease-fire negotiations beginning on 10 July – the Communist air forces went into a force-preservation strategy, husbanding their resources and continuing training activities, content to wait until they had sufficient strength to better challenge the UNC air superiority.[218]

Shooting Down 'Bedcheck Charlie'

While the success at Suwon encouraged further KPAF 'night heckling' operations, the spectacular embarrassment galvanized FEAF into doing something about the threat that, thus far, had been scoffed at as insignificant. Contrary to popular mythology, the Po-2's Shvetsov radial engine, propeller, and its steel tube frame did present a radar echo and the USAF's 606th Aircraft Control and Warning Squadron (AC&WS; based at Kimpo AB, its Tactical Air Direction Center's callsign was 'Dentist') – whose primary Western Electric AN/TPS-1B search radar (75 mile/139km effective range over land) was located 12 miles (20km) north of Seoul – actually tracked the raiders on both occasions, despite their relatively low-altitude.[219]

Six nights after the second Suwon attack, American radar controllers again detected a slow moving target in the 'ground clutter' around Seoul and called for any airborne aircraft in the vicinity 'to flush the unidentified aircraft'. USAF Capt Richard M. Heyman, a WW2 Mustang pilot now flying a B-26B night intruder (8th BS[L]/3rd BW[L]), was returning from the Wonsan area with plenty of ammo still in his 14 .50-cal machine guns.

Heyman later explained,

'As we were getting close to Kunsan (our base), we heard the controller 'Dentist', calling for any aircraft in the vicinity of Seoul that had any ammo left. We answered, and he immediately vectored us toward a low-flying bogey. As we got closer, he advised us to descend to a lower altitude (about 1,000 ft), and... [asked] us to slow down to about 100 knots! There was no way we could stay airborne at that speed!

'When we were close enough, I slowed to about 130 knots, dropped the flaps and gear and opened the cowl flaps and bomb-bay doors. All of this was to give us more drag. I shoved the RPM up to a high setting... to maintain flying speed and control. The time was slightly past midnight, and the moon was out. All three of us were straining our eyes looking for 'Charlie'. After a short while we saw this biplane, and radioed the controller to make sure it was the intruder we were after. He confirmed it.

The Po-2 was flying 180 degrees to our heading, so we whipped around and gave chase. He did a good job of evading us by turning into us so we would overshoot him. After about ten minutes of this 'cat and mouse' game, we thought we had lost him. Suddenly, we spotted him right down on the deck, flying over a river and going between the banks. I guess the pilot didn't realize that the water reflecting the moonlight made him clearly stand out. I pulled around in a steep bank and gave him a burst of .50-cal that raked all over his fuselage. He went down in seconds.'[220]

During the first two weeks in July, the 1st Night Bomber Battalion lost two more Po-2s and their crews, both to a USMC night-fighter unit, VMF[N]-513 'Flying Nightmares', equipped with the veteran F4U-5N Corsair and the new, twin-engine, two-seat Grumman F7F-3N Tigercat – both mounting airborne intercept (AI) radars and four 20mm cannon. Normally, these types were used for night interdiction missions against Communist supply lines, but when the nocturnal raiders made their occasional appearance, they were the most capable UNC aircraft available to intercept them.

The first morning in July 606th AC&WS detected another 'night heckler' north of Seoul and this time 'Dentist' had a *bonafide* night fighter to work with: an F7F-3N Tigercat piloted by USMC Capt Edwin B. Long with Warrant Officer (WO) Robert C. Buckingham working the radar. Long later related:

'The slow, very manoeuvrable biplane was next to impossible to get a clean shot at. It took three passes to get lined up. But when I did the tremendous firepower of the Tigercat did the job quickly, and he went down into the side of a mountain in a fiery crash.'[221]

Shortly after midnight eleven nights later, another Po-2LSh was intercepted over Seoul by the 'Flying Nightmares', this time by USMC Capt Donald L. Fenton flying a F4U-5N Corsair. 'Dentist' vectored Fenton to the target and he spotted it and attacked in the face of the rear gunner's machine gun fire. His four 20mm cannon blasted the little biplane – it disintegrated into a wad of wood and fabric, wings folding back, and fell to the ground.[222]

Having lost three aircraft and six crewmen in three weeks, the 1st Night Bomber Battalion stood down from combat operations for two months to rebuild and undergo further training in low altitude night flying operations.

3rd BW(L) B-26B 'sighting in' its machine guns at night. (NMUSAF)

Vought F4U-5N Corsair of VMF(N)-513 at Wonsan AB. (NMUSAF)

CHAPTER 6
THE KPAF JOINS THE JET AGE

In September 1950, 119 KPAF student pilots arrived at Yanji and Jilin to complete their flight and operational training. Eighty of these were former cadets from the People's Naval Academy at Chongjin. The KPN's strongest force – a flotilla of two motor gunboats (MGBs) and four Soviet-built G-5 motor torpedo boats (MTBs) – was wiped out by a group of USN and RN cruisers and destroyers at dawn on 2 July, as they gamely attacked the much larger and more powerful enemy warships. This disaster was followed by similar actions – mostly by USN and RN/FAA aircraft – on the west coast, the combined effect being the complete destruction of North Korean navy's combat capability.[223]

With the KPN eliminated, there really wasn't much use for a new cadre of naval officers. Chongjin, an industrialized city of 300,000 that was the centre of iron and steel production in North Korea, was virtually levelled by massive B-29 strikes (64 bombers on 22 August and 24 two days later), destroying 65 per cent of the city and killing one third of its residents.[224] After these destructive raids, the naval academy was evacuated, its 450 cadets beginning a 60 mile trek following an unfinished railroad line through the coastal mountains towards the Tumen River (border with the USSR). From this group, 80 cadets were selected (unknown to them at the time) to become pilots, and they – designated the 'Special Group' – were marched north to a railroad depot and then carried across the Chinese border to Yanji aboard trains, traveling only during darkness to escape the savage attacks of USAF B-26 night intruders.[225]

The 'Special Group'

Arriving at Yanji in late September the 'Special Group' was given two days to acclimate to their new surroundings then immediately began academic training on 'the theoretical aspects of aviation', administered by Soviet instructors. Courses lasted through October, with the new student pilots rising at 0430hrs to attend seven hours of classroom instruction, plus physical training, and then studying until 2200hrs each night – only having time off for meals – seven days a week. The instruction covered aerodynamics, reciprocating engine theory and operation, navigation, instrumentation, radio theory, basic weaponry, and flying regulations.

After passing a final examination, flight training – also with Soviet instructors – in the Yak-18 began 1 November, the students being trucked daily some 30 miles (48km) to Yanji's satellite field to practice flying. Upon completion, in mid-December the 'Special Group' was transferred to Jilin, where they learned to fly the more powerful Yak-11. This PLAAF base had a very large, flat dirt flying field so that take-offs and landings could be made in any direction, depending on the wind, and had a collection of ten one- and two-story concrete buildings arrayed along the south side. Flying training took three months and the students graduated in early March, 1951, with an average of about 60 flying hours on the two Yakovlev trainers.[226]

Not all the young North Koreans completed the demanding flying training course, and not all of graduates were considered candidates for learning to fly jet fighters. A number of the newly-minted KPAF pilots – based more on assessments of their questionable 'political reliability' rather than poor piloting skills – were sent to Vozzhayevka airfield, the Soviet V-VS bomber base in the Amur Oblast, for training on Tupolev Tu-2 twin-engine bombers, or to Fengcheng to learn to fly the Il-10 with the 11th AAD. To the remainder were added a number of more experienced pilots – some were 'other propeller pilots' who had survived their early experience as KPAF aviators while others were 'senior student pilots' who had graduated ahead of the 'special group'. This process created a class of 70 pilots to train on the MiG-15 jet fighter.[227]

After graduation the 'Special Group' travelled by train to Anshan, China, a heavily industrialized city 57 miles (92km) southwest of Shenyang, arriving 8 March. The airfield, the North Koreans soon discovered, 'was a completely Soviet jet fighter base on Chinese territory'. It had a long concrete runway, fully developed flight line, modern control tower, large hangars and several operations and maintenance buildings. The barracks, composed of 20 three-story concrete buildings, was located on the opposite side of the city.[228]

Waiting for the North Korean trainees was the V-VS 324th IAD's 196th IAP, which had arrived in mid-February and were conducting combat training themselves. Under the direction of the division's Inspector for Flight Technique and Flight Theory, Lt Col Vishnyakov, the KPAF students were provided with additional academic training, covering 'the design, defects, and natural effects' of the MiG-15 and Yak-17 aircraft and the RD-45F and RD-10a jet engines. There were also three additional hours of flying instruction in the Yak-11. Called 'clean up' this was to ascertain each student's proficiency and was designed to lead directly to flying the two-seat, straight-wing Yak-17UTI jet trainer.[229]

However, before the KPAF students could graduate to flying jets, the 324th IAD was 'suddenly ordered into combat against the American Sabres to replace the inexperienced Soviet MiG pilots [of the 151st GvIAD]'. Flying from Langtao airfield in February and March, the 151st GvIAD lost four MiG-15s in combat with straight-wing F-80Cs[230] and, now that the USAF's 4th FIW had returned to the Korean Peninsula, they lost a fifth jet to a swept-wing F-86. Obviously, 'the earlier Russian MiG pilots became an embarrassment' and had to be replaced on the front lines with the elite 324th IAD, the division's two regiments deploying to Langtao on 2 and 3 April.[231]

Consequently, while other arrangements with the Soviets were being made for their flying training, the class was shipped northeast to Dongfeng airfield where North Korean engineers (this was where the MiG-15s, arriving by rail from the USSR, were assembled and test flown) and instructors provided academic instruction on gas turbine principles and RD-45F jet engine design, systems and operation.

In mid-April the class was shipped far to the south, to Tianjin and Qingdao for their initial jet training. By this time the class was organized into two regiments – the 59th and 60th FARs[232] – each to be composed of three eight-aircraft squadrons. The 59th FAR was commanded by Col Yang Du-Hi[233] and the 60th was led by Col Tae Kuk-Sung, a former Yak-9P pilot that had survived several battles with America jet fighters and was credited with three aerial victories.[234]

The 59th FAR was shipped to Qingdao (formerly the colonial Tsingtao) where the 28th IAD's 139th GvIAP conducted the North Koreans' 'jet transition training'. Similarly the 60th FAR was stationed at Tianjin (formerly Tientsin) where the 67th IAP provided jet training.[235] From 1 May until late June, the two Soviet regiments provided four hours of flying instruction to each student on the two-seat Yak-17UTI jet trainer, then soloed them on the MiG-15.[236]

For operational training, on 25 June 1951, the KPAF's first two jet fighter regiments were shipped back to Anshan where the 151st GvIAD's 28th and 72nd GvIAPs were now organized to provide their instruction. These were equipped with 56 'old but clean' MiG-15s. Being some of the earliest models built by Factory No. 1 at Kuybyshev in 1949, they had originally been issued to the 324th IAD at Kubinka air base near Moscow and this unit brought 65 of them to China. However, after clashing with the F-86s, they were found to be inferior – eight were lost in combat – and at the end of April 1951 the remaining aircraft were traded to the 151st GvIAD for its improved MiG-15bis.[237]

Ensign No Kum-Sok,[238] who later defected by flying a MiG-15bis to Kimpo AB, thought that the Soviet instructor pilots were 'cheerful, humorous, and exciting. They were easy-going, leisure-minded, and rather frank talkers… civil, well-educated, and good humoured. I felt more comfortable with these Russians than I did with the North Koreans.'[239]

'Training was fierce,' he added, 'with tight formation flights, navigation, aerobatics, and simulated dogfights every morning. After lunch we took two-hour naps[240] followed by the debriefing and instructions on the next day's flight'. MiG-15 training was indeed tough. Two MiG-15s and their pilots were lost in training: one, flown by Lt Ahn Eng (formerly a Yak-11 IP) 'mysteriously dived into the ground during aerobatics' on 20 August 1951, and the second crashed during landing (pilot name and date unknown).

During August, the KPAF students received one hour 'clean up' on the Yak-17UTI and averaged four hours 24 minutes flying the MiG-15, with a similar amount of time airborne in the MiG the next month. As the 'Special Group' neared graduation, the class was gathered into the base theatre for a briefing presented by an experienced 'combat pilot' from the 324th IAD. After having to listen to 'seemingly endless political harangues by North Korean officers,' the Soviet told the new KPAF MiG-15 pilots 'to avoid a horizontal fight, for the F-86 turns with a smaller radius. Always maintain higher altitude. Attack F-86s and regain altitude, which he called a "vertical fight".'[241]

Finally, the two regiments were 'graded out' by their Soviet instructors as 'ready to conduct squadron-level combat operations in daylight hours in good flying weather, and night missions in flights [four-aeroplane formations] up to altitudes of 8,000-10,000 meters [26,247-32,808ft]. [Each] regiment's technical staff have been prepared to service and repair the equipment [aircraft] independently, and the command staff [were prepared] to lead combat operations.'[242]

After much adversity, training was completed in September and, on 7 October; the 151st GvIAD transferred its 54 well-worn MiG-15s to the two KPAF regiments and, together, they formed the 1st Air Division (AD),[243] commanded by Brig Gen Kang Dae-Yong.[244] As the North Koreans prepared to deploy to the front lines, the Soviets boarded trains and returned to 'Mother Russia' where the unit joined the 10th PVO Air Army at Arkhangelsk. There it was supplied with new MiG-15bis fighters, and began its new mission of protecting the great Soviet naval bases on the Kola Peninsula for the better part of the Cold War.[245]

Yak-17UTI primary jet trainer. (Author's Collection)

Soviet MiG-15 #125 taxiing out for flight at Langtao, April 1951. (Tom Cooper Collection)

KPAF MiG-15 line up at PLAAF training base. (Albert Grandolini Collection)

22-yr old Lt No Kum-Sok. (NMUSAF)

Typical KPAF MiG-15 pilot in flight gear, full view. (NMUSAF)

Typical KPAF MiG-15 pilot in flight gear, close frontal view. (NMUSAF)

More Modern Equipment, Expansion and Reorganization

By 10 June 1951, Soviet advisors reported that the KPAF now numbered 136 combat aircraft and had 60 'well-trained pilots'. It appears that the '136' aircraft accounts for those of the 1st CAD at Sinuiju (56th GFAR and 57th AAR, flying La-9s, Yak-9Ps, and Il-10s from Sinuiju), 58th FAR (La-9s) at Fengcheng, 1st Night Bomber Battalion (Po-2s), plus the MiG-15s possessed by the 1st AD, even though this unit was still in training. The 60 'well-trained pilots', however, do not include those under instruction at the time, but appear to count only those manning the two primary combat-ready units: the 1st CAD (approximately 40 pilots) and 58th FAR (approximately 20 pilots).[246]

Just as the KPAF was finally prepared to increase its investment in the Communist coalition's air arm the PLAAF began transforming Chinese-Korean joint air HQ into a combat air command. Evidently, after the attempted Il-10 attack on Sinmi-do Island was dramatically and disastrously repulsed in June – losing as much as half the strike force to F-51 Mustangs – KPAF leadership decided to substitute its La-9s for the slow and inherently vulnerable *Shturmoviki*. With four Nudelman-Suranov NS-23 23mm cannon, the post-war development of the successful WW2 Lavochkin fighter had a much heavier forward-firing armament than the KPAF's Il-10s (two 23mm cannon and a pair of rifle-calibre machine guns), making it excellent for strafing enemy positions and unarmoured vehicles. Additionally, being a fighter, unlike the heavy, two-place, bomb-carrying 'assault aircraft', the La-9 was manoeuvrable enough to defend itself against the USAF's Mustangs and straight-wing jets.[247]

Consequently, while stationed at Fengcheng that autumn, the 58th FAR's La-9s began conducting 'ground-attack training', learning to strafe ground targets with their NS-23 cannon. According to the USAF's 'Project Suede' signals intelligence (SIGINT) reports 14 KPAF La-9s flew to Sinuiju airfield on 8 and 10 October, after completing ground attack training at Fengcheng. By the end of November, these were followed by a second group, consisting of another seven La-9s. These arrivals gave the 1st CAD three operational regiments, one air defence (56th GFAR), one assault (57th AAR), and one dual-role (air defence and ground attack; 58th FAR). This additive combat strength is confirmed by FEAF photo-reconnaissance which identified an increase from 38 propeller-driven aircraft at Sinuiju to 64 at this same time.[248]

On 7 November, the KPAF joined their allies' Andong air defence organization by deploying the 1st AD's 60th FAR to the newly-completed airfield at Uiju, North Korea. Built only a half-mile south of the Yalu River, ten miles (16km) upstream from Sinuiju, Uiju was a completely new airfield that had a 7,218ft (2,200m) concrete runway paralleling the Yalu, with large concrete pads at each end for alert aircraft, connected by a long straight concrete taxiway – that could be used in an emergency as a runway – paralleling the runway on its southeast side. Along this taxiway were 20 sandbagged revetments, each large enough for two MiG-15s. The alert pads were protected by sandbagged AA gun emplacements, two on each side, with additional AA guns scattered around the perimeter. South of the runway, taxiway, and revetments was a collection of wooden buildings providing administrative, supply, and barracks facilities. The pilots, however, were billeted five miles (eight km) northeast, in a cluster of farmhouses.[249]

With the 1st AD's arrival on the 'front lines' it appears (according to CIA/USAF SIGINT files) that the 1st CAD was at that time re-designated the 10th CAD 'thus eliminating confusion due to having identical numbers'. However, because this unit had undergone a confusing series of designation changes already (55th CAD, then 1st CAD, now 10th CAD), and due to the fact that by this time the unit was predominantly comprised of La-9 fighters, to reduce this confusion, it was colloquially known simply as the 'LA-division' (i.e., 'Lavochkin division', as opposed to 'the MiG division'), especially in KPAF message traffic.[250]

Part I: Aircraft Profile Artworks

56th 'Guards Taejon' Fighter Aviation Regiment

Originally the KPAF received 12 old Yak-9s and 42 newer Yak-9Ps; these were issued to the 56th FAR at P'yongyang's Heijo AB. Two of the regiment's three battalions (squadrons) were still in training when Kim Il-Sung started the Korean War. All examples were painted in air superiority grey overall, with national markings (the size and placement of which varied from aircraft to aircraft) in six positions and 'tail numbers' applied in differing fonts in black on the fin. (Artwork by Tom Cooper)

During June-July 1950, the 56th FAR's single operational squadron deployed 8-10 Yak-9Ps to Kimpo AB, near Seoul, extending the unit's radius of action south as far as Taejon. These three examples were amongst the five found destroyed, badly damaged, or derelict when UNC forces recaptured Kimpo that September. Notably all 'tail numbers' were neatly applied using the same font, some of which were outlined in white. (Artwork by Tom Cooper)

Yak-9P "Black 27" was found largely intact and undamaged in the hangar at Kimpo AB and, by adding pieces and parts from the five derelict Yak-9Ps, it became the basis for a flyable example of the type. It was shipped to the USA where – after repainting (see inset) – it was evaluated by the USAF Air Technical Intelligence Center at Wright-Patterson AFB at Dayton, Ohio. (Artwork by Tom Cooper)

57th Assault Aviation Regiment

The KPAF initially received 54 Il-10 'assault aircraft' and 13 UIl-10 trainers, forming the 57th AAR in January 1950. As far as is known, they retained their V-VS livery: olive drab upper surfaces and sides, with light blue undersides. Their national insignia were applied in only four positions: on undersides of the wings and on the rear fuselage sides. By June 1950 two of the unit's squadrons were operational, one of which was based at Heijo and supported the KPA's main attacks southwards towards Seoul. (Artwork by Tom Cooper)

The 57th AAR's other operational squadron (along with its training unit) was initially based at Yonpo on the east coast and supported KPA units advancing through the central highlands and along the east coast where the rough terrain inhibited the normal use of artillery. These examples were amongst the many found abandoned at Yonpo and Wonsan by advancing UNC forces during their initially successful counter-offensive in September 1950. (Artwork by Tom Cooper)

The 57th AAR deployed a squadron of 6-8 Il-10s to Kimpo to help support the KPA's advance towards Taejon. Aircraft #54 was badly damaged in a 'wheels up' crash-landing and found in a wrecked condition. Aircraft #44 and #54 were discovered intact in a destroyed hangar at Kimpo; they were repaired and shipped to the USA for technical evaluation. Notable is the different size and position of national markings: most of them quite large on the wing undersurfaces, while the placement of the roundels on the rear fuselage varied by nearly a meter. (Artwork by Tom Cooper)

58th Training Aviation Regiment

The 58th TAR began its operational service in December 1950 with two of its three squadrons equipped with two dozen Yak-18 primary trainers. Contrary to many reports published over the years, these were painted in dark green overall (and some may have had their undersides painted light blue). As is so frequently the case, their 'tail numbers' were applied in differing fonts, but always in white, on the fin. Several aircraft are known to have worn a 'pilotki' – apparently in red – on the top of their fin. (Artwork by Tom Cooper)

The 58th TAR also had one squadron equipped with Yak-11 advanced trainers, eight of which were provided in 1949, with another 14 being received the next year. As far as is known, all were painted in light blue overall and wore the national insignia at least on the rear fuselage. Only one serial number was definitely confirmed – 'tail number' 06 – illustrated here, which was shot down by a USAF F-82G Twin Mustang on 27 June 1950. (Artwork by Tom Cooper)

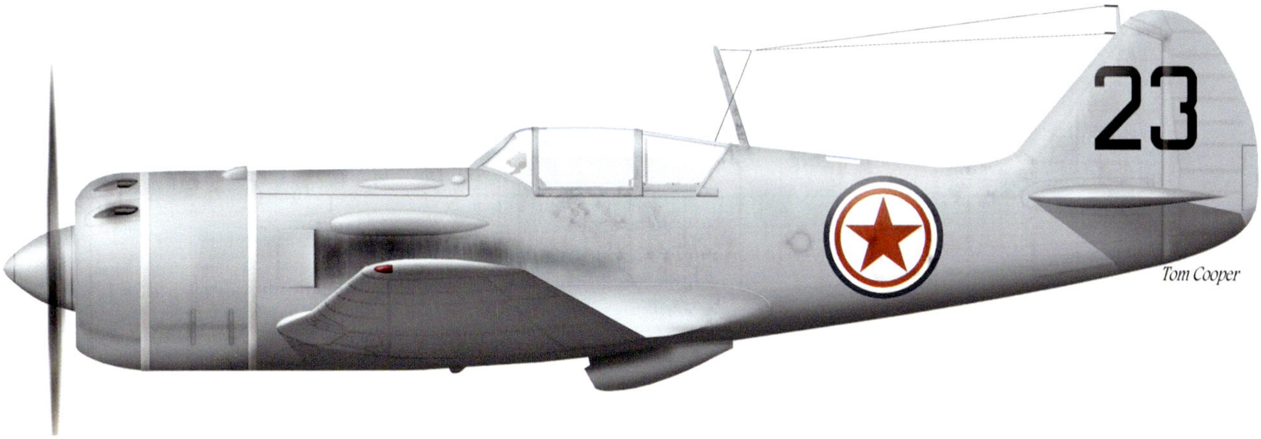

In autumn 1950, when the KPAF training programme was re-established at Yanji, PRC, the 58th TAR became the KPAF's 'Manchurian Air Academy' (also known as the PLAAF's 10th Aviation School). The TAR's designation was then used in early 1951 to establish a second fighter regiment, the 58th FAR, a 28-aircraft unit equipped with La-9s. As far as is known, KPAF's La-9s were all painted in air superiority grey overall and bore the usual KPAF 'tail numbers' on their fins. (Artwork by Tom Cooper)

3rd Night Bomber Regiment

By the time the KPAF re-established its training programme at Yanji, the service's 15 surviving Po-2 biplanes had become redundant and were grouped together in a 'liaison battalion'. Unable to strike UNC forces in any other way, this squadron started training in night bombing attacks and – despite heavy losses (initially more than 50%) – began sporadic nocturnal harassment (called 'night heckler') raids that largely frustrated USAF night intercept attempts. The unit's Po-2s were painted black overall, with 'tail numbers' applied in white or red. (Artwork by Tom Cooper)

The success of the 1st Night Bomber Battalion resulted in the formation of a second squadron, thus creating the 3rd Night Bomber Regiment. This unit was initially equipped with seven Yak-18s modified to carry two 50kg (110lb) bombs and was initially based near Sinuiju. Aircraft #15 participated in several of the more successful night attacks during 1952-53 and was eventually used, in June 1955, by Capt Lee Um-Yong (former 2nd AD MiG-15 pilot with one 'kill' to his credit) in his defection to South Korea. (Artwork by Tom Cooper)

By the spring of 1952, the 56th GFAR was re-formed as a night-fighter unit equipped with La-11s. When the 'Guards Taejon' converted to the MiG-15bis later that year, 12-14 of these were passed to the night bombing regiment, forming a third squadron. One Russian history records that 'several La-11 were painted with dark green bands wrapped all the way around the aircraft's surfaces and bands of light grey in between them'. The dark green 'wrap-around' bands were probably painted over the type's usual light grey 'air superiority' finish using the same olive green applied to KPA vehicles. (Artwork by Tom Cooper)

Mixed Aviation Regiment

One ex-IJAAF Tachikawa Ki-54c (Army Type 1 Model C) 'Hickory' twin-engine light transport was known to have been operated by the Mixed Aviation Regiment (MAR, number designation unknown), the KPAF's original transport and liaison unit. In October 1950, it was found abandoned at Heijo during the KPAF's hurried withdrawal after the UNC's successful landings at Inch'on. Note the unique insignia applied on the fin, depicting a squirrel and acorn on a thick tree branch, probably the symbol of the IJAAF's 'Heijo Air Arsenal', and the Korean national colours applied over the entire rudder. (Artwork by Tom Cooper)

When the KPA began Kim Il-Sung's invasion of South Korea, USAF Intelligence erroneously believed that the KPAF had some 22 Yak-16 10-passenger light transports in its inventory (only two Yak-16 prototypes were ever produced). Actually the MAR had about a half dozen of the similar looking, but much smaller, four-passenger Yak-6s, which were used for liaison duties and as twin-engine trainers, preparing the KPAF's initial cadre of pilots, the 'First Swallows', to fly the much larger Douglas C-47/Lusinov Li-2 medium transports. (Artwork by Tom Cooper)

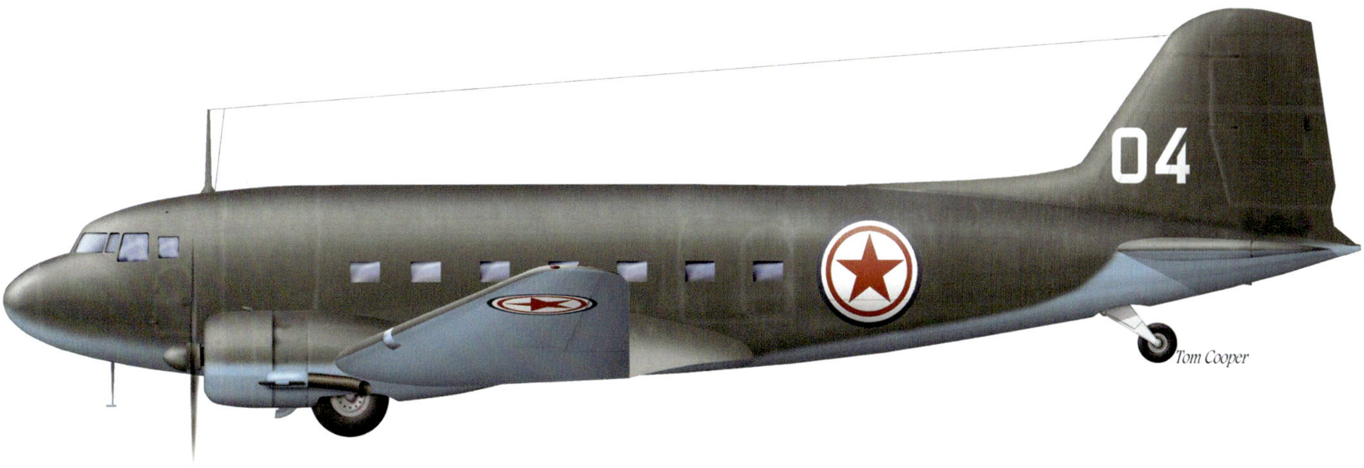

The MAR's primary equipment was initially about a half dozen Douglas C-47s and their Lisunov Li-2 clones. As far as is known, all MAR aircraft wore the same livery, consisting of dark olive green upper surfaces and sides, and light blue undersurfaces. National insignia is known to have been applied in at least four positions (wing undersurfaces and the rear fuselage sides), while large 'tail numbers' were applied in white on the fin. Some of these aircraft may have received a more complex camouflage pattern later during the war. (Artwork by Tom Cooper)

1st Aviation Division

During 1950-51 MiG-15 111025 ('Bort number' Red 125) was flown by Snr Lt Gogolev of the 2nd Squadron, 176th GvIAP, 324th IAD, who was credited with two victories in April 1951. To distinguish their MiG-15s from the similar looking F-86A Sabre, the Soviets applied what they called 'elements of fast recognition' (*elementy bystrogo raspoznavaniya*) in red to their aircraft noses (324th IAD) or the tops of their tails (303rd IAD). 'Red 125' was one of 54 'old but clean' MiG-15s transferred to the KPAF's 1st Aviation Division at Anshan airfield, PRC, in October 1951. (Artwork by Tom Cooper)

When the KPAF received the ex-V-VS MiG-15s, they added a red band around the fuselage mid-section to distinguish their MiGs from the Soviets (red noses/upper tails) and PLAAF (red rudders). 'Red 008' was another of the KPAF's early MiG-15s, flown by Lt No Kum-Sok of the 60th FAR during 1951-52. According to No, 'all MiG-15 noses were painted red all the way back to the canopy [and] had a red ring around the fuselage behind the wings'. In October 1952 this aircraft was transferred to the newly-formed 3rd Aviation Division and was lost in a fatal crash, due to engine failure, in early 1953. (Artwork by Tom Cooper)

In October 1952, the 1st Aviation Division received 50 improved MiG-15bis, 'Red 408' being assigned to (now) Snr Lt No. Like the earlier model, they were painted with two layers of clear lacquer, the first mixed with 10% aluminium powder and the second mixed with 5% aluminium powder, to present an overall 'bare metal' appearance. By this time all Communist Coalition MiGs had their red markings removed 'to make [their] air units indistinguishable to Sabre pilots.' According to No, 'The red ring on planes in my regiment seemed to say to Sabre pilots "Here's easy pickings"'. (Artwork by Tom Cooper)

Additional Combat Aircraft

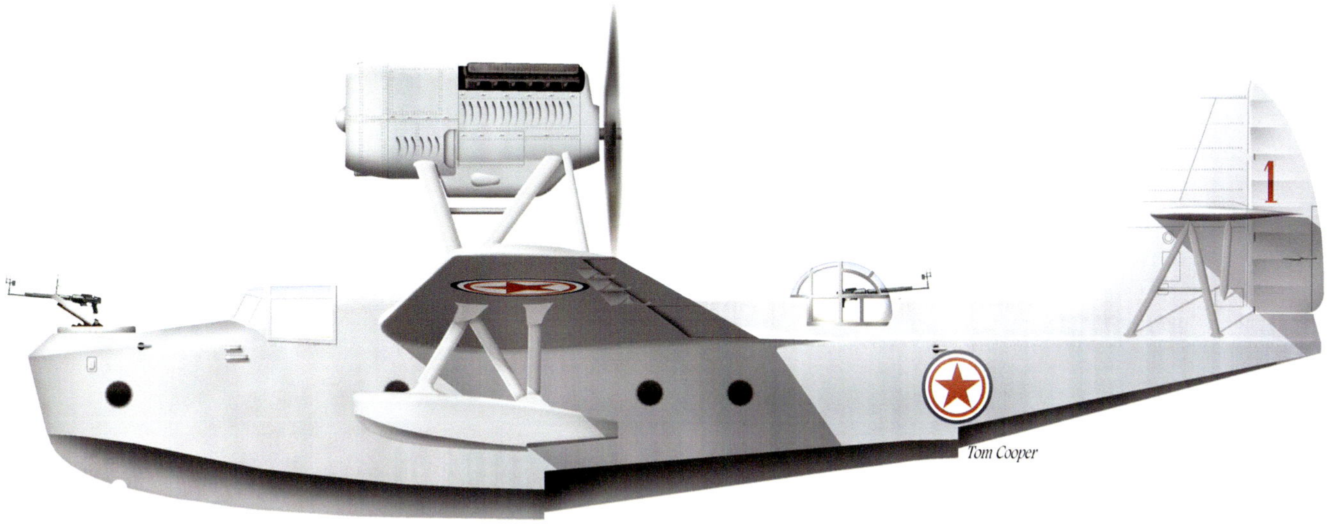

A unique participant in the Korean War was the Beriev MBE-2bis pusher-type biplane flying boat. This type was known to be used for nocturnal transportation duties, alighting in the water offshore the KPAF coastal airfields of Onjong-ni and Haeju, probably 'delivering critically needed material or personnel'. It was also reportedly used to strafe Kimpo AB on the night of 15/16 June 1951. It is not known if the MBE-2bis was a KPAF, PLAAF, or Soviet aircraft. (Artwork by Tom Cooper)

Despite prolonged training, the KPAF bomber force equipped with Tu-2s saw very little action; by the time it was operational in October 1952, its Tu-2s were being replaced by jet-powered Il-28s. Consequently, little is known about KPAF Tu-2 camouflage or markings. This example is one of several Tu-2s preserved at China's Datangshan Aviation Museum, representing PLAAF Tu-2s used by the 1st United Air Army during the Pansŏng Island campaign in November 1951; KPAF Tu-2s probably looked very much like this Chinese example. (Artwork by Tom Cooper)

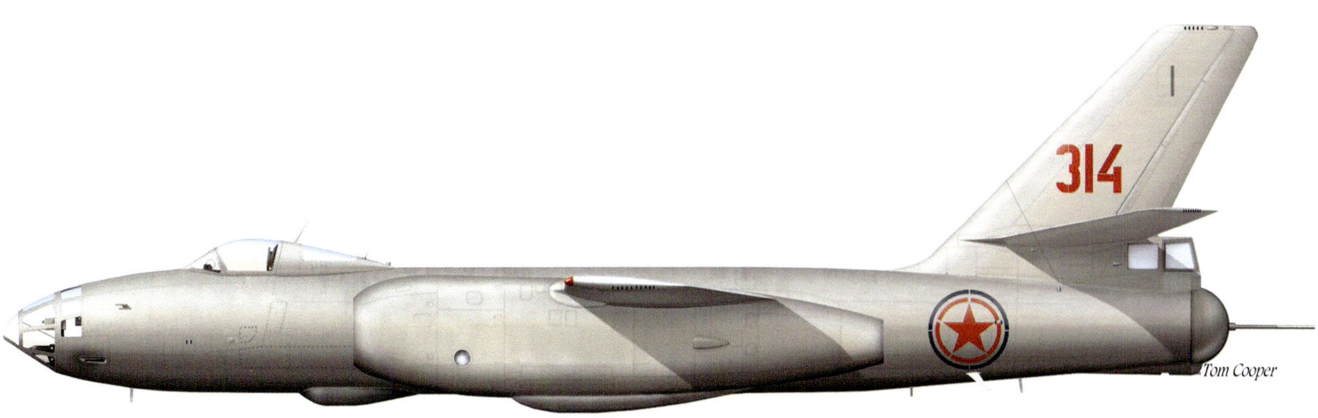

In November 1952, the KPAF's newly-established 4th Aviation Division received at least 42 new Il-28s at Kungchuling (now Gongzhuling), PRC, 39 of which were still operational at the end of the war. As far as is known, all were left in their 'bare metal overall' paint scheme (as described previously). While their 'tail numbers' were eventually moved to the nose, they were initially carried the on the fin; national insignia were applied at least on the rear fuselage and, later on, were also applied to top and bottom wing surfaces. (Artwork by Tom Cooper)

KPAF Aircraft of 1953

The 1st Aviation Division's MiG-15bis 'Red 1032' currently displayed in P'yongyang's Victorious Fatherland Liberation War Museum commemorates Hero of the DPRK Captain Gan Gyong-Duk who is credited with 10 victories (seven 'kills' and three damaged) against USN and SAAF aircraft in October 1952. By this time, red national identification markings – in this case the red 'inlet ring' – had returned. It is also decorated with ten victory markings, applied in form of seven solid ('kills') and three open ('damaged') red stars in a line down the left side of the cockpit. (Artwork by Tom Cooper)

Splendidly reconstructed and wearing its original insignia and markings, 'Red 2057' was the MiG-15bis used by No Kum-Sok in his defection to South Korea in September 1953. This jet was one of the 'at least 200 MiG-15s' the Soviets supplied at the very end of the Korean War to reinforce the KPAF as it moved into its own country following the Armistice. Today 'Red 2057' is displayed at the National Museum of the US Air Force at Wright-Patterson AFB, Dayton, Ohio. (Artwork by Tom Cooper)

Towards the end of the war, the USSR supplied a few new Il-12T troop transports to what became the 5th Aviation Division which was soon based at Sunan, just north of P'yongyang. Shortly afterwards the KPAF also received five Il-14P airliners and a single Il-14S VIP transport that became Kim Il-Sung's personal aircraft. It was used to fly him to Moscow and various Eastern Bloc nations on 'state visits' following the Victorious Fatherland Liberation War. Painted in Koryo Airlines livery, it is currently displayed at P'yongyang-Sunan International Airport. (Artwork by Tom Cooper)

Yak-9P 'White 12' – the DPRK's 'Victorious Fatherland Liberation Museum' (VFLM) contains five Korean War KPAF aircraft as well as a motor gunboat and a number of KPA tanks and vehicles. The museum staff are proud of the fact that over half a million foreigners have visited the VFLM in the 65 years since it opened in 1953, but until lately photography has been prohibited. However, the aircraft are shoehorned into such confined spaces that photography of the entire subject is difficult. (Author's Collection)

Yak-18 'White 03' represents the KPAF's pride in its sporadic, but still bothersome, light night bombing, or 'heckling', campaign – note the bomb shackles mounted on the belly between the undercarriage. It is painted in a medium green over sky blue scheme typical of KPAF training aircraft, so while it may have been used by the 3rd Night Bomber Regiment, it most likely came from the KPAF's flight training division where it could have been used to teach bombing procedures. (Author's Collection)

Although not as numerically significant as the Yak-9P in KPAF service, La-9 'White 102' was one of the approximately 20 examples that survived the conflict and were landed at Sinuiju during the last few days of the war. It is painted in the (later) standard 'air superiority' light grey over sky blue, with a red prop spinner, dark green wheel covers, and white numerals on the vertical stabilizer and rudder. (Author's Collection)

The VFLM placard for KPAF La-9 'White 102' reads: 'Fighter Plane 102, La-9: During the War for the Liberation of Korea, in the Sinuiju sky fights and other air battles this plane accomplished amazing achievements as a fighter plane.' (Author's Collection)

The VFLM contains two MiG-15s. Early model MiG-15 'Red 009' is painted to represent KPAF markings – actually left over from Soviet service – while it was assigned to the 60th FAR during the winter of 1951-52. The placard reads: 'Fighter Plane 009, MiG-15: June 22, 1952, Kim Il Sung and Kim Jung Il personally demonstrated the method of operating the fighter plane to combat the enemies.' Compare with propaganda photo on page 44. (Author's Collection)

As mentioned, the almost bunker-like construction of the VFLM building results in 'threading' the displayed aircraft between numerous concrete pillars. In this case the front-centre pillar blocks the view of the MiG-15's mid-section, which has a red ring around the fuselage just aft of the wings' trailing edge. Note that the KPAF did not apply national markings to the topsides of the MiG-15s' wings. (Author's Collection)

Close up of the forward left side of MiG-15 'Red 009' with pilot boarding ladder. (Author's Collection)

MiG-15bis 'Red 1032' was one of the 100 improved versions supplied to the KPAF and represents the one flown by Capt Gan Gyong-Duk when he led the 59th FAR against USN aircraft off North Korea's east coast in October 1952. Note the ten red 'victory stars' beneath the canopy rail. The placard reads: 'Fighter Plane 1032, MiG-15: During the War for the Liberation of Korea, this plane flew over the East Sea off the coast Hamhung and Ryunpo. The plane had an impressive record of shooting down seven and heavily damaging three enemy fighters in just one month.' (Author's Collection)

The South Korean 'War Memorial of Korea' (WMK) museum contains two North Korean aircraft, both reported to have been in the KPAF's inventory during the 1950s. Built in the Soviet Union, MiG-15UTI 'Black 128' was supplied to the KPAF after the Korean War and, according to the ROKAF Curator of the WMK, was acquired through an 'independent Korean trading company' in 1994. (Author's Collection)

Reported to have participated in the Korean War, the WMK's Yak-18 was purchased at the same time as the MiG-15UTI. Note that this example does not have the two small 'bomb racks' beneath the fuselage/wing centre-section. Also, lacking the usual 'tail number', it has no national insignia on the wing's top or bottom surfaces and is finished in olive drab over light blue. (Author's Collection)

MiG-15bis 'Red 2057' was used by Snr Lt No Kum-Sok to defect to South Korea on 21 September 1953, landing at Kimpo AB near Seoul. It was quickly hidden in a hangar where it was dismantled and then shipped to Kadena AB, Okinawa (part of Japan), where it was reassembled and flown 11 times by Maj Chuck Yeager and Capt H. E. 'Tom' Collins before being sent to Wright-Patterson AFB for further evaluation by the Air Technical Intelligence Center. It is now restored to its original markings and is currently on display at the National Museum of the USAF at Wright-Patterson. (NMUSAF Photo)

Half the world away, at P'yongyang-Sunan International Airport Kim Il-Sung's Il-14S VIP transport 'Black 535' is resplendent in its Koryu Airlines livery. This aircraft was used during the 1950s-60s – until replaced by a turbo-prop powered Il-18S 'Salon' in 1968 – to fly Kim Il-Sung to Moscow and other Eastern Bloc capitals on 'state visits'. (Andrés Ramirez via Author)

Air Bases & Airfields of Korean War 1950
Yanji
Vladivostok
USSR
Dongfeng
Hoeryong
Shenyang
Tonghua
Chongjin
Liaoyang
PR China
Anshan
Fengcheng
Andong
Langtao
Sinuiju
North Korea
Hamhung
Hungnam
Sinanju
Yonpo
Xiansilipu
Sunan
P'yongyang
Kangdong
Dalian
Heijo
Mirim-ri
Wonsan
Onjong-ni
Chinnampo
Hwang-yu
Sea of Japan (East Sea)
Pyonggang
Korea Bay
Sinmak
Kansong
Haeju
Kumchon
38°
38°
Kaesong
Chunchon
Kangnung
Kimpo/K-14
Seoul
PR China
Youi-do/K-16
Suwon/K-13
Osan
Pyongtaek/K-6
Ch'onan
South Korea
Taejon
Pohang/K-3
Kunsan/K-8
Taegu/K-2
Yellow Sea
Pusan Pocket
Pusan East/K-9
Kwangju/K-7
Pusan/K-1
major urban centres
improved ('metalled') airfields
unimproved (grass/dirt) airfields
Sachon/K-4
Miho
Korea Strait
Iwakuni
Hofu
Ashiya
Cheju/K-40
Itazuke
Japan
East China Sea
Kadena

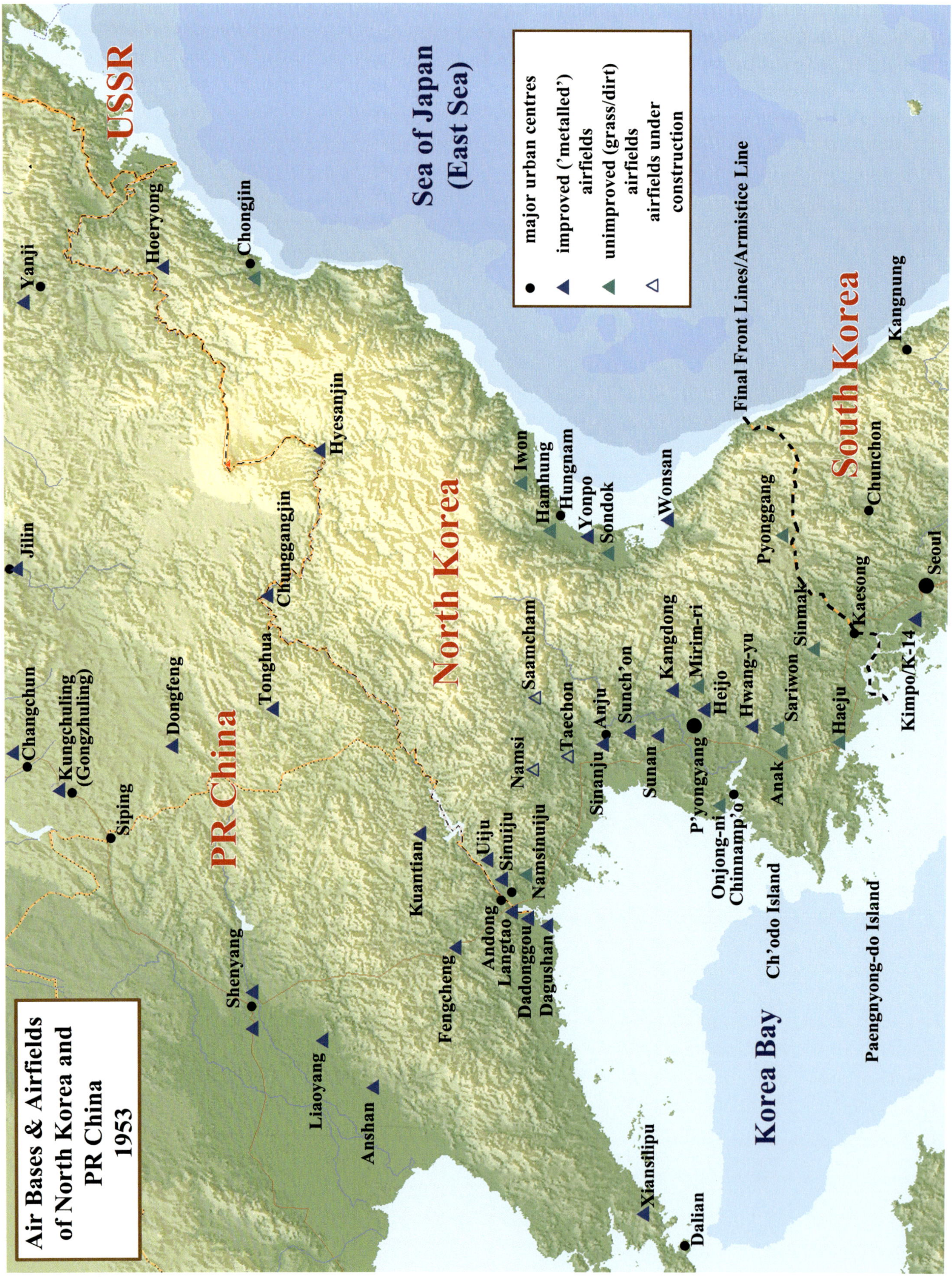

Air Bases & Airfields of North Korea and PR China 1953
major urban centres
improved ('metalled') airfields
unimproved (grass/dirt) airfields
airfields under construction
USSR
PR China
North Korea
South Korea
Sea of Japan (East Sea)
Korea Bay
Final Front Lines/Armistice Line
Yanji
Hoeryong
Chongjin
Hyesanjin
Jilin
Chunggangjin
Tonghua
Changchun
Kungchuling (Gongzhuling)
Siping
Dongfeng
Shenyang
Liaoyang
Anshan
Kuantian
Fengcheng
Andong
Langtao
Dadonggou
Dagushan
Uiju
Sinuiju
Namsinuiju
Namsi
Taechon
Saamcham
Iwon
Hamhung
Hungnam
Yonpo
Sondok
Wonsan
Sinanju
Anju
Sunch'on
Sunan
Kangdong
Mirim-ri
P'yongyang
Heijo
Hwang-yu
Onjong-ni
Chinnamp'o
Anak
Sariwon
Sinmak
Pyonggang
Haeju
Kaesong
Kimpo/K-14
Seoul
Chunchon
Kangnung
Ch'odo Island
Paengnyong-do Island
Xianshlipu
Dalian

In fact, by the end of the year FEAF Intelligence learned that in the previous two months the KPAF had grown from a 'single conventional aircraft and ground-attack division' (10th CAD) to three aviation divisions, 'one of which was jet-equipped' (1st AD). These, the Americans knew were based at 'three air stations – two in Korea [Sinuiju and Uiju] and one in Manchuria [11th AAD at Fengcheng]'.[251]

With the restoration of the KPAF's combat capability, on 4 November Maj Gen Wang Yong moved his operational HQ from P'yongyang to Sinuiju, re-establishing his command of combat units with a conference one month later attended by his subordinate commanders from P'yongyang, Sariwon, and Kangdong. Missing was Col Kim Tal-Hion, from Fengcheng, 'the popular commander of the 11th AAD'. Following the sharp defeat of his *Shturmoviki* in June – which repeated the type's heavy losses to USAF fighters one year earlier – Kim may have indiscreetly expressed some dissatisfaction with the management of the war. In an air force-wide purge of 'defeatist elements', on 27 September he was arrested for 'disloyalty', accused of 'planning to defect to the West' and summarily executed by firing squad. By the end of October the paranoia-fed purge had spread to the KPAF's training organization at Yanji, where further arrests, imprisonments and executions followed 'to clear the party of bad members.'[252]

Table 2: KPAF ORBAT, November 1951

Unit	Sub-Unit	Base	Aircraft Type	Notes
Korean People's Armed Forces Air Corps Commander: General Van Len Korean People's Air Force Commander: Major-General Wang Yong				
Operational Units				
1st Air Division				CO Brigadier–General Kang Dae-Yong
	59th Fighter Aviation Regiment	Uiju	26 MiG-15	CO Colonel Yang Du-Hi
	60th Fighter Aviation Regiment	Uiju	26 MiG-15	CO Colonel Tae Kuk-Sung
10th Combined Aviation Division				CO Brigadier-General Lee Whal
	56th Guards Fighter Aviation Regiment	Sinuiju	9 Yak-9Ps (1st Battalion), 10 La-9s (2nd Battalion)	
	57th Assault Aviation Regiment	Sinuiju	18 Il-10	
	58th Fighter Aviation Regiment	Sinuiju	21 La-9	
11th Assault Aviation Division				CO Colonel Kim Tal-Hion
	Unk. Assault Aviation Regiment	Feng-cheng (PRC)	12 Il-10s, 8 UIl-10s, unk. Yak-18s	
	57th Assault Aviation Regiment			assigned to 10th CAD at Sinuiju
3rd Night Bomber Regiment				CO Colonel Pak Den-Sik
	1st Battalion	Sariwon	6 Po-8	later augmented by Yak-18s
	2nd Battalion	Yanji (PRC)	training on Yak-18s	
Combat Units in Training				
Undesignated Bomber Aviation Division				in training
	36th Bomber Aviation Regiment	Khorol'sk (USSR)		in training on Tu-2s
	37th Bomber Aviation Regiment	Khorol'sk (USSR)		in training on Tu-2s
Other Aviation Units				
	Unk. Training Aviation Regiment	Yanji (PRC)	up to 30 Yak-18[253]	
	Unk. Training Aviation Regiment	Jilin (PRC)	up to 28 Yak-11[254]	
	Transport Regiment		C-47/Li-2, Il-12, Yak-6	

Il-10 crews resting near their aircraft. (Albert Grandolini Collection)

And Yet They Still Used Biplanes

While La-9s replaced Il-10s as the KPAF's primary daytime ground attack aircraft, after taking a two-month hiatus to regroup following its losses in June, Pak Den-Sik's 1st Night Bombing Battalion returned to combat operations in mid-September 1951.

This time the American-led UNC air force was better prepared to deal with them.

Embarrassed by the persistent small-scale successes of the KPAF 'night hecklers', on 25 July Fifth AF established a crude but effective integrated air defence system using the tactical (i.e., bombing and ground-attack) control network of the 502nd Tactical Control Group (TCG), headquartered at Seoul. The group's collocated 605th Tactical Control Squadron coordinated overall air defence operations with ground control intercept (GCI) 'local control' being exercised by the Tactical Air Direction Centers (TADCs) of the 606th AC&WS (stationed atop a large hill near Kimpo) and 608th AC&WS (eventually based on the 4,000ft high Hyangbyong-san mountain 30 miles/48km northeast of Gangneung) covering the northwest and northeast sectors, respectively.[255]

At the time FEAF's night-fighter force consisted of six North American F-82 Twin-Mustangs (68th FIS[256]) sitting strip alert in pairs at Seoul-area airfields, four NAA T-6D Texan armed trainers mounting .30-caliber machine guns at Kimpo AB, and the USMC's rather depleted VMF(N)-513 with F4U-5N Corsairs and F7F-3N Tigercats. These were augmented by Fifth AF requiring some 45 day fighters (F-80Cs, F-84Es, and F-86As) to be on 'readiness alert' at dawn and 30 more at dusk, at the main air bases.[257]

Only a week into their renewed operations, on 23 September one of Pak Den-Sik's Po-2LSh biplanes was spotted by 'Dentist' as it flew south to Kimpo AB and dropped two 44lb bombs on the 4th FIG parking area, damaging two F-86s. The US Army's 40mm and quad-.50-cal automatic-weapon batteries at Kimpo [865th AAA(AW) Bn] failed to bring down the intruder, so 'Dentist' scrambled a Tigercat to intercept the 'heckler' as it headed back north.[258]

Maj Eugene A. Van Gundy took off from Kunsan with Master Sergeant (MSgt) Thomas J. Ullom as his radar operator. Flying northeast of Kimpo at 10,000ft, Van Gundy contacted the 'Dentist' GCI controller who (as stated in his combat report)

> 'changed our altitude to 5,000ft and commenced controlling the intercept…'
>
> 'Although the bogey [target aircraft] made frequent changes in headings the controller accurately changed our vectors to correspond. As we began to close on our target our controller instructed us to reduce to 160 knots, then to 140 knots, then to 120 knots. At 140 knots we lowered our gear and flaps in order to get as slow as possible. MSgt Ullom then established contact on our own radar gear. He directed me to a point where I established a visual contact with the bogey at approximately 500 feet [range]. I made a firing pass expending 100 rounds of 20-mm ammunition. The bogey instantly burst into flames. As we pulled away we observed that the entire enemy aircraft was ablaze… The total interception took about 25 minutes, and was completed at 3,000 feet altitude.'[259]

KPAF Po-9 tail number 12 with 7.62mm ShKAS rear machine gun. (Albert Grandolini Collection)

Nine days later (2 October) the army 40mm guns at Inch'on port facilities [933rd AAA(AW) Bn] had better luck, shooting down another Po-2.[260] Reduced to only a half dozen aircraft, Pak Den-Sik's small squadron once again discontinued their night harassment attacks. With the Communist coalition's establishment of its combat air command the first week in November, the 1st Night Bombing Battalion was ordered north to participate in the Communists' first offensive air operations since the KPAF's aborted Il-10 attack on Sinmi-do Island in June.

Fighting with the Chinese

The main reason Wang moved his operational HQ to Sinuiju was for closer coordination with and – now that his air force could contribute more significantly – to personally play a much greater role in joint Chinese-North Korean operations being organized by the combined CVPAAF/KPAF headquarters at Langtao. During the preceding seven months, the Chinese-North Korean HQ had been staffed predominantly by PLAAF officers who were transferred from their air force's HQ in Beijing. Although a few KPAF officers were around, too, they 'rarely showed up

USMC F7F-3N Tigercat night fighter of VMF(N)-531. (DoD/USMC)

in their joint air force headquarters at Andong'. Originally, the combined air staff was responsible for planning (primarily signals network and aerial navigation), political, engineering, and logistics functions. However, with several PLAAF and KPAF flying units having completed their operational training, on 1 November, planning and coordinating combat operations was added to its responsibilities, upgrading it from a support staff to an operational air command headquarters that was designated the 1st United Air Army (normally rendered without its numerical designation, it was more commonly known as simply the 'UAA' – the Soviets referred to it as *Ob'yedinyennaya Vozhdushnaya Armiya* or OVA).[261]

The new combined air HQ had three components: Air Defence, Bomber, and Assault Aviation Commands, each consisting of two or more aviation divisions. At the time operational PLAAF units included three MiG-9 ADs, two MiG-15 ADs, one mixed (La-11/MiG-15) AD, one Tu-2 AD and an Il-10 AD[262] with eight more PLAAF air divisions attaining combat-ready status later that year. Because the MiG-9 was considered unsuited for combat against opposing Western fighters, they were reserved for interior air defence bomber-intercept duties only. Consequently, UAA HQ initially directed the operations of five PLAAF and three KPAF aviation divisions (1st AD, 10th CAD, and 11th AAD).

The 1st UAA began combat operations on its very first day in existence, launching four MiG-15s from the PLAAF's 3rd AD at Langtao on a photo-reconnaissance mission over the nearby off-shore islands of Ka-do, T'an-do, Sohwa-do, and Taehwa-do. That same afternoon a similar scouting mission was flown by La-11 piston-engined fighters of the PLAAF 4th FAR, launching from Fengcheng airfield.[263]

The targets of these two missions were small islands of the Pansŏng Archipelago, located just off the North Korean coast about 40 miles southeast of the Yalu River's mouth. Three of these islands were garrisoned by two battalions of the 2nd KMC regiment, ROK commandos, CIA-trained insurgent/guerrilla elements, and 159 USAF personnel. The Americans operated a radio relay station, direction finding station, navigations beacons, and a radio listening post gathering intelligence on a variety of Chinese and North Korean military activities. Taehwa-do was the most significant of the Pansŏng islands, and the furthest off-shore, defended by 1,200 South Korean marines – who regularly undertook commando, guerrilla-support, and intelligence-gathering raids along the coasts. Ka-do, the largest and closest to the coast, and the nearby T'an-do, were garrisoned to guard Taehwa-do.[264]

With the battle-lines on the peninsula becoming stagnant and ground combat settling into grim WW1-style trench warfare, during the cease-fire negotiations that began on 10 July 1951, these islands quickly became a contentious issue. Held by South Korean forces, but north of the 38th Parallel, the UNC refused to consider returning the islands to North Korean control unless the Communists agreed to territorial concessions in the Kaesŏng area. Therefore, to strengthen their 'bargaining position' the CPVA's Fiftieth Army was ordered to retake the islands in November. Eager to prove their ability to support to the ground troops, the PLAAF concentrated its three operational Tu-2 regiments at airfields near Shenyang.[265]

On the night of 5 November, CPVA units landed on Ka-do Island, subduing the small garrison in a three-hour battle. The next day PLAAF Tu-2s (8th AD's 22nd BAR), escorted by 16 La-11s (4th FAR) with 24 MiG-15s (3rd AD), attacked Taehwa-do to prevent the ROK commandos there from staging a counter-attack.[266]

PLAAF Tu-2 bombers in flight. (Author's Collection)

Eight days later, it was T'an-do Island's turn. By this time, the UAA's offensive air power had been modestly reinforced with the arrival of Pak Den-Sik's small 1st Night Bomber Battalion. During the first week in November, this unit – complete with its dedicated aircraft maintenance, administration and support organization (815th AFU) – deployed to Namsinuiju, just south of Sinuiju. The second phase of the campaign began on 14 November when KPAF Yak-9Ps reportedly strafed defensive positions on Taehwa-do and smaller islands of the Pansŏng Archipelago allowing CVPA forces to complete the capture of T'an-do.[267]

Next day Taehwa-do Island was once again attacked by PLAAF bombers, the raid successfully hitting the ROK command post, ammunition dump, and food stores, killing 60 troops and wounding another 122. That night KPAF's Po-2s joined the attacks against the defenders on Taehwa-do Island, continuing 'almost nightly bombing raids' until the end of the month.[268]

The main assault on Taehwa-do came just before midnight on 29 November, with Chinese troops coming ashore in collapsible boats, supported by a new KPN PC-class motor gunboat (mounting one 76mm, one 40mm and three 20mm guns) and mortar fire from a number of North Korean junks. They were also supported by a PLAAF night bomber raid, but according to one Russian history, 'the results of the attack were considered unsatisfactory'. At about 0100hrs six KPAF night bombers joined the battle, attacking the defenders' positions as best they could in the dark.[269]

Resistance was fierce, so to help complete the seizure of the beleaguered island, the PLAAF launched another Tu-2 attack that afternoon. This time the PLAAF bombing mission was intercepted by 31 F-86s (4th FIW), resulting in the loss of four Tu-2 bombers, three escorting La-11s and one MiG-15. ROK forces evacuated Taehwa-do the following day.[270]

Overall, the Pansŏng Islands campaign was a success, but the PLAAF's initial operational experience was disheartening. Realizing that their dreams of conducting offensive air operations had no future in the face of USAF aerial superiority, in December General Liu disbanded both the Bomber and Assault Aviation Commands, their component units returning to their respective national air arms for continued training. From this point on, the Chinese-led UAA would only attempt air defence operations along the Yalu River.[271]

CHAPTER 7
A WINTER OF JETS AND BIPLANES

When the PLAAF and KPAF established the joint UAA HQ on 1 November 1951, the Communist coalition's new Air Defence Command was assigned three Chinese MiG-15 divisions – with two more arriving in December[272] – and one North Korean MiG-15 division (1st AD), plus the mixed Yak-9P/La-9-equipped 56th GFAR. The PLAAF provided 116 MiG-15s in November, increasing to 204 the next month, and the KPAF contributed another 52 MiGs. Together the two new air arms substantially reinforced the approximately 150 MiG-15bis being flown by the Soviet's 64th IAK. The front-line MiG force – about 400 MiGs by the end of the year – now operated mainly from three 'Andong-complex' airfields, just north of the Yalu River between Andong and the coast. The newest of these was Dagushan, a brand-new jet-capable airfield with a 7,000ft (2,133m) concrete runway located near the coast about 50 miles (80km) west of Andong.[273]

PLAAF General Liu also invited the Soviets to join in the UAA, hoping that the V-VS 64th IAK, now under (now) Lt-Gen Georgiy Lobov (HSU and 19-victory ace from WW2, most recently the commander of the 303rd IAD), would participate as a full partner in the Communist coalition's air defence operations. However, Stalin would not consent to having his units under Chinese authority. Consequently, while a separate 1st UAA/CP (command post) was established only 60 yards from the 64th IAK/KP (command post) at Langtao, coordination consisted only of the UAA passing information to the Soviets so that the latter could time their launches to cover the withdrawal and return of Chinese and Korean fighters.[274]

Because of the high speeds and extreme altitudes involved in modern jet combat, both sides were dependent upon early warning (EW) radars and ground control intercept (GCI) vectors, by radio, to successfully intercept their adversaries. Early in 1951, the 64th IAK deployed its first V-VS *Pegmantit 3M* (P-3M) VHF-band EW radar at Andong. Called 'Dumbo' by the UK/US, the P-3 was developed from Massachusetts Institute of Technology (MIT) data provided to the USSR during WW2; its low power output (80-100kW) limited coverage to only 56-72 mile-range (90-115km), so it was soon replaced with the new, modern, semi-mobile, E/F-band P-20 *Periskop* ('Periscope', called 'Token' by the UK/US and later 'Bar Lock' by NATO) EW/GCI radar which was positioned at Langtao airfield, mounted on a small hill between the 64th IAK's and 1st UAA's command posts. Ten-times more powerful, the P-20 had an operational range of 90 miles (166km) and its better accuracy and faster scan rates made it better suited for ground control of MiG-15s intercepting incoming UNC formations.

To build a comprehensive EW network, the Langtao-based P-20 was augmented by four P-3M and newer P-8 (NATO 'Knife Rest') shorter-ranged 'gap fillers' deployed into North Korea at auxiliary command posts called a *Vynosnyy Punkt Upravleniya* (VPUs).[275] Together with eight visual reporting posts – two tied to each VPU – all linked to the 64th IAK/KP via an HF radio network, the entire system provided early warning and GCI capability out to 160 miles (250-270km) south-southeast of the Yalu River.[276]

Because none of the Soviet GCI controllers spoke Korean and almost none of the KPAF pilots understood Russian, language difficulties precluded an effective working relationship within the intense and dynamic environment of aerial combat. Therefore, in November 1951, the KPAF established its own EW/GCI network. Using an Andong-based radar and a Soviet-supplied P-3M erected at Uiju, Brig Gen Kang Dae-Yong, commanding the 1st AD, developed a local system that provided GCI control for his MiGs and radar assistance for returning aircraft to locate and land at Uiju and Sinuiju at night and in bad weather.[277]

Additionally, with the aid of Soviet technicians and advisors (three officers and 200 men from the 114th Radio-Technical Regiment), in late November Kang extended his EW system southwards, establishing two 'radar outposts' at Mirim-ri (called P'yongyang-East [K-24] by FEAF Intelligence, just east of P'yongyang's Heijo airbase) and Sariwon airfields. The Sariwon EW radar was connected to P'yongyang by a dedicated land-line and provided radar coverage all the way south to Kaesŏng and the battle lines north of Seoul.[278]

At Langtao, using a portable PS-03 'repeater scope' from the 64th IAK/KP, once his MiGs were airborne, Kang would relay instructions through KPAF radar controllers, directing them where to position his MiGs for attack, and continuously issued various orders during their intercepts, combat, and egress. USAF

Propaganda picture showing 'MiG-15s' taking over for Yak-9s in defending DPRK. (Detlef Billig Collection)

Kim Il-Sung and son inspecting KPAF MiG-15 at Uiju, October 1950. (Korean Central News Agency)

communications intercepts soon detected the Korean-language GCI radio vectors, resulting in FEAF Intelligence assessments that 'this net[work] is integrated with, or at least parallels, the Soviet GCI radar net in Korea.'[279]

MiG-15 retracting its landing gear on take-off. (NMUSAF)

The KPAF's 1st AD Joins the Fight

The KPAF's 1st AD joined the UAA's Air Defence Command when Kang deployed Col Tae Kuk-Sung's 60th FAR – now reinforced to 30 MiG-15s – from Anshan to Uiju on 7 November.[280] Upon arrival, Tae established an air defence alert posture of three levels. Usually eight aircraft, parked on the alert pad at the downwind end of the runway, were at Alert One: pilots in their cockpits, ground crew immediately available. At Alert Two, the pilots and ground crew had to be in the revetments with their aircraft. Alert Three was more relaxed, with the pilots available in the rest area southeast of the airfield.[281]

Scramble orders came from the 1st UAA/CP at Langtao to the regiment's mobile control vehicle parked on the alert pad. Tae could order his MiGs to launch from any of the three alert postures, shooting flares into the air to signal the Alert One and Two jets to start engines and calling the Alert Three pilots via telephone. Once airborne, the MiGs would angle northwards across the Yalu and climb steeply within the 'Manchurian sanctuary' to get above the approaching Sabres' altitudes before turning southeast, back into DPRK airspace. After take-off they switched to GCI radio frequency and would be vectored under Kang's direction.

The North Korean MiGs flew their first combat mission the day after arrival, on 8 November, 1951. The 24 MiG-15s turned south across the Yalu at high altitude, but there were no F-86s in 'MiG Alley'. Several of these familiarization flights were flown during the first week to increase the experience of the young KPAF pilots. At this point, the inexperienced North Koreans had approximately 50 hours of jet time, yet they faced battle-hardened American Sabre pilots, most of whom were WW2 veterans, all of which had more than two years flying jets and many were approaching a year of combat experience in Korea.

These sorties were valuable for increasing the KPAF pilots' formation skills, orientation to the local area, and confidence of flying in the 'combat zone'. However, they were not without risk: On the fourth mission, one pilot experienced a flameout of his RD-45 turbojet and could not get it restarted. He attempted a 'dead stick' landing at Uiju, but overshot the runway, crashing into an AA gun emplacement at the far end and was killed.

The KPAF's first encounter with F-86 Sabres was on 15 November when eight MiG-15s headed south towards P'yongyang at 39,370ft (12,000m) flying through thin cirrus clouds. A pair of F-86s managed to climb unseen to near their service ceiling (about 42,500ft/12,955m depending on conditions) and curved in behind the MiGs, attacking from the six-o'clock. The surprised Koreans scattered while the Sabres 'blew through', diving away southwards. As the MiGs climbed back to rejoin, four other F-86s

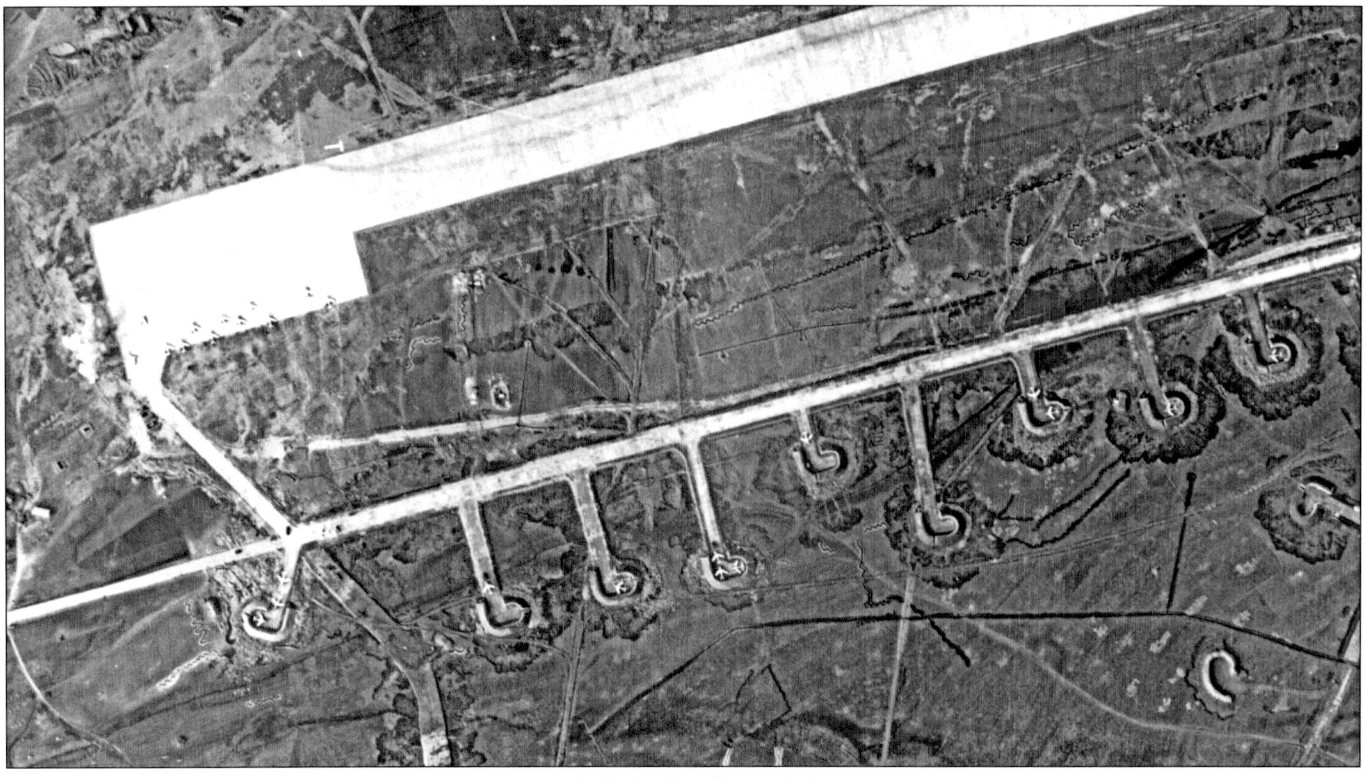

Overhead photo of Uiju Airfield showing MiG-15s on alert pad. (University of Kentucky)

appeared below them but could not match the MiGs' climb-rate or ceiling. Both sides disengaged and returned to base.[282]

American photo-reconnaissance discovered the presence of 20 MiG-15s at Uiju three days after their arrival and FEAF Bomber Command and Fifth AF began organizing a coordinated strike using B-29s, B-26s, and fighter-bombers. Meanwhile, a week later Capt Kenneth D. Chandler (336th FIS/4th FIW) and his wingman, 1st Lt Dayton W. Ragland, spotted the eight silver MiGs parked on the alert pad at the southwest end of Uiju's runway and dived down to strafe them.[283]

The strafers caught the North Koreans completely by surprise. One of the parked MiG-15s was hit in the fuel tank and burst into flames (the pilot had just climbed out for shift change), and was totally destroyed, while two more were badly damaged. One pilot, Senior Lieutenant (Snr Lt) Chung Young-Tae, was killed in his cockpit and another wounded.[284]

During the next few nights FEAF Bomber Command dispatched a dozen B-29s (98th BG), dropping some 80 tons of bombs, to knock out Uiju. Flying singly and using the new AN/APN-3 SHORAN (SHOrt RAnge Navigation) electronic navigation and bombing aid system, these missions delivered 100lb and 500lb bombs to crater the runways and blanketed the dispersal areas with air-burst 500-pounders. A particularly devastating raid on the night of 24/25 November put 474 craters in the runway, precluding further jet operations.[285]

With the USAF bombers effectively grounding the regiment, on 15 December, Kang decided to withdraw his unit to Langtao. It took 5,000 civilian labourers three days to fill the 20-foot craters and clear the rubble from the runway, after which the 60th FAR departed for their new base, in the 'sanctuary' north of the Yalu.[286]

During their time at Uiju, the 60th FAR claimed to have shot down a USAF Shooting Star and an ROKAF Mustang for the loss of three MiG-15s in combat. The first incident correlates best with the loss of F-80C (49-531) on 27 November when a four-ship from the 36th FBS (8th FBG) was reportedly attacked by 18 MiG-15s. 1st Lt Rafael A. De Breuil's jet was last seen in a 45 degree dive, jinking to avoid a pursuing MiG's cannon fire. De Breuil's crash was not observed and he was listed as MIA. The ROKAF F-51D (serial unknown), piloted by Maj Sin Cheol-Su, was lost on 15 December, reportedly to AA fire.[287]

At Langtao the KPAF's 60th FAR joined the two regiments of the V-VS 324th IAD at the west end of the airfield while the PLAAF's 3rd AD was based at the east end. Because it was considered too time-consuming to taxi to the other end of the airfield, the Soviets and Koreans always took off to the east and the Chinese took off to the west, regardless of the wind.[288]

One Soviet Korean War veteran, Guards Colonel (retired) Boris S. Abakumov, recalled that in the winter of 1951/52:

> During that time Chinese and Koreans flew from our airfield... They would go up first – then we would; we would all reverse course and form up our group on the way to the covering force area [CAP area] in the sky. The Chinese, by their own choice, flew without our top cover [and consequently suffered heavy losses to USAF F-86s]. The North Korean pilots also suffered heavy losses and after their first battle in these conditions [against the F-86s] our command decided to support them; as a result we would fly as their second echelon where teaching them was difficult, but the cadre that would form the air forces of the DPRK was created in this manner.[289]

The first significant mission flown from Langtao by KPAF MiGs was on New Year's Day, 1952. Knowing that the USAF was going to 'stand down' on the holiday, just as they had on Christmas, Tae led two dozen MiG-15s (all three squadrons) aloft to patrol southwards. Climbing to 42,650ft (13,000m), the 'train' of six four-ship formations in trail/line astern turned south, passed over P'yongyang, and flew to overhead Sariwon airfield, about halfway between the DPRK capital and the front lines. There, Tae pointed out Seoul in the distance. Lt No Kum-Sok, a member of the regiment's 2nd Battalion, flew in this mission and recalled later, 'What a strange way to celebrate New Year's Day, I viewed the two warring capitals from the sky.'[290]

KPAF Forms the 3rd Night Bomber Regiment

Once the CVPA's Pansŏng Island campaign was concluded, in early December the 1st Night Bomber Battalion returned to Sariwon where it prepared to support the KPA's night-time assaults on the off-shore islands near the Ongjin Peninsula. The KPA's 'island liberation campaign' began on 17/18 December with 80-man amphibious assault units from the 23rd Infantry Brigade taking Ch'angyang-do (now Ch'angrin-do) island, located in the entrance Ongjin Bay. Ten nights later, supported by Pak Den-Sil's night bombers, they captured Sosuap-do. Two nights afterwards an unidentified aircraft – probably a Po-2LSh – strafed USS *Eversole* (DD-789) while patrolling south of Sŏk-to Island.[291]

The 1st Night Bomber Battalion ended 1951 by sending three Po-2s south at midnight on New Year's Eve to drop bombs on Kimpo AB and Inch'on harbour facilities. During the early morning hours, one raider hit Inch'on with two bombs doing no damage while another dropped two bombs on Kimpo, destroying 16 external fuel tanks ('drop tanks') and damaging one F-86.[292]

While the KPAF's night bomber squadron was absent from Sariwon for the Pansŏng Island campaign, base commander Ch'oe Kun-Pil began a construction program, building several small dispersal airfields, each well camouflaged and capable of supporting up to three small aircraft. On 11 January he reported to KPAF HQ that three 'practice fields' were completed and suitable for the delivery of 'training planes'. Ten days later, five Yak-18 trainers – modified as light bombers – were ferried from Yanji to Sariwon, via Changchun and Shenyang. Initially, they were to be dismantled and 'stored in operating condition'.[293]

Interestingly, the North Koreans use of the terms 'training planes' and 'practice fields' completely fooled the USAF/CIA SIGINT analysts, who found, 'this move to begin training on UN-interdicted North Korean airfields [to be] incomprehensible'. Actually the Yak-18s were badly needed reinforcements for Pak Den-Sik's depleted 1st Night Bomber Battalion.

Additionally, during the first week in April, a second squadron, with seven Yak-18s, arrived in the Sinuiju area (probably the small sod field called Namsinuiju). Together, these two units constituted what USAF SIGINT discovered to be the KPAF's 3rd Bomber Regiment. Following a single aircraft night bombing

KPAF Yak-18 with pilots preparing for navigation flight. (Jin Ho Collection)

attack on Ch'o-do on 14 February, the two squadrons were not particularly active during the spring months of 1952, their aircraft were dismantled, dispersed and concealed to prevent discovery and destruction by roving UNC fighter-bombers.[294]

KPAF MiG-15 Operations – January–April 1952

During winter and spring 1952, the KPAF's 60th FAR frequently launched from Langtao airfield, flying into the 'combat zone' (the Communists' term for 'MiG Alley') to build experience, but they almost always refrained from engaging American F-86s under anything but the most favourable circumstances. No later said that:

> Whenever our local radar showed that the skies were clear of danger we were sent aloft. We had to fly and fight sometime, or we would prove useless... I was sent aloft every day at Dandong [*sic*], often twice a day. Most of these flights were relatively quiet. Occasionally a Sabre would pass me head-on at high speed. Then we would squirt off a brief shot at each other and lose contact as we raced past. By the time we could turn, we would be ten miles apart.[295]

No reported that he encountered F-86s on only 'one out of every three missions'. Because the MiGs normally entered the 'Alley' at 42,650 to 45,930ft (13-14,000m), well above the Sabres' patrol altitude (typically below the 'contrail level' 36,000ft/10,973m), 'seldom, then, did the opposing fighters clash with an exchange of gunfire.'[296]

This is confirmed by one Soviet history which reported that when the North Koreans – which normally flew with the Soviet MiG units providing cover – attempted to operate independently, without the support of their 'Big Friends,' 'they were not very eager to join in battle with the enemy'. In fact, during this three-month period, there were only four known engagements between KPAF MiGs and the F-86s. In three of these cases two dozen MiG-15s engaged four Sabres and each encounter proved inconclusive with no losses suffered by either side.[297]

The fourth instance, however, occurring on 25 January, 1952, was a completely different situation with a decidedly different outcome.[298]

Led by Maj Pak Soon-Kan (3rd Battalion commander) and directed from the ground by their air division commander, GCI turned the 'train' of 24 MiGs southwards at 26,250ft (8,000m), anxious to have them join a large dogfight – between PLAAF 4th AD MiGs and USAF 4th FIW F-86As – that had already developed about 60 miles south. However, the premature turn across the Yalu gave approaching F-86Es from the 51st FIW an altitude advantage and they quickly exploited it.[299]

While two Sabres closed from directly ahead ('12 o'clock level'), their guns blazing, another pair attacked the MiGs from above and behind ('high six o'clock'). The MiG formation was shattered and the Sabres had a field day. The Americans claimed nine MiG-15s destroyed that day; four of these were North Koreans. Pak and another KPAF pilot were shot down and killed while a third, Lt Lee Nam-Tae ejected and survived. Badly damaged, a fourth, flown by Lt Hu Bak-Yong made a 'dead stick' crash-landing at the battered Sinuiju airfield. (It is unknown how many PLAAF MiGs were lost in the battle; two F-86As failed to RTB.)[300]

Finally, the first week in April brought heavy clouds, rainstorms and thick fogs into the Yalu basin. During the next two weeks two of the 60th FAR MiG-15s were lost in weather-related accidents. Lt Hu Bak-Yong became disoriented in cloud and dived into the ground, killing him. Unable to find his airfield, Maj Lee Choon-Tuk attempted to divert to Dalian but crashed on final approach, probably from fuel exhaustion; luckily he was unhurt.[301]

Subsequently during this initial period of combat operations, nine MiG-15s were lost to all causes and five pilots killed. The aircraft losses were readily replaced. Towards the end of March, USAF 'Suede' SIGINT intercepts confirmed that the 1st AD had one regiment (60th FAR) deployed to Langtao airfield with 26

MiG-15 'Red 008' was Lt No Kum-Sok's assigned aircraft. (Albert Grandolini Collection)

Gun camera photo of USAF F-86s shooting at MiG-15. (Larry Davis)

MiG-15s and another (59th FAR) based at Anshan with 24 MiG-15s.[302] While only two UNC aircraft had been destroyed during this period, at least the aim of increasing the young KPAF pilots' experience by flying in the 'combat zone' was achieved.

To provide similar experience for Yang Du-Hi's 59th FAR, in mid-April, Kang rotated his fighter regiments between Langtao and Anshan, sending Yang's unit forward and withdrawing Tae's regiment to the rear for rest and further training. However, the spring's bad weather prevented the 59th FAR from having combat experiences similar to those of the 60th FAR.[303]

The KPAF 2nd AD Also Joins the Battle

Representing the first 'sign of the presence of at least elements of the North Korean 2nd Air Division (LA-equipped) at Sinuiju', on 12 January USAF SIGINT intercepts indicated that another '14 LA-9 flight leaders' had arrived at Sinuiju. This signified that the KPAF's propeller-driven fighter force was undergoing a substantial reorganization. Evidently the La-9-equipped squadron of the 56th GFAR, having been transferred to Fengcheng for ground attack training in November, had now returned to join the 58th FAR, their arrival providing a 35-aircraft dual-role fighter regiment at Sinuiju and freed the depleted 56th GFAR (six Yak-9Ps had been lost in combat during 1951) for reorganization and reassignment. By the end of the month the 'Guards Taejon' – now down to one squadron of nine Yak-9Ps – was withdrawn via Anshan to Dongfeng to train as a night-fighter unit.[304]

Evidently, about this time that Wang completely reorganized the KPAF division-level designations. Consisting of the 57th AAR and 58th FAR, the 'new' 2nd Air Division was a renumbering of the 10th CAD. The last mention of the '10th Air Division' in KPAF messages intercepted by American COMINT and SIGINT units was in March. In May, intercepts of PLAAF and KPAF messages revealed that the latter's training organization at Yanji was now known as the '10th Aviation School' or, more colloquially, as the '10th Manchurian Air Academy', under the direct control of the KPAF rear-echelon HQ at Yanji.[305]

Since the disastrous attempt at raiding Sinmi-do Island the previous summer, very few operations by the 57th AAR's Il-10 '*Shturmoviki*' had been observed, but by the beginning of 1952 there were some indications that Wang was considering expanding the type's role, especially on North Korea's east coast. On 12 March, several unidentified single-engine aircraft were discovered parked on the ramp at Wonsan airfield and some 2,800 feet of its runway was undamaged and considered useable. Six weeks later (21 April) USN F4U Corsairs, flying inland to direct naval gunfire bombardment, identified an Il-10 on the field and immediately attacked, strafing and destroying the '*Shturmovik*'.[306]

The next day a pair of USAF F-86E Sabres (51st FIW) made a similar strafing attack on Sinuiju airfield, Maj Elmer W. Harris and Capt Iven C. Kincheloe being credited with destroying two 'Yak-9s' on the ground.[307] Returning two weeks later, on 4 May, these two 25th FIS pilots destroyed another five 'Yak-9s' while other Sabres flew 'top cover'. Spotting two single-engine propeller aircraft taking-off from Sinuiju, two 16th FIS Sabres dove to attack, Capt Richard H. Schoeneman leading 1st Lt James A. McCully in shooting down both of them. Schoeneman was credited with an Il-10 destroyed and McCully with a 'Yak-3'.[308]

About this time, KPAF leadership began preparations to convert the 2nd AD to MiG-15s and directed the Sinuiju-based division to begin flying tactical training missions. According to one Russian history, 'They flew their most experienced pilots from the battles of 1950 to Antung [*sic*] in fours of La-9s so that they could become masters of the best flying skills. The[ir] primary mission was the study of the tactics of air combat with the latest change in Soviet pilots, since in the near future they themselves would be led into combat in groups of MiG-15s.'[309]

During a training flight near Langtao on 20 June four La-9s – led by Hero of the DPRK Maj Baek Gi-Rak and flown by 'four North Korean aces [with] solid combat experience' – were spotted by Sabres from the 4th FIW. High overhead, Col Royal N. Baker, was leading a fighter sweep of 'MiG Alley' with four four-ship formations from the 336th FIS. Leaving three four-ships as 'high cover', Baker led his formation down to attack the trailing pair of La-9s. He and wingman, 1st Lt George J. Wood, claimed the two La-9 wingmen shot down on the first pass. Indeed, Snr Lt Kang Sung-Hung was shot down and killed; Lt Kim Hwa-Ren's fighter was set afire, but he was able to crash-land his burning aircraft in a field.[310]

The other pair went into defensive turns and try as they might, Baker and his wingmen could not get their speeding Sabres inside the Lavochkins' tight turning circles long enough to score a telling burst. Hearing the mêlée on the radio Capt Frederick C. Blesse, led his four-ship (334th FIS) to the fight and from 18,000ft altitude watched the spectacle of the F-86s 'coming in extremely fast, taking a couple of quick shots, then chandelling up another 5,000 feet to await their next turn. One of the enemy pilots was

KPAF La-9s taxiing out for takeoff. (Jin Ho Collection)

KPAF La-9 pilot Major Baek Gi-Rak, 'Hero of DPRK'. (Tom Cooper Collection)

playing them like a piano, knowing exactly what each F-86 was going to do. Just before each Sabre was within firing range, the La-9 would go into a tight little turn. The '86 pilot's shots were nowhere near the mark, and they would zoom back up.'[311]

Finally Blesse asked if he could make a pass and 'the frustrated Col Baker approved'. Leaving his three wingmen to 'give me a little cover', Blesse 'peeled off' to attack Baek Gi-Rak:

'Down almost in the weeds, I [pulled up at him and] popped my speedbrakes, pulled the throttle all the way back to idle and started coming up at him. He saw me and put the Lavochkin into that real tight turn but I just kept going up. He rolled out just like he had been doing, thinking he was perfectly safe. I rolled over, came up about 400 feet (150m) behind him, constantly closing the gap...'

'Firing on him, I didn't want to overshoot. He would have been very dangerous, since he had better manoeuvring performance, better turn capability and better everything except acceleration. As I slid up on him, there were several hits and the La-9 blew up with me about 200 feet underneath... [and] went into a steep turn and crashed'.[312]

Baek was killed, but Hero of the DPRK Capt Kim Gi-Ohk returned to claim two Sabres shot down. Russian sources stated, 'According to the KPA [High] Command, three La-9s were downed and two pilots killed [but] their pilots shot down three F-86s and one American Sabre pilot, named Farler, was taken prisoner.'[313]

This was the last known operation by the KPAF's propeller-driven fighter and ground attack units from Sinuiju airfield for several months. On 15 October, the Chinese reported that the North Koreans evacuated '69 conventional aircraft [La-9s and Il-10s] from combat airfields in the Yalu River complex, including Sinuiju, to airfields in the Manchurian interior.'[314]

CHAPTER 8
THE SPRING OF CHANGE

As 1952 began the Communist coalition started a gradual, though profound, shift in its conduct of aerial operations. It began with the fact that Stalin's initial commitment to Mao Zedong – promising to provide air cover over the CVPA's supply lines crossing the Yalu River until the PLAAF could do so – had largely been fulfilled and the two premier Soviet V-VS MiG-15 air divisions (303rd and 324th IADs) returned to 'Mother Russia' after the end of January, 1952.[315]

Because the PLAAF was not yet ready to fully assume the air defence mission at Andong, Stalin consented to continue providing two MiG-15 IADs to form the backbone of the Communist air defence system along the Yalu. Replacing the 324th IAD at Langtao, at the end of January the Soviets' newly-trained two-regiment 97th IAD arrived from the Moscow Military District and, at nearby Dadonggou, two weeks later the equally inexperienced three-regiment 190th IAD moved from the Primorsky Krai to replace the 303rd IAD. In both cases, it was only the pilots and division staffs involved in the exchange, the new units' pilots taking over the departing divisions' aircraft and ground crews *in sitsu*.[316]

Both of these units had only recently completed conversion to the MiG-15 and almost all the pilots – just like their Chinese and North Korean contemporaries – were brand-new to the jet, few of them had more than 50-60 hours in type and only 10 per cent were WW2 veterans; none of them had flown in Korea. Selected for combat duty because they 'had received the best training marks from the supreme military authorities', instead of being tactical fighter units like their predecessors, the two new IADs were from the *Provito Vozdushnaya Oborona Strany* ('Anti-Air Defence of the Nation', commonly called 'PVO-Strany') the Soviet Union's independent air defence force.[317] Being dedicated strategic air defence units, their training concentrated on instrument flying, radar-directed GCI procedures, and attacking bomber formations; they had no training or practice in air-to-air combat against opposing fighters. This lack of proper training and their wholesale inexperience showed themselves immediately: in their first two months of combat they lost 27 MiGs destroyed and 62 damaged, with ten pilots killed. In the same period only five F-86s were lost to Soviet MiGs – three pilots were KIA, one MIA – plus two others damaged.[318]

Additionally, in the springtime the Soviet 'instructor divisions' also departed China, returning home to re-equip with new MiG-15bis and even newer MiG-17 fighters. In addition to converting four MiG-9 ADs to the far more advanced and effective MiG-15 during 1951, they also taught 'from scratch' two new Chinese MiG-15 units. During the first three months of 1952, four of the new PLAAF ADs[319] were added to the CPVAF's order of battle. Some of these were stationed at more distant Manchurian bases, but all of them regularly rotated their regiments through the Andong-complex airfields – which now formally included Fengcheng – in order to experience 'five to seven large-scale air battles' after which they returned to their rear area bases to rest, regroup, and replace losses.[320]

Sabres Dominate MiG Alley

By this time the Soviets were also experiencing severe problems. In addition to their inadequate training and immense inexperience, the Soviets were overwhelmed by recent changes in the USAF's

F-86s from 335th FIS flying to 'MiG Alley'. (Warren Thompson Collection)

F-86 force. First was the activation of a second Sabre unit – the 51st Fighter Interceptor Wing (51st FIW) commanded by 28-victory WW2 ace Colonel Francis 'Gabby' Gabreski – bringing to 127 the number of F-86s in Korea. Second, FEAF HQ relaxed the rule forbidding flight into Chinese airspace, allowing 'hot pursuit' north of the Yalu as long as the pursuer was in a position to complete the destruction of the enemy fighter. Gabreski quickly took advantage of this exception, and routinely sent his Sabres north of the river to patrol above (or 'hawk') the Andong airfields, ready to pounce on any attempts to take-off or fly the final approach for landing.[321]

The Soviets called these 'airfield blockading' [*blokirovanie*] operations. The inexperienced MiG pilots were at a serious disadvantage because the MiG's low-altitude performance was markedly inferior to the Sabre's, resulting in alarming losses. From February through April the two new Soviet IADs reported having 'lost 48 MiG-15bis aircraft and 16 pilots, of which 23 aircraft and seven pilots, that is, about 50 per cent, were shot down by American fighters over our airfields.'[322]

The unauthorized F-86 operations also caused the loss of at least one KPAF MiG-15. Capt Park Chun-Hak was shot down 'in the traffic pattern' at Langtao and crash-landed on the dirt strip alongside the runway, hitting his head on the canopy bow and gunsight, causing a severe concussion. Park was treated at the Soviet hospital in Harbin, but he never fully recovered and was medically discharged sometime afterwards. Incensed, once the weather allowed renewed operations, Kang became adamant about 'breaking' the F-86s' 'airfield blockading' operations. Early each morning, before sunrise on the clear days in May and June, two or four Sabres would fly to the mouth of the Yalu River and orbit (CAP) there in the contrail level (36,000 to 42,000 feet – 10,973-12,802m) so that they would be seen 'hawking' the three forward Andong airfields in what the North Korean pilots assumed 'was meant to lure us up to fight'. One June morning Kang ordered Tae Kuk-Sung to 'go after them' with two dozen MiG-15s.[323]

Taking off from Anshan in pre-dawn twilight, Tae's formation climbed as it headed south to the Yalu and then 'flew toward the contrails south of the river'. By then the F-86s were running low on fuel and headed south, the 24 MiG-15s following their contrails towards Seoul. Passing the Ch'ongch'on River the MiGs, too, became low on fuel – 'barely enough to return and land,' No reported.

> 'We gradually descended, heading north, where fresh squadrons of F-86s awaited us near the Yalu River and jumped us from all quarters, even from above.'
>
> 'Some MiG pilots sat helplessly in their cockpits until the F-86s shot them to pieces, taking no evasive action... preferring to rely on the armoured plate behind the seat. Two of them bailed out and survived. One MiG pilot made an abrupt and steep climbing manoeuvre and was shot in the head by a pursuing F-86. Three MiG-15s went down near the airfield on that fateful summer day, and most of the others were shot up.'[324]

The defeat was the second major reverse suffered by the 1st AD at the hands of the USAF Sabres – losing seven MiG-15s in two

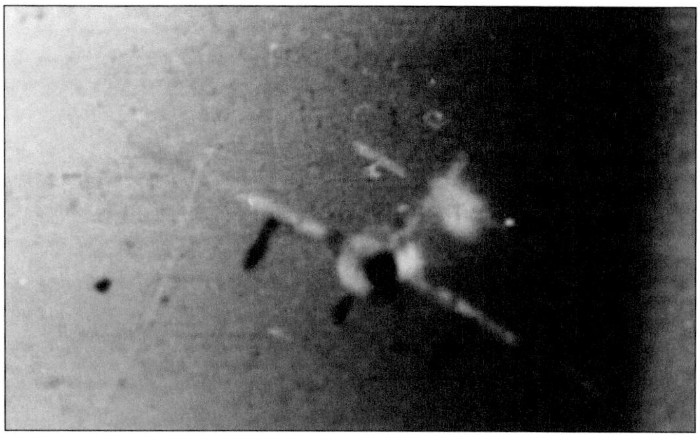

F-86 Gun camera still of MiG-15 with wheels down. (Larry Davis)

Gun camera still of MiG-15 being shot down. (NMUSAF)

engagements that were directed by Kang – and it cost him his job. No relates that around 3/4 July Kang was 'relieved of all duties, demoted to "nonperson", and discharged from the People's Army... In a militaristic and warmongering country like North Korea, the General's status had plummeted to that of a beggar.'[325]

Kang was replaced by Col Kim Hi-Kiung, a veteran KPAF fighter pilot who had flown Yak-9Ps with the 56th GFAR from Heijo airbase at P'yongyang in 1949-50. In fact, during the USN's famous raid in July 1950 Kim was one of two Yak-9P pilots (Tae Kuk-Sung was the other) that attempted to defend the KPAF's 'home field' from carrier-based Corsairs and Skyraiders. Both were shot down, bailed out and survived, but not before Kim could fictitiously claim to have shot down three of the attackers (as 'F-80s').[326]

A New Mission

Kim had different ideas about how to 'get back at' the Sabres that so brazenly 'hawked' the Andong airfields. At Anshan, he ordered Tae to begin training his regiment for a special mission. Gathering his pilots into a briefing room and Tae explained, 'Much of the Sabre strength is at Kimpo, We [will] train you to destroy the Sabres before they get into the air.' For six weeks the MiG-15 pilots trained to strafe ground targets, using the air-to-ground gunnery ranges at Fengcheng, where KPAF La-9s had practiced strafing during the preceding autumn.[327] According to No,

> We practiced by strafing ground targets with live ammunition, buzzing in line, one after another. This promised to be an effective tactic, and we hoped to do on the ground what we could not do in the air. Unfortunately, fragments from our

> cannon rounds, which ricocheted off the ground damaged a few MiGs. We were soon ready to perform the mission, flying from Andong, but, the word to attack never came. At the last minute, the mission to Kimpo was cancelled because the Soviet high command… feared the Americans would retaliate by strafing MiGs in Manchuria.[328]

While the 60th FAR practiced airfield strafing missions, Yang's regiment took on an entirely new and different mission. During this period UNC carrier-based naval aircraft augmented USAF and RAAF straight-wing jet fighter-bombers (F-80Cs, F-84Es, and Meteor F.8s) flying interdiction missions against CPVA supply lines and reserve forces in and around the area of P'yongyang and Chinnamp'o. At the time these missions – averaging 60-75 sorties per day – were being flown by the US Marines' VMA-312 'Checkerboards', which was embarked with two dozen F4U-4Bs Corsairs aboard the 11,000-ton escort carrier USS *Sicily* (CVE 118).[329]

The first MiG-15s to encounter carrier-based attack aircraft were those of the PLAAF, which had become intent 'to push the line of battle to the south of the Ch'ongch'on River, so [they] could avoid battles over their own bases. Another goal was to send MiGs deep into the P'yongyang and Chinnamp'o areas, protecting ground troops from enemy fighter-bombers'. Accordingly, the PLAAF sent flights of four or eight (occasionally 12) MiG-15s, usually under cloud cover, 'to Chinnamp'o and even to Sariwon to engage fighter-bombers… attacking ground targets south of P'yongyang'. From July to October, the Chinese pilots operating in this area claimed 30 'USAF fighter-bombers and conventional navy planes' shot down for the loss of only two MiG-15s.[330]

Learning of the apparent Chinese success, the 59th FAR also began 'hunting' naval attack aircraft. Soviet MiGs were prohibited to fly over the water, for fear that the loss of a Soviet pilot and his rescue (alive) or recovery (of the dead body) would expose Stalin's charade, and Chinese MiGs did not venture off-shore due to the lack of an air-sea rescue capability. KPAF units, however, were not subject to these concerns and, in fact, previously Il-10s had made a number of attacks 'well out to sea'. This is confirmed by one Russian history which states, 'during that summer [*sic*] more and more of the Koreans were flying out over the sea, and a squadron of KPAFAC MiGs led by Teng Doo-Ho [probably actually 59th FAR Commander Yang Du-Hi] fought a September battle with six naval aircraft.'[331]

Following an inconclusive attack on two VMA-312 flights near Chinnamp'o on 9 September, the next day KPAF MiG-15s engaged USMC Corsairs twice. The first attack, against four Kimpo-based VMA-323 F4Us, was unsuccessful despite ten firing passes, but the second – made by eight MiG-15s – resulted in losses on both sides.

At the time VMA-312 was flying 'maximum effort' interdiction and CAS missions attacking a troop concentration south of the Taedong Estuary, opposite Chinnamp'o. Leading two F4U-4Bs, Capt Jesse G. Folmar recalled,

> as we crossed the coast and headed into enemy territory, we began executing a tactical weave at 10,000ft. Arriving over the target area, we observed no activity, so we continued to fly reconnaissance in the area of the Taedong Estuary. As we started to bank over a small island [Sŏk-to] off the coast, I caught a glimpse of two MiG-15s in the early stages of setting up for a firing pass on us. They were in loose echelon formation, so I steepened my banking turn into them, while at the same time increasing power. I jettisoned all external ordnance and fuel tanks and then switched to guard channel [on the radio] to report that we were being attacked by MiGs. I told Lt [Walter E.] Daniels to fly a much tighter weave, and not to let the Communist jets out of his sight.
>
> Seconds later, I spotted two more of them closing rapidly from my 'eight o'clock'. I turned hard to the left, trying to bring my guns to bear before they could open fire, but due to their rapid closure, I was unable to do so. Their tracers were overshooting us, so I reversed my bank to the right and turned inside one of the MiGs as he started a climbing left turn. I pulled up and got him squarely in my gunsights, then I triggered off a long five-second burst with my four 20mm cannon. I could tell that I had him boresighted by the blinking flashes along the left side of his fuselage. A grey trail of fuel vapour began to stream from the MiG, and this quickly turned into billowing black smoke. He nosed over slightly and seemed to lose acceleration. Seconds later the pilot ejected, and he tumbled through the air in what appeared to be a ball of smoke… I glanced down and saw the flaming MiG hit the water vertically.[332]

Folmar and Daniels reformed their formation and resumed their defensive weave just as a second four-ship of MiG-15s set up to attack in 'a loose column of two sections'. Folmar ordered a slicing left-hand break turn to head out to sea.

VMA-312 'Checkerboards' F4U Corsair in flight. (Warren Thompson)

Three MiG-15s making high speed firing passes. (NMUSAF)

I had just started picking up good diving speed when I saw balls of tracer passing on my left. At that instant I felt a severe jolt and explosion in my left wing. My aircraft began to shudder as if in a high speed stall. I glanced over and saw that my left aileron and about four feet of my left wing were gone. Also, the top of the left wing was gutted to the inboard side of my inboard 20mm gun. My damaged aeroplane was trying to roll to the left, although the control column was placed in the full right position. This led to my decision that it would be too hazardous to attempt a landing back on *Sicily*, so I decided to bail out.'

The wingmen also made firing passes on the stricken Corsair as Folmar 'rolled out of the right side of the cockpit and fell clear'. From his parachute he watched as the seven MiGs circled the area, but headed back to the north after he landed in the water. Remarkably, 15 minutes later he was rescued by a USAF Grumman SA-16 Albatross twin-engine amphibian.[333] One Russian history states, 'According to North Korean records, in this action squadron commander Teng [*sic*] shot down one carrier bomber, while his wingmen downed an enemy fighter that was trying to cause him to break off his attack.'[334]

Fighting Task Force 77

For months, flying from two to four aircraft carriers off the peninsula's east coast, USN aircraft had been operating over the eastern part of North Korea with total impunity. Primarily these were propeller-driven F4U-4 Corsairs and AD-4 Skyraiders, but by September – because of the total lack of airborne opposition – even the jet-powered F9F-2 Panthers were flying ground attack missions. Consequently – unlike battling Sabres in MiG Alley – fighter sweeps of North Korea's east coast against USN carrier aircraft promised great rewards for little risk.[335]

By this time the KPAF had expanded and improved its air defence radar network. In addition to establishing a fourth GCI/EW radar site at Such'ŏn (40 miles [64km] south Sinuiju, covering the area between the Yalu and Ch'ongch'on Rivers), with Soviet help an EW radar was established at Huichon, in the central highlands. In July a sixth EW radar site was established near Chongjin and was reportedly was able to look into the Sea of Japan 'as far south as required'. Additionally, the proficiency of KPAF radar controllers had increased remarkably, regularly controlling MiG-15s in day combat using Korean, Chinese, and Russian, depending on which nation's units they were directing. In a notable achievement, during a two-week period in mid-February, the parallel and independent KPAF GCI directed 142 [flights of] fighter aircraft.[336] With the confidence provided by 'positive radar control', it was thought that the chances of successfully locating and engaging the USN attack aircraft were vastly improved, and the qualitative superiority of the MiG-15 should result in 'easy kills'.

For this mission Yang chose the squadron led by Capt Gan Gyong-Duk, which Kim reinforced with the 60th FAR's 2nd Battalion, this squadron deploying eight MiG-15s to Langtao airfield. The two squadrons formed what was known as the 'special attack group'. Gan's squadron flew as the 'strike group' – to locate and attack USN formations – while the 60th FAR's squadron followed, flying at high altitude to cover the strike group. Following training flights to hone the MiG pilots' long-range navigation skills, in mid-September the two squadrons began flying 'sweeps' to the east-southeast, usually to the huge semi-circular Wonsan Bay that was the USN's main area of air operations.[337]

After a few inconclusive encounters, on 4 October, in an attack that appeared to be under 'positive GCI control prior to and during the attack' four MiG-15s engaged a formation of seven F4Us that had been pounding Yonpo airfield. The Corsairs (VF-884/USS *Kearsarge*) were headed back to their carrier and were completely surprised by the speeding jets slashing through their formation, firing their 23mm and 37mm cannon. Before the Corsair pilots could react, Gan Gyong-Duk shot down one of them; the crippled Corsair went into a steep dive into the sea, killing Lt Eugene F. Johnson. The attack lasted only 90 seconds before the MiGs turned northwards and egressed unscathed.[338]

Three days later the KPAF MiGs repeated their fighter sweeps engaging USN attack aircraft three times. On the first occasion four MiG-15s attacked a flight of four Corsairs near Hungnam in an inconclusive engagement. On a second mission to the same area it appears that the four-ship 'strike group' split with one pair attacking eight Skyraiders – the ADs returned fire but 'no damage was inflicted by either side and the MiGs retired to the west'. The others – led by Gan – attacked four F4Us (VF-193/USS *Princeton*) just south of Hungnam, 'destroying one F4U'. Ensign John R. Shaughnessy bailed out and was rescued by a destroyer (USS *Boyd*, DD-544) but died on board from his injuries. From this point on TF 77's carriers provided eight or twelve F9F Panthers to accompany each major strike in the Wonsan and Hungnam areas. Flying 1,000 to 2,000ft above and behind the ADs, with the F4Us on the flanks, the 'jet cover' was sufficient to deter further MiG attacks against USN aircraft.[339]

Nevertheless, the 'special attack group' continued its high altitude patrols over Hungnam and Wonsan Bay and on 12 October Gan's four-ship formation spotted four F-51Ds from No. 2 'Cheetah' Squadron, South African Air Force (SAAF), conducting armed reconnaissance north of the bay, between Samdong-ni and Kowŏn-ŭp. In a typical slashing cannon attack, the MiGs shot down one Mustang, Lt Trevor R. 'Chick' Fryer bailing out to become a POW.[340]

Two days later 16 MiG-15s returned to the Wonsan-Hungnam area and spotted the USS *Vesuvius* (AE 15, an ammunition replenishment ship) conducting resupply operations with the 'blockade task group's' minesweepers and destroyers. Four MiGs 'orbited over the ships but did not make hostile moves or come within gun range'. Flying 'high cover' for the 'strike group', (now) Snr Lt No Kum-Sok reported, 'On these flights we saw U.S. Seventh Fleet warships off the shore of Wonsan harbour, but we were ordered not to strafe those unsinkable warships. The attempt would be futile. One clear day I saw three shining warships about five miles off the coast. They were a cruiser [*sic*] and two large destroyers.'[341]

On 16 October, eight KPAF MiGs 'aggressively pursued' a USN strike group of 15 aircraft but 'broke off the attack before firing'. Next day eight MiG-15s returned to Wonsan but remained at altitude, making contrails high above the bay. The last time the

KPAF MiGs were observed over the area was 20 October, when two USN aircraft spotted four MiGs twice high above them.[342]

According to the principal PLAAF history, 'in early October North Korean pilots claimed 15 [enemy] aircraft destroyed or damaged' in their east coast operations. Gan was credited with 10 of these victories and was awarded the 'Hero of the DPRK' honour. With these victories added to their record, on or after 21 October the 1st AD was withdrawn from front-line duties, 34 MiG-15s flying from Langtao to join the 14 remaining at Anshan. The departure of the 1st AD, coupled with the withdrawal of the 2nd AD from Sinuiju a week earlier, 'practically empt[ied] the airfields in the Yalu River complex of North Korean air units.'[343]

F4U Corsairs flying near USS Boxer. (US Navy)

During their rest at the rear area base, the pilots who had flown 50 or more combat missions were awarded the 'Gold Medal' – the KPAF equivalent of the USAF and RAF Distinguished Flying Cross – in a 'grand' ceremony 'with the whole regiment at attention on the parade ground while a band played and senior officers made requisite patriotic speeches.'[344]

A few days later, Wang received word that new MiG-15bis fighters had arrived from the Soviet Union and the 1st AD was ordered to ferry their remaining, very tired, older model MiGs to Yanji. There these were handed over to the newly formed 3rd AD, whose 60 pilots had just soloed the Yak-11 advanced trainer and were ready to begin their training on jet fighters, before the pilots of the 1st AD departed by train to Changchun, China, to accept their new mounts.[345]

F9F Panther flying near Yonpo airfield. (US Navy)

Capt Gan Gyong-Duk, credited with 10 victories over Wonsan from 4 to 12 October 1952. (Tom Cooper Collection)

SAAF No. 2 'Cheetah' Squadron at Hoengsong airfield (K-46). (NMUSAF)

CHAPTER 9
FIGHTING AT NIGHT

Following the disastrous (for the Americans) daylight bombing raids during October 1951, in which nine B-29s were destroyed and another four damaged,[346] on 28 October FEAF HQ directed its Bomber Command to switch exclusively to night bombing attacks, flying 2,500 sorties during the first five months of night operations, augmenting Fifth AF's B-26 Invaders and significantly increasing the night attacks on – and damage to – North Korean railways and other CPVA supply lines. In response, the Soviets transferred their only night-fighter unit, Lt Col I. A. Yefrimov's 351st OIAP (*Otdel'nyy IAP*, 'independent fighter aviation regiment') with 28 pilots and 20 La-11s, from Lüda (an airfield near Dalian) to Anshan.[347]

However, only 11 knots (20km/hr) faster than the B-29s, the 351st OIAP's La-11s soon proved to be too slow to effectively intercept the four-engined night bombers, prompting Lobov to order Yefrimov's *1st Eskadra* to convert to MiG-15s. (The regiment's *2nd Eskadra* remained equipped with La-11s and concentrated on attacking the lower and slower B-26s.) By the end of 1951, the squadron's conversion to the MiG-15bis was completed and they flew their first night intercept training missions over North Korea on 29 January. Once proficiency was attained in night flying and GCI intercepts, to shorten the range and response time, on 7 May Yefrimov and his *1st Eskadra* deployed nine MiG-15bis to Langtao – the only frontline airfield with runway lights – to begin combat operations. The unit's first success was on the night of 10/11 June, when four MiG-15s intercepted a stream of eleven B-29As [19th BW(M)] bombing railroad bridges at Kwaksan (near Chongju), shooting down two Superfortresses and damaging a third so badly it force-landed at Kimpo AB with one wounded aboard.[348]

Meanwhile the regiment's *2nd Eskadra*, continuing to operate La-11s from Anshan against Fifth AF B-26 night intruders, also scored, shooting down an RB-26C in May and a B-26C in June.[349] Afterwards *2nd Eskadra* also transitioned to the MiG-15bis, handing over their 14 remaining La-11 night fighters to the KPAF's 56th GFAR.[350]

The 'Guards Taejon' Become a Night Fighter Unit

In the meantime, the KPAF's premier fighter unit, having lost six of its 15 Yak-9Ps in 1951 and transferred its La-9s to the 2nd AD, had been withdrawn to Dongfeng at the end of January. After enjoying a two-month rest, the 'Guards Taejon Regiment' were observed training in GCI-controlled night intercept operations by USAF 6920th Security Group, Johnson AB, Japan. Radio intercepts of 'North Korean air voice traffic' revealed that in April 'North Korean aircraft are making many night flights', evidently still operating their tired Yak-9Ps.[351]

For 18 months USAF B-26s (3rd and 452nd BWs) and USMC F4Us and F7Fs (VMF[N]-513) had been flying night intruder and attack missions against trains and truck convoys in North Korea with relative impunity. To provide target illumination for their nocturnal strikes, Fifth AF used six flare-dropping C-47s (called 'Fireflies', assigned to the 67th Tactical Reconnaissance Wing at Kimpo AB). Similarly, beginning in June 1951, the USN began using a combination of Corsairs and Tigercats striking truck convoys illuminated by Convair PB4Y-2 Privateers (VP-28, based at Itami, Japan) on 'Lamplighter' missions. With a loiter time of six hours and carrying 250 flares, the four 'Lamplighters' provided nightly illumination for relays of Marine night attack aircraft. Vectored towards the American intruders by the KPAF's upgraded GCI network, the Guards pilots of the 56th GFAR found the 'Lamplighter'/fighter teams to be self-illuminating targets.[352]

On the night of 7 June, a 'Lamplighter' spotted and 'lit up' a convoy of seven trucks south of Sariwon, calling in a VMF(N)-513 F4U-5NL flown by 1st Lt John W. Andre to 'work them over' with napalm and 20mm strafing. As he rolled in for another pass, Andre was suddenly surprised to see bright orange tracers – 'flaming golf balls' – streaking over his left wing, then beneath him, then over his right wing. The attacker overshot, passing the Corsair to the right, Andre quickly identifying it as a Yak-9 painted in dark camouflage, and banking right and squeezing his trigger, he riddled it with a volley of 20mm cannon fire. Flames streamed from beneath the engine cowling and the Yak dove away, Andre pulling up to keep from following it into the dark terrain below. The 'Lamplighter's' spotters reported the Yak exploding on ground impact.[353]

Undaunted by this loss, later that month the 56th GFAR transferred to Anshan where they received the 351st OIAP's 14 remaining La-11s and began night fighter training, probably with Yefrimov's *2nd Eskadra* acting as instructors.[354] The La-11 represented a major increase in long-range fighter sweep and bomber escort – as well as night fighting – capabilities, allowing the 'Guards Taejon' to once again range across the frontlines, as they had two years before. Surprising everyone (on the UN side at least), on 18 July, a USAF B-26 was 'briefly engaged [by] two conventional fighter aircraft about 25 miles (40 km) south of the front lines in central Korea.'[355]

Additionally, while 'concentrating its efforts on becoming proficient in night operations', the unit also began training in the bomber escort role. In early August, its La-11s were observed in the rear area practicing rendezvousing with and escorting bomber

MiG-15 chasing Tu-4. (FoxbatFiles.com)

La-11 long-range escort and night fighter. (Photo by Chris Pinn)

aircraft, using GCI directions to affect the join-up and then protecting the Tu-2(s) from mock fighter attacks. This exercise may have been conducted in conjunction with the '17th Mixed Aviation Battalion' stationed at Taizhou airfield in China's North Kiangsu Province. Operational since January, this unit appears to have been a tactical training organization that was 'equipped with five Yak-10 fighters [*sic*; probably Il-10s are meant], four Yak-9 fighters, two reconnaissance aircraft, and one Tu-2 bomber'. In this instance, the unit would have provided the Tu-2 to be 'escorted' and its Yak-9s would have flown as the 'enemy interceptors'.[356]

Finally, in defiance of the USAF's air superiority over most of North Korea, late in October 1952, the 'Guards Taejon' made at least one daring daytime 'fighter sweep' as far south as P'yongyang, remaining 'on station' over the North Korean capital for 15 minutes despite the presence of F-86 Sabres operating in the area.[357]

KPAF Night Bomber Operations Resume

Just as the Communist coalition's EW/GCI radar networks were expanded and improved during the winter and spring of 1952, FEAF's own air defence network also grew with increasing capabilities. In February, the 606th AC&WS established a Bell Telephone/General Electric 750kW AN/CPS-5 search radar on Ch'o-do island that had a maximum range of 200 miles (322km) and thus could 'see Communist aircraft over the airfields at Antung [*sic*]'. While not an aircraft control capability, the new facility (callsign 'Postcard') could give F-86 pilots a 'heads up' of enemy activity as they headed north to 'MiG Alley' and provided early warning of any major raids headed towards South Korea.[358]

In October, 606th AC&WS upgraded its Ch'o-do radar site by installing an AN/TPS-1B portable EW/GCI radar. Overwater, this radar could detect formations of bomber-size aircraft at 10,000 feet altitude at a distance of 120 nautical miles (222km) and its greater resolution permitted the squadron's collocated second TADC (callsign 'Dutchboy') to provide 'Sabres [with] ground-control vectors of the same kind that the Reds had enjoyed for several months'. Defended by ROK Marines, protected by a substantial force of UNC naval vessels and covered by FEAF fighters during daylight, the idea of launching an amphibious assault to capture Ch'o-do was too daunting a proposition, so – by autumn – it became a prime target for Pak Den-Sik's 3rd Night Bomber Regiment's renewed operations.[359]

To counter the KPAF's nocturnal 'heckler' attacks, in March 1951, the USAF replaced the antiquated and awkward F-82 Twin Mustangs of the Japan-based 68th FIS with 15 new jet-powered Lockheed F-94A Starfires, stationing a two-ship detachment on strip alert at Suwon. A year later, this small detachment was replaced by the 319th FIS with improved F-94Bs. Anxious to avoid having Hughes Aircraft Company's new AN/APG-33 AI radar (developed from the AN/APG-3 used by SAC's new B-36 nuclear bomber's tail gun) and E-1 fire control system fall into Communist hands, USAF HQ limited FEAF's Starfire operations to over friendly territory only.[360]

In May 1952, the USAF's F-94s were joined by 14 new Douglas F3D-2 Skyknight night-fighters assigned to VMF(N)-513, based at Kunsan. Powered by a pair of 3,400lb thrust Westinghouse J34-WE-36 turbojets, the big, boxy, straight-wing two-seater was equipped with the Westinghouse AN/APQ-35A radar and armed with four 20mm cannon. The aircraft's performance was unremarkable, but this (and its radar) allowed it to mingle with the B-29s *en route* to the target, and its rather advanced search and tracking AI radar permitted relatively autonomous operations.[361]

Throughout the springtime and early summer, Pak Den-Sik's two squadrons – one with 11 Po-2s and Yak-18s at Sariwon and the other having seven Yak-18s based near Sinuiju – remained largely inactive, their aircraft being dismantled and dispersed to prevent discovery and destruction by roving UN fighter-bombers. However, on 8 and 9 July the Yak-18 unit at Sinuiju was observed conducting night flying training that appeared to include night bombing practice.[362]

Five days later there were indications of renewed combat activity when KPA HQ warned frontline Chinese Volunteer Army units that, 'Aircraft of the [Korean] People's Army will take off to carry out their duties… behind enemy lines' and that the KPAF aircraft would be recognized by the distinctive sound of the five-cylinder Shvetsov M-11 radial engine (that powered both the Po-2 and Yak-18) which was 'similar to the motor of a truck'. To support these intended operations, 'several small dirt air strips [were built] immediately behind the front lines' to serve as forward operating locations and emergency recovery airfields. Radar evidence confirmed combat missions were resumed in late July, flying from the P'yongyang valley to east central Korea, where ROK army units reported light, sporadic and ineffectual night attacks.[363]

After another three-month hiatus, Pak Den-Sik once again resumed regular combat operations on 13 October when four Po-2LSh biplanes raided the 606th AC&WS's radar and air-direction centre on Ch'o-do. They strafed with light machine guns and dropped seven pairs of small bombs, most of them falling within 200 yards of the radar site, killing four Korean civilians in a nearby village and wounding two US servicemen and five Koreans. None of the intruders were damaged by .50-caliber machine gun fire from the local air defence unit, Battery A/933rd AAA (AW) Bn. As they departed, an intercepting F-94 achieved radar contact and made six firing passes, but each time was foiled by the biplanes' slow speed and nimble manoeuvring.[364]

A month later (12 November) an unknown number of raiders (type also unknown) bombed the island of Paengnyong-do attempting to damage the 608th AC&WS's secondary surveillance radar. The raiders caused negligible damage.[365]

Because the new radar-equipped USMC Skyknights were beginning to disrupt the 351st OIAP's night intercepts of FEAF B-29s – especially when working with 'Dutchboy' GCI controllers – later that month Pak Den-Sik's 3rd Bomber Regiment was ordered to renew its attacks on Ch'o-do Island. These began on 26 November with 'six unidentified single-engine piston aircraft' attacking in two waves of three, dropping ten or eleven bombs, but causing no damage.[366]

Shifting their objectives to the Seoul area, on the night of 5/6 December Pak Den-Sik's 3rd Bomber Regiment launched a 'maximum effort' with all of the 1st Battalion's Po-2s and Yak-18s dropping bombs in what was noted to be 'the largest enemy [air] raid of the war', while four attackers (most likely those of the Sinuiju-based 2nd Battalion) dropped ten small bombs on Ch'o-do and two more on nearby Sŏk-to. However, none of the raiders caused any damage and there were no casualties. Stationed nearby, HMCS *Crusader* – a 1,825-ton former RN WW2 C-class destroyer mounting three quick-firing 4.5inch turrets and three paired 40mm Bofors AA guns – fired 79 rounds into the night sky but failed to hit any of the raiders. Five nights later the 'night-hecklers' returned with equally ineffective results.[367]

Finally, on 10/11 December, Pak Den-Sik's 'night hecklers' – called 'Lowboys' by American GCI controllers – finally felt the effectiveness of the Marine Skyknights when Lt A. Joseph

KPAF Yak-18 (formerly KPAF 'White 15' on display at the US Smithsonian Air & Space Museum. (NMUSAF)

USAF F-94B Starfire of the 68th FIS on alert at Suwon AB. (USAF)

Corvi and Sergeant Daniel R. George were vectored against a slow moving 'bogie' flying at 2,000 feet, off the west coast of North Korea, south of (and apparently headed towards) Sinanju. Obtaining radar contact and a confirmation that the target was a 'bandit' George steered Corvi to an attack position and, still unable to see the target, he opened fire with the F3D's quartet of 20mm cannon.

Corvi later reported 'we didn't know we had made a kill until my R/O reported a wing and flaming debris flying past us'. The victory was credited as a Po-2, but was probably a Yak-18 from 3rd Bomber Regiment's 2nd Battalion returning to Sinuiju from the unit's mission of bombing Ch'o-do Island.[368]

The increased operations tempo continued to the end of the year with Po-2s and Yak-18s attacking – in two relatively large raids – Seoul, Inch'on, Kimpo, and Suwon air bases, and the rear areas of the ROK's First Army, causing minor damage and wounding some South Korean troops during the last-mentioned strike (22/23 December). In a departure from their nocturnal bombing missions, on 30/31 December Pak Den-Sik's raiders flew over Seoul, Kimpo, and Suwon dropping propaganda leaflets, welcoming the New Year.[369]

Night-Fighters Join the 3rd Night Bomber Regiment

By this time the KPAF's 3rd Night Bomber Regiment was reinforced by the addition of a third squadron, this one equipped with La-11 night-fighters. At the end of October 1952, all three of the KPAF's propeller-driven fighter and ground attack regiments (56th GFAR, 57th AAR, and 58th FAR) had been withdrawn from combat operations to reequip with versions of the MiG-15. Correspondingly to upgrade to the new jet fighter, the 'Guards Taejon' passed its remaining La-11s – along with some night-qualified pilots to fly them – to the 3rd Night Bomber Regiment to form a night-fighter squadron. With the La-11's much longer range and its three 23mm cannon – also considering the KPAF's affinity towards using the Lavochkin types as ground-attack fighters – the new 3rd Battalion was a welcomed addition to Pak Den-Sik's night bomber regiment.[370]

Meanwhile, from late December 1952 through most of January the Soviets' growing force of night fighters[371] enjoyed several successes against FEAF's B-29 heavy bombers as they attempted to destroy North Korean railway supply lines. During this period the USAF lost three B-29 bombers and one RB-29A shot down and three more Superfortresses DBR.[372] Quite obviously the slow Marine F3D-2s were becoming increasingly ineffective protecting the USAF's night bombers from the faster, GCI-guided MiG-15s.[373] Consequently, the USAF Chief of Staff, General Hoyt S. Vandenburg, became acutely concerned about the mounting B-29s losses to Communist night-fighters and, by this time, relented on his prohibition against employing the advanced Lockheed F-94B Starfire radar-equipped interceptors beyond the front lines. The Suwon-based 319th FIS began augmenting the USMC Skyknights, flying 'barrier patrols' over North Korea and at the end of January were rewarded with their first 'night kill'. But instead of being a Soviet MiG-15, the target proved to be a KPAF night raider.[374]

On the evening of 30 January Capt Ben L. Fithian and Radar Observer (R/O) Lt Sam R. Lyons were launched to assist another aircraft and headed for Ch'o-do Island, where another F-94B was having difficulty locating a low altitude target. Fithian recalled:

> When we got within about 50 miles [80km] of the activity, Ch'o-do released the other F-94 for recovery at K-13 and took control of us. We were at about 25,000 feet [7,620m]. They started giving us range and direction to the 'hostile'. It was something like 30 miles [48km] away at one o'clock [30° to the right of the aircraft's nose]. They gave us a descent order to 5,000 feet [1,525m] and a series of turns. We end up at 5,000 feet [1,525m] going southeast about ten miles [16km] west of P'yongyang; we were about six miles [10km] behind the hostile who was doing about 130 knots [241km/hr]. We swung behind the target and continued to descend. We made the first radar contact at about five miles [eight km] range.
>
> In order to get the optimum advantage with our airborne radar fire control system, we descended to tree-top level. It was a moonlight night and I could see the ground under us, but not ahead. Once I looked out and we were very close over some trees that looked like tall sycamores, so I climbed up a bit. I figured the Korean pilot probably knew the terrain and if he could get through, we could too. Also, the prize of the first 'kill' using the F-94 was worth laying it all on the line. We

made radar contact again at slightly less than five miles [eight km] and I slowed it down a bit to about 130 knots [241km/hr]. With speedbrakes extended, after getting a [radar] lock on the target, we started to climb and close. The enemy aircraft was at about 1,500 feet [457m] altitude. We had an overtake speed of about 40 knots [74lm/hr] when we got into [gun] range of 1,200 feet [366m].

I started firing on the radar scope. I fired a long burst and saw no results. We continued to close and I fired again. Still no hits! We were at about 600 feet [183m] behind the target and [when I fired again] I moved the stick around in about a six-inch [15.3cm] circle and saw some flashes. We were armed with API [armor piercing incendiary ammunition] – they made a flash upon impact. As soon as I saw a lot of flashes, I held the stick steady and continued to fire. Our .50-caliber rounds were devastating to the target, as it immediately burst into flames and nosed straight down. The light provided by the ball of fire and low altitude gave us a lasting image. The aircraft hit the ground in seconds with the cockpit still closed. We identified it as a Lavochkin...

We called 'splash one' and Ch'o-do gave us a vector towards another hostile about eight miles [13km] away. We were low on fuel [and] our altitude was very low and we ran into some intense ground fire, [so I] climbed out... On recovery at K-13 we did a victory roll and landed. We were met in the revetment area by almost everyone in our squadron. When we shut our engine off, everyone clapped hands.[375]

Recorded as a 'prop' in the official USAF Korean War victory rolls, the destroyed Lavochkin is most often reported to be a La-9. However, considering the fact that only the ADF-equipped La-11 was used by the KPAF for night operations, it most likely was one of that type, assigned to the 3rd Bomber Regiment's new night-fighter battalion.[376]

CHAPTER 10
NEW JETS FOR THE KPAF

After twelve months of unproductive negotiations, by June 1952 the warring parties in the Korean conflict were no closer to a truce than when they began their discussions. In the absence of any meaningful progress at Panmunjom and in response to the stonewall intransigence by the Chinese and North Koreans on the POW repatriation issue, on 10 July General Otto P. Weyland (CinC FEAF since 10 June 1951) issued a new strategy directive ordering maximum 'air pressure' by attacking 'targets which might motivate the Reds to accept reasonable truce terms.'[377]

FEAF Intelligence determined that P'yongyang, which had not been attacked in over a year, had 75 military targets within and around the city, and selected 30 of them – supply warehouses, troop billets, communications centres, and command posts – as being the most significant contributions to the Communist coalition's continued war effort. While their MiG-15s' limited operational range precluded any of their units from being able to contest UNC air attacks on the North Korean capital, it was defended by 48 large-calibre AA guns and over 100 smaller, automatic weapons. Only a relatively short distance behind the front-lines, the massive USAF/USN raids – totalling 1,200 daytime and 54 night bomber sorties – came as a complete surprise and utter shock to Kim Il-Sung, his government, and its military. For the loss of two USN Skyraiders and a USAF F-84D, the day-long bombing assault destroyed 1,500 buildings and caused 7,000 casualties, including killing more than 400 high-ranking government officials and communist party members.[378]

Destruction of P'yongyang and its effects

The devastation of P'yongyang on 11-12 July prompted a flurry of telegrams (15-18 July) between Kim Il-Sung, Mao Zedong and Stalin in an urgent effort to prevent further catastrophes. To Stalin, Kim appealed for the provision of additional light and medium AA guns to equip ten new AAA regiments, expanding the UAA's day fighter coverage south far enough to protect P'yongyang, and increasing PLAAF and KPAF night fighter operations. Additionally, he called for the release of the 40 aircrews training on Tu-2s at Khorol'sk 'so that they could immediately take part in active military operations and bring influence to bear on important military sites'.[379]

Kim urged Mao to have the Chinese-led UAA improve its control of fighter forces 'so that it *correctly* [author's emphasis] directs the air battles over Korean territory', extend its fighter coverage southwards to defend P'yongyang, 'and to strengthen by all measures the air defences of the capital and important industrial sites'. Acknowledging UNC daytime air supremacy, he added that 'It is necessary to send already-trained air force bomber units on night action deep in enemy [territory] to boldly carry out air battles [and] subject to bombardment a number of airfields, warehouses, barracks, and other military installations of the enemy'.[380]

With little change made regarding Kim's appeals, on 29 August, FEAF repeated its devastating attacks against P'yongyang, this time even including RN/FAA units, to mount an unprecedented 1,403 sorties. While USAF Sabres and RAAF Meteors provided 'barrier CAPs' along the Ch'ongch'on River to preclude any interference by Communist MiG-15s, the four massive waves of attackers hit numerous factories, warehouses, troop billets, and a number of public offices, including the Munitions Bureau, Ministry of Rail Transportation, and Radio P'yongyang. With his allies (as well as his own air force) being completely unable to prevent the destruction of his capital, as well as all other cities south of the Ch'ongch'on River, Kim became increasingly disillusioned with the prospects of continuing the conflict, so much so that Chinese Foreign Minister Zhou Enlai reported to Moscow that North Korea's 'Great Leader' was becoming 'panicky', which in turn led to uncertainties within the Chinese leadership.[381]

Sensing weakening resolve by his Asian allies, Stalin hosted a conference in Moscow on 4 September, attended by Kim Il-Sung, Zhou Enlai and Peng Dehuai. In this meeting Stalin formally agreed to equip ten AAA regiments and promised Kim that the USSR would 'provide the material [MiG-15bis fighters] for three air divisions.'

At the end of the meeting – which also covered the thorny POW repatriation issue, layout of frontal ground defences, fighter pilot proficiency, and a myriad of lesser military matters – Stalin promised, 'We intend to send one division of jet bombers each to Korea and China if, of course, you want this'. In chorus, Zhou Enlai and Kim Il-Sung responded with, 'Of course we want this, Comrade Stalin.'[382]

Based on these agreements, 100 new MiG-15bis jet fighters for the KPAF were sent to Kungchuling, (now Gongzhuling), near Changchun, in PRC's Jilin Province. At the end of October the first half of this consignment was accepted by the 1st AD, the unit then returning to Anshan to train on the new, more powerful model.

The newly-reorganized 2nd AD followed suit. This division once again combined the 56th GFAR with the 58th FAR, these two units passing their remaining La-9s and Yak-9Ps to the '10th Aviation School' at Yanji to equip the two-squadron 'fighter training regiment'. The 2nd AD's two fighter regiments were manned primarily with a mix of Yak-9P and La-9 veterans and recent pilot training graduates, with Hero of the DPRK Major Kim Gi-Ohk being promoted to command the 58th FAR. The KPAF's newest jet fighter division was commanded by Brig Gen Hu Min-Kuk, who had previously been the vice-commander of the KPAF's training establishment at Yanji.[383]

To ease the transition to jet fighters, a number of MiG-15-experienced pilots from 1st AD were transferred to Hu's unit, the most important being Col Tae Kuk-Sung, the former commander of the 60th FAR, who became Hu's deputy. When Tae, having added two (fictitious) victories over F-86s to his previous score, became the vice-commander of the 2nd AD; his position commanding the 60th FAR was assumed by Maj Chae San-Tae.[384]

To form the new 3rd AD – which was equipped with the 'hand-me-down' early model MiG-15s from the 1st AD – the 57th AAR relinquished its Il-10 'assault' aircraft, passing them to the 10th Aviation Schools' assault training regiment before beginning training on the MiG-15. (Correspondingly the 11th AAD was evidently disbanded at or before this time.) Additionally, the new 61st FAR was formed, providing the second regiment for the new fighter division. Due to lack of IPs available, the division's training programme was slow and arduous – the 3rd AD was not considered 'combat ready' until the end of the war.

Meanwhile, the 60th FAR returned to Langtao in November and that month launched 56 combat sorties with their new, more powerful MiG-15bis. Snr Lt No later stated:

> On our first combat mission in the new fighters we gained an altitude of 13,000 meters [43,000 feet] somewhat faster than in the older model. The advantage of a faster climb than the Sabre had been further improved. Over the Yalu River, we encountered F-86s scattered all over the so-called 'MiG Alley' and we attacked each other at a relatively high altitude. Chinese and Soviet MiGs were also involved, making the sky a confusion of aircraft. Each fighter seemed to shoot at anything that flew in front of it, at least if it seemed like a foe. My regiment became embroiled in several dogfights, and our grand formation was broken up, but I managed to remain part of a four-ship formation.[385]

Miserable winter weather ensued, reducing flying operations the next two months, limiting the 60th FAR to 24 sorties in December and only 12 in January. There were no reported engagements, victory claims or losses during these months.[386]

F-86 Gun Camera still of MiG-15bis escaping a firing pass. (NMUSAF)

Jet Bombers Join the KPAF

As Kim Il-Sung requested, the KPAF bomber unit – now upgraded to a division (with no change in its actual size) – completed their training at Khorol'sk and was transferred to Kungchuling/Gongzhuling where it began receiving the Soviets' new, fast, twin-engine jet Ilyushin Il-28 light bomber. Fulfilling Stalin's promise, approximately 100 Il-28s were delivered to northern China during November-December 1952. According to CIA COMINT reports, 'up to 45' of these went to the PLAAF, while 'at least 42' were provided to the KPAF at Kungchuling in early December, equipping the recently-trained 4th AD's 36th and 37th Bomber Aviation Regiments that arrived at this base in mid-November.[387]

Upon arrival the Tu-2 unit began operational training and local familiarization flights, but these soon gave way to Il-28 transition training conducted by Soviet IPs. The course of instruction began with type qualification and formation flying training, with 'squadron formation bombing' practice observed in January 1953. Proficiency appears to have come quickly for, on 17 December, a pair of Il-28s were seen flying over the northwestern edge of Korea, along the Yalu River. Training progressed rapidly, including cross-country navigation missions, a flight of 18 Il-28s being observed on 27 January, with as many as 28 flying cross-country sorties the next week. In March night flying training – and apparently night bombing practice – were conducted. Three bombers may have been lost (or damaged and withdrawn for repairs) during training because on 12 March the unit reported 39 Ilyushins on strength.[388]

The KPAF bomber force – or an independent reconnaissance or training unit – retained 15 propeller-driven Tu-2s as reconnaissance aircraft or for twin-engine transition and basic bomber procedures training (prior to transitioning to the jet-powered Il-28), or both. On 30 January 1953 one of these aircraft was detected by 'Dutchboy', apparently headed towards Ch'o-do island on a reconnaissance mission, or to test USAF reactions and defences. The TADC scrambled the Sabres sitting alert at Kimpo and began vectoring two four-ships of F-86s already airborne towards the radar contact.[389]

First Lt Raymond A. Kinsey (335th FIS/4th FIW) was the first pursuer to spot the 'errant… bomber' – flying at lower altitude over the sea off the coast near Chinnamp'o – and diving down he made three firing passes before the bomber caught fire, 'came apart, rolled over and dove into the Yellow Sea'. If this ill-fated mission was designed to test USAF defences, it certainly proved discouraging to the KPAF's hopes of mounting any bomber attacks during daylight.[390]

Despite this setback, Kim Il-Sung was sufficiently pleased with the bomber unit's proficiency that, at about this time, he sent Gen Nam Il, the KPA chief of staff, to Andong to meet with General Nie Fegnzhi (UAA commander since 10 July 1952). Nam urged the UAA to use the KPAF's newly trained jet bomber unit in night attacks on Seoul, as retribution for the USAF's destruction of P'yongyang. Fearing American retaliation against Chinese airfields north of the Yalu – 'and painfully aware of the PLAAF's inability to defend them' – Nie refused to consider immediate action, however, he agreed to maintain sufficient strike forces to deter a possible US/UN amphibious assault along North Korea's west coast. Nie also encouraged – and agreed to support – a renewed night bombing offensive by the KPAF's 3rd Bomber Regiment, provided only militarily significant targets were attacked.[391]

In fact, USAF Fifth AF leaders were definitely concerned about the arrival of the 400-knot Ilyushin jet bombers just across the Yalu River, saying that they posed the 'greatest possible threat to FEAF'. As early as 5 January 1953, Fifth AF Commander (since 30 May 1952) Lt Gen Glenn O. Barcus said, 'I have become greatly concerned about the possible effect of an enemy air offensive on the operational capability of this command. Our position has become more sensitive in recent months due to the continued enemy build-up and conversion to jet aircraft, particularly in such types as the Il-28 jet bomber'. From bases around Shenyang, with its 690 nautical mile range, all of South Korea could be targeted with bombloads up to 4,000lbs – a serious strike capability. Since Andong-based MiG-15s could not escort the Ilyushin even as far as the front lines, in daylight the bomber was vulnerable to interception by the 600-knot F-86s, but the type was assessed to have a 'formidable night-attack capability'. Therefore, USAF leadership feared most the very attacks – 'night action deep in enemy [territory, bombing] airfields, warehouses, barracks, and other military installations of the enemy' – that Kim Il-Sung had been urging since his July messages to Stalin and Mao.[392]

However, with the Chinese reluctance to allow such strikes from their territory, the only means the Communist coalition had for 'striking back' at the US/UN forces was in a resumption of the KPAF's 'night heckler' attacks – in increased strength and frequency.

KPAF Il-28R '0220' twin-jet medium bomber. (Tom Cooper Collection)

Table 3: KPAF ORBAT, November 1952

Unit	Sub-Unit	Base	Aircraft Type	Notes
Korean People's Armed Forces Air Corps Commander: General Van Len Korean People's Air Force Commander: Major-General Wang Yong				
Operational Units				
1st Air Division				CO Colonel Kim Hi-Kiung
	59th Fighter Aviation Regiment	Anshan (PRC)	24 MiG-15bis	CO Colonel Shin Kang-Dong
	60th Fighter Aviation Regiment	Anshan (PRC)	24 MiG-15bis	CO Colonel Chan San-Tae
2nd Fighter Aviation Division				CO Brigadier-General Hu Min-Kuk
	56th Guards Fighter Aviation Regiment	Anshan (PRC)	24 MiG-15bis	CO Major Kim Chi-San
	58th Fighter Aviation Regiment	Anshan (PRC)	24 MiG-15bis	HDPRK Major Kim Gi-Ohk
3rd Night Bomber Regiment				CO Colonel Pak Den-Sik
	1st Battalion	Sariwon	6 Po-2, 5 Yak-18	
	2nd Battalion	Sinuiju	7 Yak-18	
	3rd Battalion	Anshan (PRC)	12 La-11	
Combat Units in Training				
3rd Air Division	57th Fighter Aviation Regiment	Yanji (PRC)	45 MiG-15	

Unit	Sub-Unit	Base	Aircraft Type	Notes
	61st Fighter Aviation Regiment			
4th Air Division	36th Bomber Aviation Regiment	Kungchuling (PRC)	42 Il-28, 15 Tu-2	
	37th Bomber Aviation Regiment			
10th Aviation School	Primary Training Aviation Regiment	Yanji (PRC)	approx 30 Yak-18	
	Advanced Training Aviation Regiment	Jilin (PRC)	approx 20 Yak-11	
	Fighter Training Regiment/	Yanji (PRC)	24 La-9s	
	Assault Training Regiment	Yanji (PRC)	20 Il-10s	
	17th Mixed Aviation Battalion	Taizhou (PRC)	5 Il-10s, 4 Yak-9Ps, 1 Tu-2	
Transport Aviation Regiment			estimated at 12-20 C-47/ Li-2/Il-12/ Yak-6	

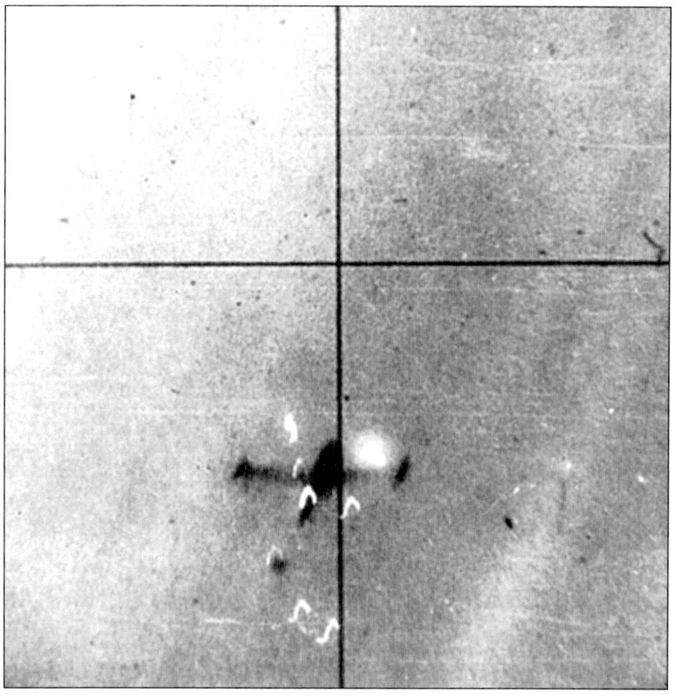

USAF F-84 being shot down by a Soviet MiG-15 and claimed as an F-94. (Tim Callaway Collection)

KPAF Fighter Operations in the New Year

By February the 2nd AD completed training on the MiG-15bis at Anshan and moved to Langtao to begin combat operations. To relieve the mounting congestion, the next month the 1st AD deployed to Kuandian, a new jet-capable airfield about 50 miles (80km) northeast of Andong, in the mountains about 25 miles behind the Yalu, north of the Suiho dam/Sup'ung hydroelectric powerplant complex. Originally a dirt airstrip at 6,560ft (2,000m) elevation, the airfield was improved in 1952 to become the base for the PLAAF's 25th FAR (9th AD), which was equipped with La-11s.[393]

On 23 June 1952, the giant hydroelectric complex had been subjected to devastating USAF/USN air attacks, damaging it so badly it was 'off line' for two months. Since half of the electrical output of this complex powered Chinese industrial centres in Shenyang and Anshan, it was vital to prevent a repeat of the successful American air attack, so Kuandian was improved into a jet-capable base by the construction of a PSP-surfaced runway, a project that was completed mid-December. This expedient modification proved unsuccessful, causing the loss of one MiG-15 during landing on the initial deployment, so two more months were taken to construct a proper concrete runway, permitting the operations of the KPAF's 1st AD and a Soviet MiG-15bis squadron.[394]

While protecting the critical hydroelectric powerplant, the division's 60th FAR – and specifically its commander, Maj Chae – received credit for destroying 'an F-94, apparently on a reconnaissance sortie'. Four MiG-15s attacked the target (most likely an RF-80), which was last seen 'to bank sharply to the left and [went] into a spiralling dive to speed away'.[395]

The regiment's first big clash of the year with USAF Sabres was on 21 March when 16 MiG-15bis launched from Kuandian to join a large air battle involving two Soviet MiG regiments and two PLAAF air divisions against both USAF Sabre fighter groups. Passing 11,000 metres (36,089ft) as they approached the Yalu, Chae spotted numerous jet contrails ahead at a much higher altitude. Worried, he radioed the GCI controllers at Langtao where General Lee Whal was directing the KPAF portion of the air battle. Lee assumed the contrails were from Soviet or PLAAF jets launched earlier and called back, 'Don't worry about them, and keep climbing'.[396]

According to No, 'We climbed higher and flew right into them. Hordes of F-86s jumped us at 13,000 metres [43,000ft], coming from left and right and from ahead. I saw a dozen Sabres scattered around the sky and knew there were many more. Every MiG went its own way, trying to escape the fatal web woven by pairs of the American fighters'.[397]

No and his wingman escaped by continuing to climb straight ahead, the more powerful VK-1 turbojets powering their new fighters above – and out of reach of – two Sabres that pursued them, but one North Korean pilot – Lt Kim Lee-Joo – had his MiG riddled by Sabre machine guns, disabling the engine and severing the control lines. His ejection seat failed and Kim was forced to bale out manually, but he impacted the horizontal stabilizer and was probably knocked unconscious (if not killed outright) and never deployed his parachute.[398]

The Sabre pilots were credited with eight victories while suffering two F-86Fs damaged. During March the UAA lost 13 Chinese and Korean MiG-15s – while the USAF lost only two F-86s.[399]

The Return of the 'Guards Taejon'

Together the KPAF's two MiG-15bis units flew 352 sorties in February, a dramatic increase in combat operations. While this is attributed largely to improved weather (at least in the Soviet histories), it also reflects the fact that a second Korean fighter division was now participating, spearheaded by the more aggressively-led 56th GFAR, commanded by Major Kim Chi-San. An elite unit with a strong combat reputation to uphold, the 'Guards Taejon' – now flying front-line jet fighters instead of second-hand WW2-era propeller aircraft – was determined to live up to its honorific title and return to the pre-eminence, and glory, of being the KPAF's premier fighter unit. Additionally, in what appears to be a departure from the Soviets' usual practice, this unit's leadership was augmented by six Soviet 'advisors' that not only coached the battalion and regimental commanders, but also led the Guards' MiG formations into battle. Known only by their surnames (or codenames), at the regimental command level they were Comrades Zaytsev and Pashkov, with Comrades Ostrosablin, Barsukov, Koryagin and Rublev as squadron 'advisors'. According to one Russian historian, 'All of these men were fighting even more illegally than the Soviet aviation units and there are no observations of their actions in combat'.[400]

Capitalizing on his successful experience committing the 59th FAR against USN Corsairs and Skyraiders, Col Tae urged his new command to avoid fighting Sabres in MiG Alley but instead sweep southwards along Korea's west coast looking for the far more vulnerable propeller-driven carrier-based aircraft. On 4 February six KPAF MiGs swept as far south as the Taedong River estuary and, apparently guided by radar controllers, intercepted a flight of four USN F4Us of VMA-312 (USS *Bataan*, CVL 29) near the small island of Sŏk-to. The Corsair pilots dodged the Korean attacks, claiming to have damaged one MiG-15 before the attackers departed northwards. Two days later a pair of KPAF MiGs intercepted four RN/FAA Fairey Firefly AS 5s from HMS *Glory* (NAS 810) off the coast near Chinnamp'o and made one firing pass, returning to Langtao to claim one destroyed. No damage was actually done.[401]

The 'Guards Taejon' first clash with USAF F-86s occurred on 28 March when Capt Han Min-Kwan attempted to lead his squadron beyond 'MiG Alley' to patrol near Sunch'ŏn at 12,000 meters (39,370 feet). The North Koreans engaged a formation of 4th FIW Sabres led by their wing commander, Col James K. Johnson. A swirling, high-altitude dogfight quickly developed and element leader Lt Kim Hyon-Hak closed to attack the American flight leaders, but was jumped by other F-86s. Kim's wingman, Lt Ho Ki-Bok, 'counter-attacked' against the pair of Sabres pursuing his leader, reportedly shooting down one F-86, while Kim switched targets, attacking F-86s chasing Han. In a high-G climbing turn Kim rolled out behind and beneath one of the Sabres and opened fire, reportedly shooting it down. As the swirling dogfight continued, the Koreans claimed a third Sabre shot down, but lost one (pilot not named) MiG-15bis to Col Johnson.[402]

Flying a new F-86F Johnson entered the fight from above, reporting that:

> I was leading my flight, patrolling the south side of the Yalu River at about 42,000 feet. Looking down and to the left [north-northwest] as we headed up the river, I spotted two MiGs below us headed south. I called [my wingman, 1Lt Robert Carter] and pointed out the MiGs. We dropped our tanks, and went into a dive coming up behind the apparently unwary MiGs. I closed on one of them, and opened fire at about 200 feet. I gave him two real good bursts. The first burst hit the left wing, and walked right up into the canopy. The second burst went right up his tailpipe. The MiG started shedding large pieces and started burning furiously. Suddenly the canopy came off and the pilot ejected. The aircraft headed down, disintegrating as it fell, and crashed just north of the Yalu River.[403]

Attempting to fulfil Kim Il-Sung's directive of expanding the UAA's air defense as far south as P'yongyang, the KPAF's 1st and 2nd ADs flew 376 MiG-15bis sorties in March, reporting in the January-March period to have lost three of their new MiG-15bis, including one that mysteriously caught fire in flight, Capt Lee Yoon-Ha ejecting safely.[404]

F-86 Gun Camera stills of MiG-15 pilot ejecting from his aircraft. (USAF)

CHAPTER 11
THE BEGINNING OF THE END

On 12 March 1953 – one week after Stalin's death – the KPAF was reported to possess 194 combat aircraft, including 97 MiG-15bis (1st and 2nd ADs), 39 Il-28s (4th AD), and 58 other, obsolete types (14 Tu-2s, 20 Il-10s and 24 La-9s) Additionally there were approximately 40 older MiG-15s (3rd AD) and 50 other types (Po-2s, Li-2s, Il-12s, and Yak-11/18s) in the training and transportation command at Yanji, PRC.[405]

In spite of re-equipping with the more powerful MiG-15bis and the new Il-28 tactical bomber, the Communist coalition had proven unable to expand the contested airspace of 'MiG Alley' southwards beyond the Ch'ongch'on River – P'yongyang remained completely exposed to UNC air attacks – and was deterred from mounting any air attacks on 'airfields, warehouses, barracks, and other military installations of the enemy' – the 'active military operations' – that Kim Il-Sung so desperately wanted.[406]

By the time Stalin suffered his debilitating and eventually fatal stroke, Kim Il-Sung and his regime were ready for a cease fire due to the horrific devastation the North Koreans had endured, and even Mao Zedong – because Chinese Communist priorities were shifting to rebuilding their nation and its economy after the ravaging civil war – also began favouring an armistice. During the ceremonies and Politburo meetings accompanying Stalin's funeral, on 19 March Chinese Premier Zhou Enlai secured the agreement of Georgy Malenkov (Stalin's heir apparent) and the Supreme Soviet to pursue a more conciliatory approach, resuming the 'peace talks' at Panmunjom. This move was publicly applauded and diplomatically encouraged by the Soviets and on 20 April the first POW exchange ('Operation Little Switch') returned 6,169 sick and wounded prisoners to their home nations.[407]

Despite the promise provided by the (now) more productive negotiations for ending the war, the fighting in 'MiG Alley' continued with increasing ferocity, fuelled primarily by the mounting 'MiG madness' and the 'ace race' amongst the now clearly superior USAF F-86F pilots.

During April through June, Soviet units lost 39 MiG-15s destroyed and 15 pilots killed.[408] With Stalin's death and the obvious change in Soviet interest in (not) prolonging the war, the Soviet MiG units lost much of their motivation for continuing the battle. The resulting lower morale, 'accumulated combat fatigue, and disadvantageous operating conditions contributed to [July's] high loss rate' – another 15 MiGs lost and four pilots killed. The Soviets' blamed the summer's 'reduction of their combat effectiveness' on 'disadvantageous operating conditions' and the introduction of inexperienced Chinese and North Korean pilots, who often 'caused a different situation and influence on results of combat operations.'[409]

According to one Russian history, 'The UAA was becoming increasingly more active, and their number of sorties increased, which compensated for the reduction in the combat activity of the 64th IAK.'[410] Increasingly the six PLAAF and two KPAF MiG-15 ADs – totalling 450 MiGs – shouldered the larger burden of meeting the Sabres in 'MiG Alley', the Chinese accepting the fact that, initially at least, theirs were primarily 'combat training missions' with potentially lethal outcomes. However, the ensuing slaughter of ill-trained and woefully inexperienced PLAAF pilots – losing as many as 62 MiGs and 20 pilots in combat with F-86s during April, May and June[411] – prompted Mao to send General Wang Bingzhang, the PLAAF's first deputy commander, to Langtao to 'rescue the situation'.[412]

56th GFAR – Fighting to (near) the End

The North Koreans, however, had more at stake in the waning months of the contest and, from Langtao airfield, the 56th GFAR "strove to show that they 'were not just boys into battle' in the deadly 'game' of aerial combat."[413]

Maj Kim Chi-San's 'Guards Taejon' flew 96 sorties in May, most of them during the three days 8-10 May. On one occasion, 'The squadron [commanded by Kim Sheng-Uk] received the

New F-86Fs of the 51st FIW in flight. (NMUSAF)

assignment to intercept enemy aircraft which had penetrated to the Ch'ongch'on River area. Arriving in the designated area, the squadron commander's wingman Lee Gil-Bok spotted a pair of enemy aircraft and reported this to the commander. The leader attacked them from above and shot one of them down. But at this point they were themselves attacked from above by a flight of four F-86s. The wingman drove off this attack, and abandoning his leader, went in hot pursuit of them. He chased them down and attacked them straightaway, downing one of the Sabres, but the other three F-86s caught him in pincers and damaged his aircraft. Things would have turned out badly for the young pilot, if his squadron hadn't hurried to his assistance. Lee Gil-Bok brought his damaged MiG back to base with difficulty and landed it.'[414]

As one Russian historian reported, 'May 1953 marked an increase in combat activity of the UAA, especially as our sources note, the North Korean pilots'. This continued in June and July, culminating with the KPAF MiG-15s flying an increased percentage of combat missions – totalling 38.24 per cent of the UAA's 1,632 sorties flown in the last two months of the war.[415] From early May until mid-July, the 56th GFAR was credited with destroying 25 enemy aircraft and damaging 5 more. Kim Chi-San was personally credited with four 'kills' and one damaged and on 17 July was awarded the title 'Hero of the DPRK'.[416]

Two days later the 'Guards Taejon' returned to combat with even greater enthusiasm. About this time, with the Panmunjom 'peace talks' appearing to make progress, FEAF began an 'airfield denial campaign' to minimize the availability of bases that KPAF aircraft could be flown into once the Armistice was signed. As part of this campaign, on 19 July, Fifth AF launched a massive fighter-bomber strike against the airfields at Sinuiju and Uiju. Participating were the 8th and 18th Fighter-Bomber Wings – by now both were completely re-equipped with F-86Fs – covered by the 4th and 51st FIWs, making a total of 168 Sabres flying in the strike. An estimated 16 MiG-15s from Kim's 56th GFAR, accompanied by 24 MiG-15s from the PLAAF's 10th and 16th FARs, attempted to repulse the raiders while Soviet MiGs covered the Chinese airfields. In the ensuing air battle no F-86s were lost, despite PLAAF and Soviet claims of shooting down one each. Sabre pilots were credited with ten MiG-15s shot down

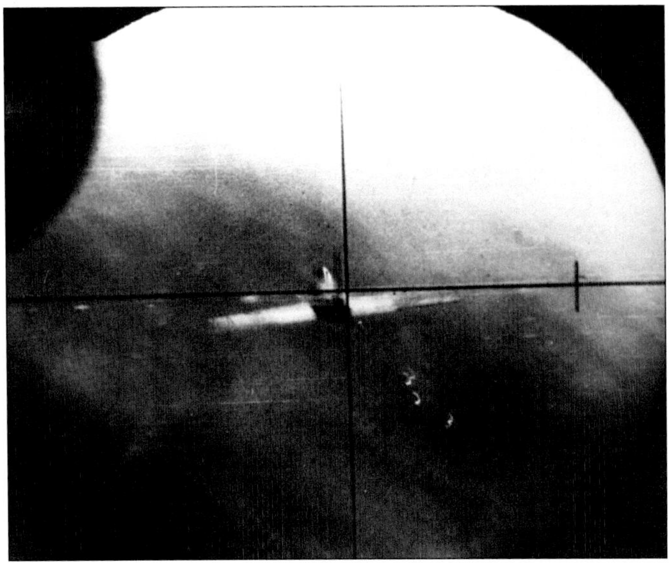

F-86 in MiG-15 Gun Camera film still. (Tim Callaway Collection)

HDPRK Major Kim Chi-San, credited with four kills he claimed to have scored between 11 March and 28 May 1953. (Tom Cooper Collection)

(two of which are known to have been Soviet jets; the PLAAF reportedly lost none this day), plus another three when the raids were repeated the next day.[417]

During the two days' air battles the 56th GFAR claimed 11 Sabres destroyed – bringing the unit's total score to 36 for the May-July period – of which Kim was credited with two additional victories, both on 20 July, bringing his personal tally to six 'kills'.[418]

KPAF 3rd Bomber Regiment Returns to Combat

Having weathered the severe Korean winter, Pak Den-Sik's night raiders – now increased to three squadrons with the addition of the former-56th GFAR La-11s – resumed combat operations. The first target on their 'hit list' was the 608th AC&WS TADC on Ch'o-do Island that provided GCI information to the Sabres constantly sweeping 'MiG Alley'. A chronic 'thorn in the side' of Soviet and UAA MiG-15 operations and an impediment to any renewed night bombing campaign, 'Dutchboy's' AN/TPS-1B radar needed to be neutralized if possible.

On 15 April, the KPAF launched its renewed 'night heckling' operations with a fairly large raid (number and types of aircraft remain unknown) against the Ch'o-do GCI site, continuing its bombing attacks for two hours. Very little damage was done – and none to the GCI unit – but bombs falling among the 608th AC&WS bivouac killed two US Army enlisted men and wounded 22.[419]

While newly acquired searchlights and Battery A/933rd AAA (AW) Battalion's tracers lit up the night sky, neither could locate the small, slow-flying raiders and none were shot down. The 319th FIS scrambled four F-94Bs but the attackers were flying so low that the Starfires' R/Os could not detect them amongst the 'ground clutter' on their AN/APG-33 radar scopes.

The next night – five week's after Stalin's funeral – Pak's raiders dropped several thousand leaflets over the Seoul and Inch'on areas proclaiming the Communists' 'peace desires'. This mission was followed by almost nightly bombing raids – against Kimpo AB, Chunchon, and US Eighth Army frontline troops – by all three types of KPAF night attack aircraft. Several American troops were wounded and a number of Korean civilians killed, but no material damage was done until the night of 23 April when the raiders struck Kimpo AB, damaging five RF-80A reconnaissance jets (45th Tactical Reconnaissance Squadron, Photographic-Jet).[420]

KPAF Yak-18 serial number 10 Taxiing out for takeoff. (Albert Grandolini Collection)

The small, low-flying raiders – because of their low radar 'signature' and slow, barely recognizable movement on the radar scopes – were frequently able to sneak in to their targets, avoiding radar detection, which completely negated the American advantage of networked ground-based radar system, GCI radio control and radar-equipped jet-powered night fighters. The attack on Kimpo was the last straw, causing Fifth AF Fighter Command to break from its long-established air defence command structure and decentralize control of night fighter operations and air raid warning systems, authorizing individual base commanders to declare air raid warnings and launch locally-based aircraft to intercept the North Korean attackers.

Kimpo AB, for instance, acquired a pair of portly radar-equipped USN Douglas AD-4W Skyraiders (usually used for electronic warfare and airborne early warning) from Marine Composite Squadron VMC-1[421] at Pohang; a 14-gun B-26B Invader; and a machine gun armed T-6D 'Mosquito' (normally a FAC aircraft) paired with a C-47 'Firefly' flare-ship, as its local night air defence force. If the base was attacked, these would be launched and flown under the direction of the base's ground control approach (GCA – a unit specializing in 'talking aircraft down' to the runway during bad weather situations, not a combat GCI unit). The GCA radars were tied into the 502nd TCG's air defence network in an attempt to increase its radar coverage and provide a more comprehensive 'air picture'.[422]

Additionally, Kimpo had a battalion of 90mm radar-directed AAA guns (68th AAA Bn) and another of automatic weapons [865th AAA (AW) Bn] spread around the airfield – the SCR-584 radars of the AAA batteries were also tied into the airbase's GCA control centre for local defence and fed information to the Seoul-based 608th AC&WS TADC for sector surveillance, in the hopes of contributing to a more comprehensive 'air picture' for the air traffic (ATC) and GCI controllers to use in attempting to direct the airbase's defence against the elusive and aggravating night raiders.[423]

Jets versus Biplanes

As the nocturnal harassment attacks continued into May, one of the small propeller-driven biplanes showed up on radar northeast of Ch'o-do in the early morning hours of 3 May and an F-94 Starfire patrolling the area was vectored to intercept. Flown by Second Lieutenant (2nd Lt) Stanton G. Wilcox, once the F-94 got low enough for R/O 2nd Lt Irwin L. Goldberg to get a radar contact, Wilcox lowered his landing gear and flaps and slowed the large, heavy interceptor to 110 knots (177km/hr) to allow Goldberg to get a radar-directed 'firing solution'. Reportedly, Wilcox called 'splash one', indicating that they had destroyed the target but, evidently, immediately afterwards the big Starfire stalled out and spun into the water. While unidentified wreckage was located floating near the F-94's last known position the next day, the aircrewmen were listed as MIA. Because of Wilcox's victorious radio call, he was posthumously credited with destroying an enemy 'prop' aircraft.[424]

Due to this loss, Fifth AF restricted the 319th FIS from attempting intercepts against enemy aircraft flying below 2,000 feet (610m) or slower than 160 knots (257km/hr). Meanwhile, undaunted, the KPAF night raiders continued their nocturnal missions, focusing their attacks mainly on Seoul. Shortly after midnight on 27 May six to eight Po-2LShs and Yak-18s scattered small bombs and artillery shells over the South Korean capital, rupturing an oil line between Inch'on and Yongdungpo. Some of these attacked Kimpo AB where they injured one man and caused minor damage to one F-86 and two RF-80As. In response, the base commander scrambled his C-47 'Firefly' and T-6G 'Mosquito' to engage the low-flying light aircraft. However, the C-47's million-candlepower magnesium flares blinded the 'Mosquito' pilot and no successes resulted.[425]

A week later three Po-2LShs attacked Ch'o-do, dropping eight light fragmentation bombs, but caused no damage or injuries, returning on 7 and 8 June with similar results. On 8/9 June a stream of the 'hecklers' flew across Seoul while USAF F-94s searched fruitlessly for them. The next night five small single-engine raiders attacked Paengnyong-do, again dropping eight bombs but causing no damage to military facilities. Continuing their nearly nightly attacks into early June, the KPAF raiders repeatedly attacked Seoul, Kimpo, and Ch'o-do.[426]

While the materiel damage caused by the 'Bedcheck Charlies' was negligible, their nearly constant nocturnal attacks were an embarrassment to the USAF and extremely frustrating for Fifth AF Fighter Command. No one felt that more than the commander of the 319th FIS, Lt Col Robert V. McHale. Having just been credited with downing at MiG-15 on 8 June,[427] McHale was eager to have a similar success against Pak's 'night hecklers'. Six nights later, on patrol near Ch'o-do with R/O Capt Samuel Hoster, McHale was vectored against a slow moving target at 5,000 feet (1,525m). Hoster acquired a radar contact on the target and GCI cleared the F-94 to fire, but evidently in doing so McHale did not recognize his high closure speed and flew into the target, destroying both aircraft and killing himself and his R/O.[428]

Send in the Marines

Beginning on 10 June 1953, one of the last Communist ground offensives was launched against the II ROK Corps and X US Corps, in the eastern and central sectors of the front. The offensive was launched for the propaganda value of claiming that the Communists were magnanimously willing to sign an armistice even though they were 'winning' the war and to secure as much territory as possible for North Korea before the cease fire went into effect.[429] To support this offensive Pak Den-Sik's 3rd Night Bomber Regiment stepped up its attacks, especially in the Seoul area. On the night of 15/16 June nine Po-2LShs and Yak-18s 'rattled Seoul', some of the raiders dropping their small bombs near the mansion of South Korean President Syngman Rhee and damaging the National Police Station, killing two and injuring eight others. Reportedly one Po-2LSh was shot down by AAA as

USMC VMC-1 AD-4W Skyraider at Pyongtaek airfield. (Warren Thompson Collection)

it crossed the front lines and Kimpo AB scrambled one VMC-1 Skyraider to intercept the raiders' second wave.[430]

The standard AD-4W was a highly modified Skyraider that mounted a powerful, long-range AN/APS-20A airborne early warning (AEW) search radar, as well as a number of electronic countermeasures (ECM) systems. For the night intercept mission, however, the APS-20 was replaced by AN/APS-31 surface search/navigation radar taken from a Martin PBM-3 Mariner maritime patrol flying boats. The APS-31 had a 'ground mapping' capability that the 'over-water' APS-20 did not, allowing the radar operator to differentiate moving (e.g., airborne) targets from the relatively stationary ground returns. In addition to the pilot, normally a radar operator and ECM specialist were carried in the cramped fuselage, but for this mission only the radar operator would be needed. The increased weight of the radar, ECM gear and additional crewmen resulted in the Skyraider's armament being reduced to two AN/M2 20mm cannon in the wings.

Taking off around midnight, Maj George H. Linnemeier and Chief Warrant Officer (CWO) Vernon S. Kramer were handed off to 'Dutchboy' and vectored to the northeast where Kramer soon made radar contact with a slow moving, low altitude intruder. Linnemeier slowed the heavy Skyraider to 90 knots (167km/hr) as they closed to firing range, and destroyed the target – evidently a Po-2LSh – with his twin 20mm cannon.[431] While the loss apparently discouraged the rest of that morning's attackers, a major effort was mounted the following night. Some 15 night raiders – including La-11s – attacked the Seoul area, starting several fires. A pair of Yak-18s dropped four bombs on a POL (petroleum, oil and lubricants) depot at Inch'on and started a blaze that consumed 5.5 million gallons (of 9.35M gallons stockpiled) of petroleum products.[432]

As the numerous raiders flooded local air defences, the increasing volume of ground observer reports added enormously to the numerous radar contacts reported by AAA batteries and Kimpo's GCA control centre. Confusion reigned as the swamped TADC again scrambled a Skyraider, this one flown by Maj Robert H. Mitchell, but everywhere they went this Marine crew soon found themselves being fired at by friendly AAA, despite the TADC's repeated orders for the gun batteries to 'hold tight'. Mitchell finally managed to locate and attack one of the raiders, but overtaking the slow-moving light aircraft too quickly, he wisely broke off the attack rather than colliding with his target.

The next day, Fifth AF did an about face, reverting to its traditional command and control arrangements, removing the local air base commander's authority to control AAA guns, returning them to the TADC. To reduce the number of 'unfiltered' radar plots, the AAA radars were removed from the center's network and the GCA radars were only allowed to report aircraft entering their airspace without a proper ATC clearance. The problem for the Americans was not the air defense radar network, but the type of interceptors being used. While the USAF's jet interceptors proved disappointing, Linnemeier's success was promising, so Fifth AF petitioned the US Navy for a detachment of four F4U-5N Corsair night-fighters from TF 77.[433]

CHAPTER 12
ENDING THE WAR

For night air defence, at this time each of the four USN carriers operating off the Korean coast embarked a four-aircraft/six-pilot night-fighter detachment from VC-3 (USN Composite Squadron Three),[434] operating radar-equipped F4U-5NLs (a winterized F4U-5N; L for 'low temperatures'). The F4U-5N mounted four AN/M3 20mm cannon and carried a Sperry AN/APS-19A search/intercept radar capable of detecting fighter-size targets within 60° of the nose out to 12 nautical miles (22km) and provided a 'firing solution' inside 1,500 yards (1.37km). One day after Fifth AF's request, 31-year old Lt Guy P. 'Lucky Pierre' Bordelon led VC-3's Det D from the USS *Princeton* (CVA 37) to Kimpo AB. After an 'inbriefing' on USAF intercept procedures and the

Joint Operations Center's[435] 'rules of engagement' (ROE) VC-3's 'Detachment Dog' flew to Pyongtaek airfield (K-6), a USMC base about 30 miles (48km) south of Seoul that was better equipped to maintain and service the unit's Corsairs.[436]

Hoping to foil the American night-fighters, the KPAF night bomber regiment waited for a dark, moonless night – 29 June – and launched two Yak-18s on a 'night heckler' mission. Flying south, the pair were detected over Asan-Man (near Seoul), and Bordelon was scrambled to intercept. The JOC's ROE required a positive visual identification before engaging any intruders.[437]

Bordelon later wrote:

> I was launched and vectored on the tail of an unknown aircraft. Closing to point-blank range, I identified the 'bogey' as a Yakovlev 18 with a rear seat gunner who sprayed the area to my left and below me with machine gun fire. I fired my four 20mm cannon and literally blew the Yak out of the sky! Reporting the kill to ground control, I was told that another bogey had popped up. I was vectored into contact with a second Yak-18 and after reporting 'enemy', and was cleared to fire. Pulling in tight I opened up with my 20mm cannon. I saw the incendiaries begin to burn the aircraft and then an explosion. The aircraft seemed to break into several large pieces, burning furiously. My controller reported the sky 'clear' and directed me to return to the field.[438]

Final Night Air Battles

Attempting to match capabilities with the USN Corsairs, the 3rd Night Bomber Regiment began using its La-11 night-fighters instead of the vulnerable Yak-18 armed trainers, launching two of them two nights later. Bordelon was airborne on a night combat air patrol when the JOC detected the south-bound intruders. He recalled:

> Arriving on station, I reported in and was vectored toward unknown targets. As I manoeuvred to come in behind the two aircraft, I identified them as Lavochkin 11 fighters. They were in loose trail formation so I pulled in behind the rear aircraft and gave a 'Tallyho' on the bogeys. I was cleared to fire and targeted one La-11. After two short bursts of cannon fire, it began to burn and dove straight down into the ground. The lead aircraft started to follow the burning aircraft down, and I closed on him and began firing. My target turned left, then right and started to climb as I gave him another burst. With that, he exploded into fire and began falling apart. I followed the largest burning mass down to 500 feet [152m] and saw him crash near my first kill.[439]

No further intruders were detected until the moonlit night of 16/17 July when a single La-11 was discovered. Bordelon and Lt (jg) Ralph 'Hoppy' Hopson were scrambled to intercept and Hopson initially acquired the target but his AN/APS-19A failed as he was closing in on the 'bogey', before he could acquire visual contact. Bordelon later recounted:

> I gave a 'tally ho' [visual contact with the target] and reported that the contact was definitely an unfriendly aircraft. JOC gave me clearance to fire just as the enemy aircraft began to bank hard to port. As we passed Kaesong, he suddenly rolled wings level and I gave him a long burst of 20mm HEI [high explosive incendiary] cannon fire. I saw a wing coming off and pulled left as he blew up with a tremendous explosion. Then, turning right and circling, I could see the bright splash of fire on the ground as the La-11 impacted.[440]

During the June night-bombing offensive and the missions intercepted by Borderlon, the KPAF 3rd Night Bomber Regiment lost the last of its Po-2LShs, two Yak-18s and three La-11s. Except for the fortuitous expedient of incorporating USN night-fighters into its air defence system, the USAF was never able to effectively deal with the KPAF's growing night bombing capability. In fact, in a 'backhanded compliment', the USAF official history allows that 'The [North Korean] 'Bed-Check Charlie' crews demonstrated that an air defence system could seldom be perfect'.[441]

FEAF's Airfield Denial Campaign

Informed that their governments would be seeking a negotiated end to the fighting in Korea, on 27 March 1953, PLAAF General Nie Fengzhi and his UAA HQ convened a 'joint conference' at Langtao, attended by four Chinese MiG-15 air division commanders, KPAF commander Wang Yong, and representatives from the Soviet 64th IAK HQ at Shenyang.[442] In discussions concerning the 'end game' for the Korean conflict's air war, the conferees agreed that as much 'aviation materiel' as possible should be positioned in North Korea by the date and time that the cease fire took effect, thus allowing the Soviets and Chinese to withdraw with some confidence that the North Koreans could defend themselves in the event of a resumption of combat.[443]

According to points already agreed to by both UNC and Communist negotiators, the draft armistice provided 'that combat aircraft in Korea cannot be reinforced following the end of hostilities, but worn out or damaged aircraft can be replaced with equipment of the same type'. Therefore, the Soviets agreed to provide as many as 600 MiG-15s (including transferring to the KPAF those already present in Soviet units in Manchuria) by flying in 100 aircraft to each of the six MiG bases being used by the UAA,[444] thus positioning them for quick movement into North Korea just before the cease fire took effect. To receive them, the KPAF and PLAAF agreed to 'rehabilitate' a number of airfields from the Yalu River to P'yongyang. While USAF and CIA communications and signals intelligence made American leaders aware of the former, Fifth AF photo-reconnaissance soon discovered the latter.[445]

In addition to the two airfields at Sinuiju, one at Uiju, Sariwon, and P'yongyang's Heijo airbase, the USAF's 67th Tactical Reconnaissance Wing (67th TRW) monitored 30 other airfield sites in North Korea. By the end of April the 67th TRW's RF-80As and RF-86As had discovered the creation of three new airfields deep in the interior, along the Chinese border, and that six others – heavily cratered and unused for months – were being repaired.[446] Also aware of the provision within the draft armistice, General Weyland and his FEAF staff also surmised that 'to get ready for the cease fire, the Communists intended to repair as many airfields as possible and then, in the last hours before the truce went into effect, to rush in a maximum number of aircraft'. To thwart this possibility and thereby deny the KPAF the ability to re-establish itself in strength on its own territory, FEAF Bomber Command planned on mounting a bombing campaign against these airfields. Specifically, the mission objectives were to destroy runways, 'cutting' them to reduce any landing surface to less than the 3,000ft (914m) needed for the MiG-15.[447]

Beginning on 10/11 June FEAF B-29 Superforts began nightly raids against these airfields, and were joined three nights later by carrier-based fighter-bombers from TF 77. By this time, American counter-measures for protecting their night bombers were proving increasingly effective. During the two months before the end of the conflict, the Soviet night-fighter MiGs (now the 298th OIAP)[448] failed to destroy a single B-29. Consequently, by 23 June all of the target airfields except one (Hoeryong [K-35], in the far north, along the PRC border) had been neutralized. However, a typical Korean summer of foul weather foiled further UNC air operations for nearly three weeks. Due to the urgency created by the last Communist offensive, when they could fly, FEAF and TF 77 were forced to turn their bombing efforts to interdiction and CAS. During this distraction – and under the cover of the bad weather – the Chinese troops and local Korean laborers 'made remarkable progress in their airfield rehabilitation efforts.'[449]

Appointed by Wang, the movement of the KPAF's 280 aircraft into North Korea was the responsibility of Maj Gen Kim Han-Jun, the service's political commissar (top political officer, with authority equal to the commander). On 17 July, 21 La-9s were flown into Sinuiju and dispersed in berm-protected revetments.[450] Two days later, using the sod 'infield' at Uiju, the KPAF's 1st AD began flying its 43 MiG-15bis into that base. According to Lt No Kum-Sok, two dozen of these were shuttled from Langtao to Uiju six at a time and 'as soon as a MiG landed, it was pushed south to the mountainside [bordering that side of the airfield] and camouflaged' and the pilots were trucked back to Langtao. Alerted to the movement, Fifth AF launched its massive fighter-bomber strike against Sinuiju and Uiju, attacks beginning at 1615hrs that afternoon. The initial attacks destroyed six La-9s (the survivors were dispersed off the airfield) at Sinuiju and damaged four MiG-15s at Uiju. The attacks continued, with lesser intensity, every day that the weather allowed.[451]

While Fifth AF fighter-bombers tried to destroy KPAF aircraft as soon as they arrived, FEAF B-29s resumed their attempts close the North Korean airfields to any additional arrivals. Beginning at 0100hrs on 20 July, 15 Superforts (19th and 307th BWs) attacked airfields at Sinuiju and Uiju, with nine more (98th BW) attacking the next morning. At Uiju, the arriving MiGs were towed off the airfield and dispersed and hidden 'in fields and hills adjoining the hard-surfaced highway between Uiju and Sinuiju'. The next night 18 B-29s 'blanketed Uiju's dispersal areas' with fragmentation bombs and incendiaries. FEAF reconnaissance and intelligence estimated 21 MiG-15s destroyed, but No reported that only six jet fighters were destroyed in these attacks. FEAF's B-29s also hit Namsi, Taechon, Sunchon, P'yongyang, and Saamcham, dropping 500lb (226.8kg) bombs to crater the runways and infields, and 100lb (45.4kg) fragmentation bombs and incendiary clusters to destroy aircraft.[452]

While bad weather thwarted Fifth AF operations in the northwest, in the east, beginning on 22 July TF 77 launched three large strikes, hitting Yonpo, Wonsan, Hamhung, Sondok, Hoeryong, Hoemun, and Hyesanjin airfields. The weather finally relented the last day, allowing FEAF to launch a final 'maximum effort' to neutralize the KPAF's airfields in the northwest while TF 77 cratered five runways from Hyesanjin to Hamhung. Follow-up reconnaissance by 67th TRW showed 'every airfield in North Korea was unserviceable for jet aircraft landings'. According to No, this was true for all except Uiju.[453]

The Rush to Peace

The 1st AD completed transferring its MiG-15s to Uiju on 22 July and the 60th FAR pilots returned to Langtao to take over the jets of the 56th GFAR, allowing that unit a well-earned rest. The visiting regiment manned 16 MiG-15bis at Alert Posture No. 1 (pilots in cockpits). According to Lt No Kum-Sok, 'I looked up and saw about six F-86s crisscrossing the sky above. They were not very high. We took off into that perilous situation that had destroyed many MiGs in the past. Two by two the MiGs rolled down the scarred runway and into the air'. One pair of MiGs returned immediately because Capt Kim Jung-Sup's landing gear would not retract, Kim leading his wingman, No, back to the runway for landing while the others climbed southwards in two or three formations to engage two flights of Sabres.[454]

One of the American flights was a formation of three F-86s (25th FIS/51st FIW) led by USMC Maj John H. Glenn, Jr., (later NASA astronaut and US Senator). The fourth Sabre had aborted the mission due to mechanical problems, leaving Glenn with his wingman, 2nd Lt Sam P. Young, Jr., and the second element leader, six-victory 'ace' 1st Lt Henry Buttelmann. As Young later recalled:

> We were about ready to complete our patrol over 'MiG Alley', with no activity, when [Glenn] spotted several MiGs below us. Evidently they had also been out on patrol and were headed north, back to their base at Antung [*sic*]. We immediately went after them and in the fight that followed, Major Glenn destroyed his third and Lieutenant Buttelmann shot down his seventh.[455]
>
> Shortly after the two MiGs were shot down, I spotted one below me and chased him to a very low altitude. With the high speed I had gained in the pursuit, I almost overshot him. Since I was so close and we were at such a very low altitude, the radar gunsight would not 'lock-on', so I switched to fixed sight and gave him a quick burst. When those .50-calibre rounds hit him, they sparkled just like fireworks on the 4th of July. I later discovered that the residue of small pieces of metal from the MiG had come back and embedded in my windscreen; that's how close we were. This MiG pilot was very aggressive, but not very good. His only tactic was to break one way then the other as we skimmed through the mountains. My second burst caused an explosion, starting at the right wing root...[456]

From the MiG-15 parking area at Langtao airfield, No had a 'ringside seat' to this, the final aerial duel of the Korean War:

> No sooner had I taxied the aircraft to the waiting mechanics than I saw a MiG-15 being pursued by an F-86 at close range just above the runway. The MiG was headed southwest lower than the traffic pattern when the Sabre opened fire. I could see the tracers crashing into the fuselage of the MiG, piloted by Lieutenant Su Chul-Ha. Too low to eject, Lieutenant Su attempted a crash-landing with his disabled aircraft but overshot the runway and flew into the ground at a high angle. His jet exploded as the Sabre climbed away.[457]

According to No, due to the FEAF's success in neutralizing North Korean airfields:

> General Wang suddenly switched tactics. He decided it would be more practical to violate the truce than take further losses from bombings at Uiju… On July 26 and 27 everyone at Dandong [*sic*] – Soviet, Chinese, North Korean pilots, mechanics, and commanding officers – worked around the clock dismantling and crating MiGs. On the night of the 27th, the field was lit like day by searchlights while we worked frantically in cool, drizzly weather.

A PLAAF history confirms: 'At Andong, ground crews from three Chinese air divisions were mobilized to dismantle and crate MiGs and Il-10s. At the hour when the ceasefire went into effect, some one hundred crated planes had been loaded onto trains and river barges ready for shipment across the Yalu River'.[458]

Most of these went by train across the Yalu railroad bridge to sidings in Sinuiju and at the airfield; the marshalling yards packed with flatcars bearing crated MiG-15s provided a lucrative target for FEAF Bomber Command's last raid. However, according to one Russian history, 'the final airstrike against Sinuiju airfield took place on 27 July, shortly before 2200hrs, when the truce was set to begin… a large group of B-29s heavily bombed the airfield with large bombs and napalm [*sic*], and burned up a large portion of the shipped MiGs while still in their containers.'[459]

Another 17 crated MiGs were sent across the river aboard four large barges. According to No:

> About three hours before the deadline, my battalion was finished [dismantling and packing the MiG-15s] and large tractors loaded our crated planes onto river barges for shipment across the Yalu River. At 10 P.M., July 27, the effective hour of the cease-fire, I was in a mist on a long barge carrying five crates across the Yalu. Three other barges carried a dozen other crated jets and equipment. [We] arrived in North Korea the next morning, docking at a small harbor near a rail line.[460]

The last mission flown by the KPAF during the Korean War was launched from one of the Andong-complex airfields at 2055hrs that evening, when two Tu-2s took off, crossed the Yalu River into their homeland airspace and landed at Uiju. The cease-fire agreement – finally ending more than three years of active hostilities – went into effect at 2200hrs that night.[461]

Conclusion

The KPAF ended the Korean War with, according to Russian sources, 412 aircraft, including 'at least 200 MiG-15s', 39 Ilyushin Il-28 twin-jet bombers, 13 Tupolev Tu-2 twin-engine night-bombers, and 40 Il-10s and La-9s.[462]

More importantly, the KPAF emerged from the conflict with a cadre of combat experienced fighter pilots and a number of experienced (but not combat veteran) bomber aircrews. While most Soviet and Chinese histories denigrate and minimize the KPAF's contribution to the air war in Korea, many Soviet pilots who fought in the Korean War praised their Asian comrades, saying 'they fought bravely and selflessly'. Chinese and Korean alike were commended

> for their courage and pluck in battle. If they latched onto the tail of an enemy fighter, it was a fight to the finish with no breaking off… [however] North Korean pilots often rushed at the enemy without checking their rear first, which led to heavy losses on their part. They paid no attention to whatever was going on behind them, and the American pilots often took advantage of this… and frequently punished them for their carelessness.[463]

Almost all American and British historians present the North Korean air force as a tiny and insignificant – at most emblematic – organization that put forth only a token effort during the three-year long conflict that Kim Il-Sung initiated. In Russian histories the KPAF is typically maligned as being small, weak, and less than half-hearted in its efforts to defend its own nation, almost totally discounting what little the small air arm was able to do. True, compared to the enormous and extensive aerial operations flown by the USAF, USN, and associated UNC units – and even in comparison with the lesser, though still substantial Soviet and Chinese efforts – the KPAF's participation in the Korean War is relatively insignificant.

However, when considered on its own, what was attempted and what was accomplished represents a notable set of achievements. These include: its establishment of an air force – out of almost nothing – in only a few months, the complete rebuilding – in another few months – of itself after being virtually annihilated by the USAF and USN in the opening weeks of the war, and its increasingly considerable contribution to the Communist coalition's air operations in the closing months of the Korean War. All DPRK propaganda aside, these notable achievements represent the high points of the KPAF's history in that conflict.

Enhancing the KPAF's limited success in air-to-air combat, DPRK propaganda – which invariably exaggerated the air arm's 'victory claims' – boasted that, over the course of the war, its fighter units shot down 164 enemy aircraft, including 44 F-86 Sabres, 11 B-29 Superfortresses, and 11 B-26 Invaders. They also claimed that KPAF airfield attacks destroyed 287 enemy aircraft on the ground, including 12 B-29s and 10 B-26s. The highest scoring unit, of course, was the 56th 'Guards Taejon' GFAR which, after being credited with destroying 60 enemy aircraft during the first two months of the war, was reported to have destroyed another 42 American aircraft, including 36 Sabres, while flying the MiG-15bis.[464]

There is no denying that the North Korean pilots flew with remarkable – some might say 'foolhardy' – courage, resulting in 14 pilots being credited with downing five or more enemy aircraft and being awarded the honor of Hero of the DPRK. Of these five were killed in combat. Most notable was Kim Gi-Ohk who began the war as a 24-year old Yak-9P pilot and survived the war and numerous combats. Credited with 'shooting down' (destroying or damaging) as many as 17 UN propeller-driven aircraft, by the end of the war he was promoted to colonel and became commander of the 3rd AD. Representing the very best of KPAF's fighter pilots, immediately after the cease-fire, in August 1953 Kim – along with two other HDPRKs – was sent to the prestigious Soviet Air Academy at Monino.[465]

Not to be left out of the propaganda pronouncements, the 57th AAR is claimed to have destroyed 40 enemy aircraft total, primarily in its Il-10 airfield attacks, but also reportedly shot down 'at least' seven in aerial combat. Additionally the KPA anti-aircraft units were officially credited with destroying 5,729 enemy aircraft and damaging 6,484 more – numbers far exceeding the 1,986 UNC aircraft losses to all causes – while KPA ground units reportedly captured 11 enemy aircraft.[466]

While completely unable to support KPA units in the ground war after the first six weeks of combat, the KPAF's recurring 'night heckling' operations continually frustrated USAF air defence systems and was a persistent embarrassment to Fifth AF. Even though the material damage and casualties it caused were militarily insignificant, its repeated successes as an instrument of harassment eventually proved to be a point of pride in the history of the KPAF.

The truly remarkable aspect of the KPAF's participation in the Korean War is not its performance or accomplishments, but the fact – in Western historical literature at any rate – it remained almost completely unmentioned and its combat experiences virtually unknown. Having collected numerous 'snipets' from a wide variety of American, Chinese, and Russian sources, this account tells that story – as flawed as it must necessarily be – until research into DPRK and KPAF archives reveal the true nature and extent of the North Korean air force's role in the 'Victorious Fatherland Liberation War'.

A happy DPRK Premier Kim Il-Sung during a State Visit to East Germany after the Korean War. (NARA)

Table 4: KPAF ORBAT, August 1953

Unit	Sub Unit	Aircraft Type	Notes
Korean People's Armed Forces Air Corps Commander: General Van Len Korean People's Air Force Commander: Major-General Wang Yong			
Operational Units			
1st Air Division		43 MiG-15bis	CO Colonel Kim Hi-Kiung
	59th Fighter Aviation Regiment		CO Colonel Shin Kang-Dong
	60th Fighter Aviation Regiment		CO Colonel chae San-Tae
2nd Air Division		45 MiG-15ibs	CO HDPRK Major Kim Ji-Sang
	56th Guards Fighter Aviation Regiment		
	58th Fighter Aviation Regiment		
3rd Air Division		40 MiG-15	CO HDPRK Colonel Kim Gi-Ohk
	57th Fighter Aviation Regiment		
	61st Fighter Aviation Regiment		
4th Air Division		40 Il-28, 2 Il-28U, 5 Tu-2	
	36th Bomber Aviation Regiment		
	37th Bomber Aviation Regiment		
5th Air Division	Flying Training Regiment	20 Yak-18, 10 Yak-11	
	Assault Training Regiment	30 Il-10s, 2 UIl-10	
	Fighter Training Regiment	15 La-9, 2 La-9UTI, 10 Yak-9P, 2 Yak-9V	
Other Aviation Units			
	Transport Aviation Regiment	estimated at 12 Li-2/ Il-12	

BIBLIOGRAPHY

Abakumov, B. S., 'Soviet Flyers in the Skies of Korea', 1/93, *Voprosy Istorii*, (in Russian, translated by Stephen L Sewell)

Air Intelligence Information Report (AIIR) No. 195-9-52, 'Ro Kum Suk, North Korean People's Army Air Force, MIG-15 Pilot', compiled by Donald Nichols, 24 September 1953, located in the US National Archives and Research Administration (College Park, MD), Record Group 341, Records of HQ USAF, Intelligence Documents Branch, Air Intelligence Reports, 1942-53, AF 591549-592236, Box 1758, 631/52/53/6,

Appleman, R. E., *South to the Naktong*, (Washington DC: U.S. Army Center of Military History, 1961)

Bermudez, J. S. Jr., 'Korean People's (North Korean) Air Force', *The Korean War: An Encyclopedia*, ed. Stanley Sandler, (New York: Garland Publishing, 1995)

Bordelon, Guy P., Jr., Cdr USN (Ret.), 'Night-Fighters Rule Korean Skies After Dark', *Naval Aviation News*, July-August 2003

Brown, E., 'Memories of Great Fighter Pilots: Frederick C. 'Boots' Blesse', published on *SabreJet Classics* website, http://sabre-pilots.org

Carey, A. C., *Twin Mustang: the North American F-82 at War* (Barnsley: Pen & Sword, 2014)

Churpin, K., *Stalin's Last Fortress: Military Secrets of North Korea* (ZAO 'Izdatel'stov Tsentroligraf': Moscow, 2012)

Cull, V., & Newton, D., *With the Yanks in Korea, Volume 1* (London: Grub Street, 2000)

Daugherty III, L. J.,*Train Wreckers and Ghost Killers: Allied Marines in the Korean War* (Washington DC: US Marine Corps Historical Center, 2003)

Davis, L., *The 4th Fighter Wing in the Korean War* (Atglen, PA: Schiffer Publishing Ltd, 2001)

Demin, A. 'In the Skies of Korea: The Eagles of Mao Zedong Against the Hawks of Uncle Sam', *Mir Aviatsii* magazine, series of articles, 2004 (translated by Stephen L Sewell, 2010)

Dorr, R. F., *B-29 Superfortress Units of the Korean War* (Oxford: Osprey Publishing Ltd., 2003)

Dorr, R. F., Lake, J. & Thompson, W. E., *Korean War Aces* (Oxford: Osprey Publishing Ltd., 1995)

Farrar-Hockley, Gen Sir A., *The British Part in the Korean War, Volume 1: A Distant Obligation* (London: HMSO, 1990)

Futrell, R. F., *The United States Air Force in Korea, 1950-1953*, (Washington DC: Office of Air Force History, 1981)

Hagedorn, D., *North American's T-6: A Definitive History of the World's Most Famous Trainer* (North Branch, MN: Specialty Press, 2009)

Halliday, J., 'Air Operations in Korea: The Soviet Side of the Story', *A Revolutionary War: Korea and the Transformation of the Postwar World*, ed. William J. Williams (papers and lectures presented at the 14-16 October 1992 USAF Academy Military History Symposium, published by Imprint Publications: Chicago, 1993)

Hallion, Richard P., Dr., *The Naval Air War in Korea* (Baltimore: The Nautical & Aviation Publishing Company of America, 1986)

Hallion, Richard P., Dr., 'T-33 and F-94… more stars in the Lockheed galaxy', *Air Enthusiast* No. 12, (April-July 1980)

Harden, B., *The Great Leader and the Fighter Pilot: The True Story of the Tyrant Who Created North Korea and the Young Lieutenant Who Stole His Way to Freedom* (NY: Viking Penguin, 2015).

Hastings, Max, *The Korean War* (Simon and Schuster, NY: 1987).

Hegarty, J., Lt Cdr, RN, 'HMS Jamaica: Korean War Service 1950', http://www.britains-smallwars.com, 2008.

History of Air Technical Intelligence Center, 1 January 1952 – 30 June 1952 (Wright-Patterson AFB, OH: USAF Air Material Command Air Technical Intelligence Center).

Jackiewicz, J & Fleischer, S., *Japanese Aircraft in Foreign Service, Volume 1* (Warsaw: Atelier Kecay, 2011)

Jackson, R., *Air War over Korea* (New York: Charles Scribner's Sons, 1973)

Korean War: Chronology of US Pacific Fleet Operations (Washington Naval Yard: Naval Historical Center, posted on website https://www.history.navy.mil) in seven parts. Part 1: *June-December 1950*; Part 2: *January-June 1951*; Part 3: *July-December 1951*; Part 4: *January-April 1952*; Part 5: *May-August 1952*; Part 6: *September-December 1952*; Part 7: *January-April 1953*; Part 8: *May-July 1953*

KORWALD, 'Korean War Aircraft Loss Database: Date of Aircraft Loss Report', (Washington, DC: Defense Prisoner of War/Missing Personnel Office) as posted on Department of Defense, Defense Technical Information Center (DTIC) website: http://www.dtic.mil

Kramarenko, S., *Air Combat over the Eastern Front and Korea: A Soviet Fighter Pilot Remembers* (Barnsley: Pen & Sword Books Ltd, 2008)

Krylov, L. & Tepsurkaev, Y., *Soviet MiG-15 Aces of the Korean War*, (Oxford: Osprey Publishing Ltd, 2002)

Lansdown, J. R. P., *With the Carriers in Korea: The Fleet Air Arm Story, 1950-1953*, (Wilmslow: Crécy Publishing Limited, 1997)

Leary, W. M., *Anything, Anywhere, Any Time: Combat Cargo in the Korean War* (Washington DC: USGPO, 2000)

Mansurov, A. Y., 'Stalin, Mao, Kim and China's Decision to Enter the Korean War, September 16 – October 15, 1950: New Evidence from the Russian Archives', *Cold War International History Project Bulletin*, No. 6-7, Winter 1995/1996, 107, 108, 117.

McLaren, D., *Mustangs Over Korea: The North American F-51 at War 1950-1953*, (Atglen, PA: Schiffer Publishing Ltd, 1999)

McLaren, D., *Double Menace: P/F-82 Twin Mustang* (Colorado Springs, CO: ViP Publishers, 1994)

Morozov, V., & Uskov, S., 'On Guard for Peace and Labor', *Mir Aviatsii* magazine, February 1997 (in Russian, translated by Stephen L. Sewell)

Naboka, V. A., *NATO's Hawks in the Sights of Stalin's Falcons: Soviet Flyers in the Protection of the Skies of China and Korea (1950-1951)*, (Krasnodar: Sovietskaya Kuban Publishing, 1999), (in Russian, translation by Stephen L Sewell)

No Kum-Suk, *A MiG-15 to Freedom: Memoir of the Wartime North Korean Defector Who First Delivered the Secret Fighter Jet to the Americans in 1953* (Jefferson, NC: McFarland & Company Inc., 1996)

Odgers, G., *Across the Parallel: The Australian 77th Squadron with the United States Air Force in the Korean War* (Melbourne: William Heinemann Ltd., 1952)

Paul, J. & Sprit, M., 'HMS Triumph: Tour 25/6/1950-29/9/1950', http://www.britains-smallwars.com, 2008

Person, J. (editor), *New Evidence on the Korean War* (Independence, MO: The Harry S Truman Presidential Library, 2010)

Politella, D., *Operation Grasshopper* (Tyler, TX: Robert R Longo Co Inc., 1958)

Rastrenin, O. V., 'Il-10 Ground Attack Aircraft, Part 2', *Modelist-Konstruktor* magazine, 2005 (in Russian, translated by Stephen L Sewell)

Rottman, G., *Inch'on 1950: The last great Amphibious Assault* (Oxford: Osprey Publishing Ltd., 2006)

Rottman, G., *Korean War Order of Battle: United States, United Nations, and Communist Ground, Naval, and Air Forces, 1950-1953* (Westport, CT: Praeger Publishers, 2002)

Sambito, William J., Major, *A History of Marine Fighter Attack Squadron 312* (Washington, DC: HQ USMC, History and Museums Division, 1978).

Seidov, Igor, *Red Devils over the Yalu*, translated and edited by Stuart Britton (Solihull: Helion & Company Limited, 2013)

Thompson, W. E., *B-26 Invader Units Over Korea*, (Oxford: Osprey Publishing Ltd, 2000)

Thompson, W. E., *F4U Corsair Units of the Korean War* (Oxford: Osprey Publishing Ltd., 2009)

Thompson, W. E., *F-51 Mustang Units of the Korean War* (Oxford: Osprey Publishing Ltd., 2015)

Thompson, W. E., *F-80 Shooting Star Units Over Korea*, (Oxford: Osprey Publishing Ltd, 2001)

Thompson, W. E., *F-84 Thunderjet Units Over Korea*, (Oxford: Osprey Publishing Ltd., 2000)

Thompson, W. E., 'Fighter Combat over Korea, Part 1: First Kills', *Wings of Fame*, Vol. 1, 1995

Thompson, W. E., 'Fighter Combat over Korea, Part 2: Jet Aces', *Wings of Fame*, Vol. 2, 1996

Thompson, W. E., 'Fighter Combat over Korea, Part 3: A Year of MiGs', *Wings of Fame*, Vol. 3, 1996

Thompson, W. E., *Naval Aviation in the Korea War: Aircraft, Ships and Men* (Barnsley: Pen & Sword Aviation, 2012)

Thompson, W. E., & McLaren, D. R., *MiG Alley: Sabres vs MiGs Over Korea* (North Branch, MN: Specialty Press, 2002)

USAF Historical Study No. 81: USAF Credits for the Destruction of Enemy Aircraft Korean War, (Maxwell AFB, AL: USAF Historical Division Aerospace Studies Institute, 1963)

USAF Korean War Victories by Date (Maxwell AFB, AL, Air Force Historical Research Agency) as posted on National Museum of the US Air Force website: http://www.nationalmuseum.af.mil

Volkovskiy, N. L. (editor), *The War in Korea 1950-1953* (St. Petersburg: OOO Izdatel'stvo Poligon, 2000), (in Russian, translation by Stephen L Sewell)

Weathersby, Kathryn, 'New Russian Documents on the Korean War', *Cold War International History Project Bulletin, No. 6-7*, Winter 1995/1996, pp. 30-125.

Werrell, Dr. Kenneth P., *Sabres Over MiG Alley: F-86 And The Battle For Air Superiority In Korea* (Annapolis, MD: Naval Institute Press, 2005)

Williams, W. J., 'Bedcheck Charlie and the An-2', *Air Power History*, Winter 1996, Vol. 43, No. 4

Wurster, Charles A., '1Lt Charles A. Wurster, Pilot, 36th Tactical Fighter Bomber Squadron, Combat Operations in Korea, 1950', an unpublished biographical manuscript provided to the author by Warren Thompson.

Zhang, Xiaoming, *Red Wings over the Yalu: China, the Soviet Union, and the Air War in Korea* (College Station, TX.: Texas A&M University Press, 2002)

Zolotarev, Maj-Gen V. A., Yaremenko, V. A., Pochtarev, A. N., & Usikov, A. V., *Russia (USSR) in Local Wars and Regional Conflicts in the Second Half of the 20th Century* (Moscow: Kuchkovo Polye Publishing, 2000), (in Russian, translation by Stephen L Sewell)

NOTES

1 Hastings, pp.40-43.

2 Harden, pp.16-19, 24-27, 31-36. Kim Il-Sung's original name was Kim Song-Chu, but feeling that this was too bland, while fighting Japanese occupation forces in 1935 'The Great Leader' adopted the name of a dead – and non-Communist – Korean guerrilla leader (whose name meant 'become the sun') as his own. Persecuted by the Chinese Communists as well as being hunted by Japanese occupation forces in Manchuria, Kim eventually fled to the USSR where he was trained by the Red Army and reportedly commanded the battalion-size 88th Special Independent Sniper Brigade beginning in April 1942. This 600-man multi-racial (Korean, Chinese, and Asian Russian) unit's mission was to infiltrate enemy-occupied zones to gather military intelligence. Kim returned to Korea on 25 September 1945, leading a band of 60 of his former unit members ashore at Wonsan as a Soviet army *Kapitan*.

3 Rottman, *Korean ORBAT*, p.161.

4 Lee's name is also rendered as Lee Hwal.

5 *Ibid.*, pp.161 & 169 & 161, 169; & Bermudez, p.179.

6 Rottman, *Korean ORBAT*, p.169. The Yakovlev UT-2 (*uchebno-trenirovochnyi* meaning 'primary/advanced trainer') was an open cockpit, fixed gear, all-wood monoplane powered by a 125hp Shvetsov M-11D five-cylinder radial engine. It was originally designated the AIR-10 by the Yakovlev design bureau. The Po-2 was originally designated U-2 (*uchebnyy* for 'instruction') in Soviet service.

7 *Ibid.*, pp.161-162.

8 Bermudez, p.179.

9 Wang Yong's name is also rendered as Wan Yong, Wang Young, Wang Yung, Wang Yen, or Wang Yun.

10 Rottman, *Korean ORBAT*, p.170, Zhang, pp.18 & 25 & Hallion, *Naval Air War*, p.28.

11 Seidov, p.40 & No Kum-Sok, pp.12-13.

12 Bermudez, p.179.

13 Futrell, p.19.

14 Demin, p.2.

15 Person, pp.24-25 & Document No.4, Memorandum from T. Shtykov to Chairman of the USSR Council of Ministers, 15 September 1949. This message also contains the first indication to Moscow of Kim Il-Sung's intent to reunite the Korean people through military means.

16 Although separate from KPA, the North Korean air force was structured in the classic army pattern: corps, division, regiment, battalion, and company. The battalion was the equivalent of a squadron in other air arms and was composed of three companies, or 'flights'. Due to the greater familiarity with the term 'squadron' as an air force organizational unit, in this work it will be used instead of 'battalion' except in formal unit designations.

17 Initially, each KPAF squadron had an authorized strength of 12 aircraft, with the regiment possessing another eight (total 44) in maintenance and reserve.

18 Morozov *et al*, pp.29-30 & Bermudez, pp.179-180.

19 Seidov, p.21.

20 Morozov *et al*, p.30 & Churpin, p.16.

21 These were Heijo airfield at P'yongyang, Hamhŭng, Chŏngjin, and Hoeryŏng. – as per Morozov *et al*, p.29.

22 *Ibid.* The Soviet unit involved in these flights was the 344th Transport Aviation Regiment based at Vladivostok, PR.

23 McLaren, *Mustangs*, p.16.

24 Rastrenin, p.29.

25 Zhang, pp.21, 41-43.

26 Person, pp.24-25 & Document No.4, Memorandum from T. Shtykov to Chairman of the USSR Council of Ministers, 15 September 1949.

27 *Ibid.*, p.30 & Volikovkiy, p.30. Bermudez, on p.180, cites the KPAF had some 76 officer pilots, which translates to the 32 combat-ready Yak-9P and Il-10 pilots and another 44 qualified pilots assigned to training and transport (non-combat) units. Of the 120 pilots reported on strength by Soviet documents, that means another 44 were in combat units still undergoing operational training.

28 Heijo was the Japanese name for P'yongyang. Because the airfield was a major IJAAF base, depot, and arsenal, to distinguish this former Japanese military complex from facilities inside the city, it will be referred to in this work by its original IJAAF name. USAF Intelligence called it 'Pyongyang Main' airfield or K-23.

29 Futrell, pp.19, 308. In addition to the former flying club fields, other former-IJAAF airfields that were available but unused at this point included Namyong-ni (Kangdong), Sunan, Sinanju, and Yongyu (Hwangyu).

30 Futrell, p.184 & Hallion, *Naval Air War*, p.35. See also United States Army Air Forces (USAAF) Air Objective Folders: Korean Area, dated 12 August 1944, pp.5, 6, 21, 24, 25.

31 Jackiewicz *et al*, p.98.

32 Rottman, *Inch'on*, p.38.

33 Bermudez, p.180; Morozov *et al*, p.30; Rottman, *Korean ORBAT*, p.170 & Seidov, p.21.

34 Aircraft inventory numbers represent approximates/maximums possible at the time.

35 Farrar-Hockley, p.5. A Korean War veteran, General Farrar-Hockley had a distinguished military career, rising to become NATO's Commander-in-Chief Allied Forces Northern Europe before retiring in 1982, after which he became a noted military historian.

36 Person, pp.26-27; Document No.4, Memorandum from T. Shtykov to Chairman of the USSR Council of Ministers, 15 September 1949, & Document No.5, Telegram from Stalin to Mao Zedong, 26 September 1949.
37 *Ibid.* and Harden, pp.49, 52, 55-56. What Stalin did not know, apparently, was that in the first few months of 1950, the Truman administration, heavily criticized for 'losing China' to Communism, had reassessed its policy towards the Soviet Union in light of Stalin's opportunist efforts – using surrogate Communist forces – to expand the USSR's 'sphere of influence'. National Security Council Report 68 (NSC-68) 'United States Objectives and Programs for National Security', which Truman approved, established US foreign policy as 'the Soviets should be challenged wherever in the world they next embarked upon an assault on freedom'. Kim's invasion of South Korea was that 'next… assault on freedom' and Truman promptly acted in complete accord with his Administration's published policy. Unfortunately, the classified nature of the document worked against it and Stalin had no idea that the American response would be so sudden, sharp, or strong. If he had known the content of NSC-68, 'it is profoundly unlikely that Moscow would have ever allowed the North Korean invasion of June 1950 to take place' – see Hastings, pp.50-51.
38 Person, pp.29-30 & Document No.6, Telegram from Shtykov to Vyshinsky, 19 January 1950, and Document No.7, Telegram from Stalin to Shtykov, 30 January 1950. The Soviet credits amounted to 70.7 million rubles, but Kim also sent nine tons of gold, 40 tons of silver and 15,000 tons of ore containing rare earth metals and radioactive materials, the total valued at 133 million rubles.
39 Volkogonov's statement was originally made in an interview with the Yonhap News Agency, broadcast by BBC, 23 June 1993, and is referenced by Halliday, pp.163-164. See also Weathersby, pp.36-37.
40 Weathersby, pp.30, 37-38 & Harden, pp.54-59.
41 The Soviet advisor to KPAFAC Commander, General Van Len, was Col A. Petrachev.
42 Zolotarev *et al*, pp.67-68 & Weathersby, p.39.
43 Weathersby, pp.31, 39.
44 Person, pp.47-49 & Document No.12, Cable from Shtykov to Vyshinsky, 30 May 1950.
45 Harden, p.59, quoted from Evgeniy P. and Natalia Bajanova, 'The Korean Conflict, 1950-1953: The Most Mysterious War of the 20th Century—Based on Secret Soviet Archives', an unpublished manuscript, 59, 60.
46 Appleman, pp.19, 24 & Volkovskiy, p.58.
47 Appleman, p.19.
48 Morozov *et al*, p.38.
49 These were at Sinmak (K-20), Pyonggang (K-21), Kansong (K-50), and Kumchon (K-52). Futrell, pp.19.
50 Hagedorn, p.207.
51 Morozov *et al*, p.30.
52 These were Taegu (K-2), Kwangju (K-7), Suwon (K-13), Kunsan (K-8), and Cheju-do (K-39). Youi-do airfield was K-16 and Kimpo AB was K-14. For ROKAF's initial force structure and aircraft inventory, see Futrell, p.17; Cull *et al*, p.10 & Morozov *et al*, pp.30, 38.
53 Later redesignated Pacific Air Forces (PACAF).
54 Futrell, pp.2-4, 58.
55 Futrell, pp.68-69 & Davis, p.6.
56 Cull *et al*, pp.6-8.
57 These were the, the 27th Air Army defending Sakhalin Island, 29th Air Army responsible for the Khabarovsk District and the 54th Air Army protecting Vladivostok and the Primorsky District.
58 Lansdown, p.37 & Halliday, p.150.
59 Seidov, p.23.
60 Zhang, p.22. The 29th GvIAP was transferred from the Soviets' premier MiG-15 unit, the 324th IAD, traveling all the way from Moscow, while the 351st IAP was stationed at Dalian as part of the 153rd IAD. The 829th ShAP was formed using battalions from the Tu-2 and Il-10 regiments also stationed in the Dalian area. Zhang, p.81 & Krylov *et al*, p.11.
61 Zhang, pp.46-47, 83, 237.
62 Arriving at Xiansilipu AB (near Dalian) on 3 October, the 29th GvIAP joined the 177th IAP, which had been transferred from the 303rd IAD after it arrived at Vladivostok. The two units were issued 80 new MiG-15bis and one week later formed the 50th IAD, the division staff being provided by renumbering the 106th IAD HQ.
63 Demin, p.1 & Zhang, p.35, 217 & 237.
64 The prestigious guards fighter division was originally the 5th GvIAD, a component of the Moscow Military District Air Force and the third to be equipped with MiG-15. For the secret deployment to China, its designation was changed to the 151st GvIAD as a security measure; Seidov, pp.35-36.
65 Harden, p.143. Lee joined the ROKAF and fought in the ensuing war, helping to liberate P'yongyang (and rescue his wife, children, and parents), eventually rising to the rank of colonel to become vice-commander of the ROKAF Academy. His Il-10 was later flown to Kimpo and was reportedly found there by KPA troops capturing the base; its subsequent fate is unknown. No Kum-Sok, pp.12-13 & Rastrenin, p.29.
66 Harden, p.143 & McLaren, *Mustangs*, p.16.
67 Harden, p.59 & Bajanova, pp.59-60.
68 Appleman, pp.23-28; Rottman, *Inch'on*, p.38; Volkovskiy, pp.58-60 & Zolotarev *et al*, p.68.
69 Rastrenin, p.29.
70 Absent was Harvard IIB #101. All ten of the ROKAF's trainers at Youi-do were eventually lost – either destroyed or abandoned – during the opening phase of the war.
71 Futrell, p.14; Morozov *et al*, p.31 & Seidov, p.23. The USAF lost four C-54s during the first week of the war: the MATS C-54D (serial number unknown) at Kimpo on 25 June, a 6th TCS C-54D (serial unknown) DBR by Yak-9Ps at Suwon on 28 June, a 22nd TCS C-54D (42-72648) destroyed by Yak-9P strafing at Suwon on 28 June (officially written off on 30 June), and a 22nd TCS C-54G (45-415) which crashed into a 2,000ft hill five miles NW of Pusan (now Busan) on 30 June, killing the crew and 19 members of the US Army 71st Signal Battalion. In this work US aircraft loss information is predominantly derived from KORWALD. However, in this case KORWALD only includes the latter two aircraft, and then attributes the loss of 23 lives aboard the C-54G to the loss of the C-54D by strafing. Where possible, in this study all information from KORWALD has been verified and confirmed – or corrected if necessary – by individual unit or command operations and loss reports. See also Leary, pp 1-5.
72 Rastrenin, p.29.
73 The 68th FAWS was stationed at Itazuke and had 12 F-82s operational. The 339th FAWS was based at Johnson AB, near Tokyo, and immediately dispatched six serviceable F-82s to Itazuke, retaining its remaining four combat-ready aircraft for air defence alert duties protecting the Japanese capital. At Itazuke these 18 were joined by 10 F-82Gs from 4th FAWS to form the 347th Provisional Fighter Group (All Weather) under Lt Col John F. Sharp. This temporary unit controlled F-82 operations over Korea until 5 July when it was inactivated. See Futrell, p.8 & McLaren, *Double Menace*, pp.32-33.
74 Futrell, pp.8-9 & 12.
75 '8th Fighter-Bomber Group: Historical Data for the Months of May and June 1950' (henceforth cited as '8th FBG History'), p.7; Carey, p.74; Futrell, pp.9, 19; McLaren, *Double Menace*, pp.33-34; Seidov, p.23 & Thompson, First Kills, pp.6-7.
76 Appleman, pp.28-31, 39; Futrell, pp.9, 12; McLaren, *Double Menace*, p.33; Seidov, p.24 & Volkovskiy, pp.59-60.
77 8th FBG History, p.7, Futrell, pp.12 & McLaren, *Double Menace*, 35, 36.
78 Thompson, First Kills, p.8. See also Carey, pp.77-79; 8th FBG History, p.7 & McLaren, *Double Menace*, pp.35-37. The Yak pilot was killed on the ground in a shoot-out with ROKA troops near Kimpo while the rear seat observer was killed in the ensuing crash.
79 8th FBG History, pp.7-8; Carey, pp.78-79 & 81; Cull *et al*, pp.11-12; McLaren, *Double Menace*, p.36; Seidov, pp.23-24 & Thompson, First Kills, pp.6-8.
80 Thompson, F-80, pp.36-37.
81 Demin, p.2.

82 8th FBG History, pp.7-8; Futrell, p.13 & Seidov, pp.23-24. Russian sources also claim 'one Mustang' shot down by a rear gunner; Rastrenin, p.29.
83 Appleman, pp.32, 34; Futrell, pp.12 & 24; Volkovskiy, p.63.
84 The B-26B (44-34379) of the 13th BS(L) had been badly damaged during the morning's low-level attack on the Munsan railway yards just south of the 38th Parallel. The F-82G (46-364 of the 68th FAWS) was the one damaged by its jettisoned drop tanks on 26 June. Additionally, the C-54D (42-72648 of the 22nd TCS), which had arrived with parts and mechanics to repair the F-82G, was destroyed by fire resulting from the day's attacks and was written off on 30 June, the date typically given for its destruction; Futrell, p.27.
85 Leary, p.1. In total, the DPRK High Command reported to the Soviets that 'approximately ten enemy aircraft were destroyed at Suwon', including 'four American four-engine aircrafts [*sic*]'. Enhancing the story, the KPAF credited the Yak pilots with destroying B-29 bombers instead of troop transports – see Person, p.52; Document No.15, Report of the High Command of the DPRK People's Army, 30 June 1950, p.52; Futrell, p.28 & Seidov, pp.24, 26.
86 Futrell, p.28; Seidov, pp.24, 26; Dorr, p.11. Despite the fact that USAF bombing missions did not begin until 28 June, the DPRK High Command reported to the Soviets that, 'At 1100, 26 June nine American aircrafts [*sic*] attacked the city of Kaesŏng, which had been liberated by the People's Army. Our aircrafts [*sic*] put them to flight and, pursuing the American aircrafts [*sic*], shot down two B-29s over Seoul'. So began the grossly inflated claims of the DPRK and its air force – see Person, p.52 & Document No.15, Report of the High Command of the DPRK People's Army, 30 June 1950.
87 8th FBG History, p.9. The Il-10 was credited to Lt Roy W. Marsh (80th FBS) but the 'La-7' – which was probably another Il-10 (Soviet archives confirm the loss of two Il-10s attacking Suwon on this date) – was not credited to any individual pilot. According to Thompson, F-80, p.22, 'All pilots in Norris's (9th FBS) flight scored hits, and as Norris was raking the aircraft, it burst into flames... Norris was never given official credit for the 'kill', however, as too many of the flight had scored hits'. This was in keeping with FEAF policy, 'In no case was a [victory] credit divided among more than two persons'. See also USAF Historical Study No. 81, p.3.
88 Because the 8th FBW had only recently converted from the F-51D to the F-80C, many of its pilots were very experienced and still familiar with the Mustang. Because MacArthur's C-54 needed the best escort possible, in addition to jet-powered F-80Cs sweeping the flight path ahead of the VIP transport and a pair of F-82Gs as close escort, the Mustangs were added, following MacArthur's Skymaster to provide additional close escort. Futrell, pp.31, 68, 89 & McLaren, *Mustangs*, p.11.
89 8th FBG History, p.9. The victories went to 2nd Lt Orrin R. Fox (two Il-10s), and to 1st Lieutenants Richard J. Burns (one Il-10) and Harry T. Sandlin (one 'La-7'). Furthermore, 1st Lt Eugene R. Hanson was credited with a 'probable' Yak-9. See 'USAF Korean War Victories by Date'.
90 Futrell, pp.31, 89 & Thompson, First Kills, p.12.
91 Futrell, p.29 & Seidov, p.26.
92 Appleman, p.44, 46. The aerial counter-attack resulted directly from the KPAF's effective raids against Suwon earlier that day, prompting MacArthur to authorize the counter-air strikes north of the 38th Parallel. The following morning he received permission from Washington to attack 'air bases, depots, tank farms, troop columns, and other purely military targets' throughout the Korean Peninsula; Futrell, pp.32, 36.
93 Futrell, p.32; Seidov, p.26; & Volkovskiy, p.61.
94 Futrell, p.33; Seidov, pp.26-27; Thompson, First Kills, p.13 & Wurster, pp.1-3.
95 Seidov, p.26, 28.
96 Appleman, p.60-68.
97 Dorr, B-29, pp.12, 16, 17 & Futrell, pp.30, 46-47, 98, 99.
98 Appleman, p.48, 50; Hallion, *Naval Air War*, p.30 & Lansdown, p.11.
99 Cull *et al*, p.258; Hallion, *Naval Air War*, p.32 & Lansdown, p.11.
100 The numbers of each RN/FAA type have been reversed in all American accounts of this operation. For the most accurate information, based on the HMS *Triumph's* logbook; see Cull *et al*, p.259, 260 & Lansdown, p.15. For the USN strike force composition, see Hallion, *Naval Air War*, p.34.
101 Lt Plog's personal account provided to the author by Thompson, 4 September 2014.
102 No Kum-Sok, pp.78-79.
103 Hallion, *Naval Air War*, p.34 & Seidov, p.29.
104 Demin, p.2. For USAF victory credits, see 'USAF Korean War Victories by Date'.
105 Appleman, pp.53, 55; Futrell, pp.84, 99 & Volkovskiy, p.66.
106 Politella, pp.13-14 & Rottman, pp.16-18. At the time each American infantry division typically had two aviation sections, one assigned to the HQ Company (equipped with up to eight L-17s), and one attached to the artillery HQ Battery (with up to ten L-4/L-5s). Later these were combined to form a 'provisional aviation company' in most divisions.
107 Futrell, p.99 & Volkovskiy, p.66. Although reported as Yak fighters, the KPAF aircraft that attacked the Osan communications facility were almost certainly Il-10s. Being pure interceptors, none of the Yak-9 versions supplied to the KPAF were equipped to carry bombs.
108 Futrell, pp.51, 65, 68, 89-91, 95, 99.
109 US records report 'Downed by Yak, 400 meters N of Pukpyong RR Station'. However, original RAAF documents, including the 77Sqn Operational Record Book (ORB) describes how the aircraft was probably hit by AAA while diving to attack, and how it impacted the ground just beyond the target. No KPAF Yaks were observed anywhere in the area. Considering the fact this action was well away from the 56th FAR's normal area of operations, and that individual unit records are commonly the closest to the action – and therefore usually the most accurate and authoritative – Sqn Ldr Strout's F-51D (A68-757) was not lost to a KPAF Yak fighter, but was hit by AAA fire. Cull *et al*, pp.16, 19, 20; Odgers, pp.56-57 & Seidov, p.29.
110 Appleman, pp.86-88, and Volkovskiy, p.66. Once Seoul was captured, the 105th Tank Brigade was upgraded to a division by the addition of one battalion of self-propelled artillery (with SU-76Ms and SU-100s) and one battalion of truck-towed (122mm) artillery; Rottman, *Korean ORBAT*, p.166.
111 The 877th Air Force Unit consisted of the 1st and 3rd Companies from the 56th FAR's Engineer Battalion (aircraft mechanics and technicians) and the Finance and Supply Companies from the 3rd Technical Battalion; Rottman, *Inch'on 1950*, p.38.
112 Futrell, pp.90, 91, 99; Rastrenin, p.29; Seidov, p.29 & Volkovskiy, p.68.
113 Futrell, p.99 & Seidov, p.30.
114 Futrell, p.99 & Politella, p.20. KORWALD reports this loss as a Stinson L-5 lost on the following day.
115 Rastrenin, pp.29, 30 & Seidov, p.30. There is no mention of this North Korean air attack in either of the US Army's histories of the defensive battles between Osan and the Naktong River in July 1950.
116 The victim of Lee's attack was B-29A 44-69866. Cull *et al*, pp.20-21; Dorr, B-29, p.12; Futrell, pp.90, 91, 99; & Seidov, p.29.
117 Dorr, B-29, pp.14-15. The victim this attack was B-29A 44-61638; the bomber survived the attack, was repaired, and remained on 19th BW(M) operations well into 1952.
118 Appleman, pp.123, 125-129; Futrell, pp.97, 99; Seidov, p.30 & Volkovskiy, pp.68- 69. DPRK propaganda reported two B-26s were shot down 'above Taejon' on 15 July, but the only actually lost was B-26B [44-34263 from 13th BS(L)] which was destroyed by US forces when they were forced to evacuate Taejon on 20 July.
119 Appleman, p.152.
120 This account was taken primarily from Thompson, *First Kills*, pp.16, 18 & Wurster, pp.4-5. See also: 8th FBG History, pp.8-9, 11; Futrell, p.101 & KORWALD. In addition to Odell's F-80C (49-698), DPRK propaganda reported that on 19 July the 56th FAR shot down one B-29 (see Note 116 above) and three other American aircraft; Seidov, p.30.
121 Politella, p.20. Seidov, p.30 incorrectly attributes this action to that which occurred on 12 July 1950. Following this loss, and the KPA's first bombardment of Taejon airfield, the 24th Infantry Division's aviation sections evacuated their surviving two L-17s, one L-4, and two L-5s to Taegu and Pohang; Politella, p.21.

122 Thompson, F-80, p.22.
123 Futrell, p.101; Thompson, F-80, pp.25-26 & First Kills, p.18.
124 Appleman, pp.152-179; Futrell, p.97 & Morozov *et al*, pp.31-32. After this politically significant victory over the Americans, Kim Il-Sung awarded the 'Guards' title to the 105th Tank Brigade, four infantry brigades, four artillery regiments and two AAA regiments.
125 Futrell, p.99.
126 *USN Chronology, Part 1*, pp.2-3 & Thompson, *Naval Aviation*, pp.25, 27.
127 Futrell, p.99 & Hallion, *Naval Air War*, pp.38-39.
128 Futrell, pp.99, 100; Wurster, pp.5-6.
129 Dorr, *B-29*, p.15 & Futrell, p.101.
130 Futrell, p.102.
131 KORWALD database shows that on 9 September 1950 one B-29 (44-62084/28th BS/19th BG) was blown out of the sky by a direct AAA hit and a second (44-27288/395th BS/92nd BG) returned with 'major battle damage'. Additionally, KORWALD lists the loss of an F-51D (44-73255/39th FBS/18th FBW) on 28 September, 1950, to a Yak fighter. This information is recorded in the unit's monthly history report. However, examination of the actual combat report shows that the loss – and the death of 1st Lt Donald L. Pitchford – was probably due to ground fire and that no enemy fighters were in the vicinity. Apparently between the mission report and the writing of the unit history the word 'flak' mutated into 'Yak'. Supporting the fact that no KPAF fighters were involved in this loss is that, unlike virtually all instances of a KPAF-caused UN aircraft loss there was no DPRK propaganda claiming responsibility for this event.
132 Cull *et al*, p.265; Lansdown, p.27; Rastrenin, p.30; Seidov, p.33, 563 & Volkovskiy, p.80. Lt Ahn Hon-Zun is also reported as being An Shen-Zun, an Il-10 pilot who was also credited with destroying two enemy aircraft (on the ground) during the first four weeks of the war. Interestingly, British sources unanimously describe this as an Il-10 attack while American sources invariably refer to it as a 'Yak attack' – as does Seidov's Russian history.
133 Rastrenin, p.30 & Seidov, p.33.
134 Total KPAF aircraft credited as destroyed in aerial combat during this period were one Yak-11, 14 Yak-9Ps (although several of these were originally credited as various Yakovlev and Lavochkin types) and nine Il-10s.
135 Bermudez, p.180; Morozov *et al*, pp.31-32, 38; No Kum-Sok, pp.70-71, Rastrenin, p.30 & Seidov, p.34.
136 Seidov, p.34 & Volkovskiy, p.80.
137 Seidov, p.31, 34.
138 Demin, p.2; Morozov *et al*, pp.32, 38 & No Kum-Sok, pp.70-71, 77. According to USAF Intelligence, the Yanji complex was known as the PLAAF's "No. 10 Aviation School"; see USAF Air Intelligence Information Report (AIIR) 'Ro Kum Suk, North Korean People's Army Air Force, MIG-15 Pilot', p.2.
139 Seidov, p.40-41. Sinkevich reported that the Yak-3s used by the special training squadron were not transferred to the KPAF. However, this unit's Yak-9Vs may have been the half dozen of this variant supplied by the Soviets to the KPAF in late 1950.
140 Mansurov, pp.107-108, 117.
141 *Ibid.* & Weathersby, p.48.
142 Demin, p.5. The manpower needed for reconstruction of the 56th GFAR (20 pilots) and creation of the 58th FAR, as well as the eight new Il-10 pilots to rebuild the 57th AAR, are believed to have come from the 44 pilots who were undergoing operational training at Heijo and Yonpo when Kim started the Korean War.
143 *Ibid.*
144 CIA 'Daily Korean Situation Summary' (aka 'Daily Bulletin', or CIADB), 20 March 1951, p.3 & Zhang, pp.253. The ex-IJAAF airfield at Fengcheng was actually named Daboa airfield, called Dapu by the Russians, and was eventually upgraded to a jet-capable airbase to become home for three regiments of Soviet MiG-15s.
145 Kim Tal-Hion's name is also rendered as Kim Tal-Won and Kim Tal-Hyon. Since the beginning of the war, Kim steadily 'moved up in the ranks', having commanded the regiment's 2nd Battalion until January 1951, then the regiment itself, and finally, the KPAF's new assault aviation division. When he was promoted to command the 11th AAD, Hero of the DPRK Ree Su-An took over command of the 57th AAR. Demin, p.2; No Kum-Sok, p.113; Seidov, p.563 & Weathersby, p.48. See also CIADB, 23 October 1951, 5, 6.
146 Weathersby, pp.50-51.
147 *Ibid.* & Seidov, p.45. Khorol'sk AB (now simply Khorol) was a joint 54th Air Army and Pacific Ocean Fleet 5th Naval Air Force bomber base located 90 miles (145km) north of Vladivostok, near Lake Khanka.
148 Futrell, p.158.
149 Rottman, *Inch'on*, pp.57, 60-64 & Daugherty, p.25.
150 Rottman, *Inch'on, pp.*64-65.
151 Paul *et al*; Hegarty; Cull *et al*, p.268; Futrell, p.158 & Volkovskiy, p.80.
152 Daugherty, pp.26-27 & Rottman, *Inch'on*, pp.65, 69.
153 Photographic evidence shows that Il-10s #24, #39, and #54 (and two unknown examples) and Yak-9Ps #2, #3, #7, #9 and #49 were found destroyed. The two intact and relatively undamaged Il-10s found in the main hangar were #44 and #55, as well as a badly damaged Yak-9P (#27) whose fuselage became the basis of the rebuilt example shipped to the USA for examination and exploitation. Seidov, p.130.
154 Dorr *et al*, *Korean War Aces*, pp.6, 22. For detailed reports on the exploration of the Il-10s and Yak-9P, see *History of ATIC* (Bibliography).
155 Mansourov, p.94 & Morozov *et al*, p.31.
156 Zhang, pp.59, 217.
157 In mid-November 1950, the Soviet 328th IAD arrived to train the unit on the straight-wing jet-powered MiG-9, expanding the unit into the 14th AD in doing so. Zhang, pp.215-217.
158 *Ibid.*, pp.32, 46.
159 Krylov *et al*, pp.11-12 & Zhang, pp.59, 217. The two new PLAAF ADs were formed in late October with the 3rd AD being initially based at Shenyang and the 4th AD being stationed at Liaoyang. To fully equip these two new ADs, Stalin ordered 100 MiG-15s shipped to Shenyang, where they arrived in December.
160 Harden, pp.81-83; Krylov *et al*, pp.11-13, 29, 30; Mansourov, pp.94, 98, 100, 103, 104, 105, 113, 118; Zolotarev, pp.69-70 & Zhang, pp.61, 62, 72-76, 84-87, 91.
161 These were the two at Sinuiju (one double-track RR bridge and a combination highway/RR bridge), a highway bridge at Chongsongjin, RR bridge at Namsan-ni, and a RR bridge and highway bridge at Manpojin. Futrell, pp.223-224.
162 *Ibid &* Weathersby, p.48.
163 The first of these, from the 72nd GvIAP, reportedly engaged three F-51 Mustangs, Snr Lt Guts claiming one shot down at 1320hrs about 15km southeast of Andong. About an hour and a half later, the third formation, also from the 72nd GvIAP, reported engaging the leading four-ship of 10 F-80Cs, Snr Lt Khominich claiming to shoot down one about 25km southeast of Andong. Neither of these claims are verified in USAF loss records for this date. Krylov *et al*, p.14 & Naboka, pp.26-27.
164 Krylov *et al*, pp.13-14; Weathersby, p.48 & Naboka, pp.26-27.
165 Thompson, *F-51*, p.32.
166 *Ibid*, pp.61-62. DPRK radio broadcast that day admitted the loss of the two Yak-9Ps – with one of the pilots bailing out – but claimed two B-29s and a Mustang shot down; Futrell, p.223 & Weathersby, p.48.
167 Futrell, p.219 & Weathersby, p.48.
168 Thompson, *F-51*, pp.32, 43.
169 *Ibid.* See also Futrell, pp.219, 222; McLaren, *Mustangs*, p.97 & Thompson, *F-51*, p.23.
170 Seidov, pp.63, 563. Kim Tal-Hion was credited with one aerial victory on this date.
171 Thompson, *F-51*, pp.45-46.
172 As of 20 December 1950, NSA 'Acorn' intercepts revealed that the KPAF had three combat regiments composed, respectively, of 15 Yak-9s (56th GFAR), 28 La-9s (58thFAR), and 33 Il-10s (57th AAR). CIADB, 22 December 1950. Evidently, shortly afterwards, the 56th GFAR's remaining Yaks were concentrated in a 10-aircraft squadron (with five aircraft in reserve), to which was added a 10-aircraft La-9 squadron to provide the KPAF with a second two-squadron fighter regiment organized like the 58th FAR.
173 Futrell, pp.220-223; Krylov *et al*, pp.14-16; Zolotarev, pp.69-71 & Zhang, pp.87-88.

174 Jackson, pp.95-96 & Morozov *et al*, p.31. Pak Den-Sik's name is also rendered as Pak Deng-Sik in some Russian histories.
175 The CPVA's massive counteroffensive against UNC forces took the form of a series of 'phase offensives'. The first four of these were:
- 1st Phase, 27 October – 2 November, a series of 'spoiling attacks' against ROK and US forces as a signal to US leadership to desist in pushing to the Yalu River.
- 2nd Phase, 25 November – 9 December, a massive counter-offensive operation to drive UNC forces from North Korea.
- 3rd Phase, 31 December – 14 January, invasion of South Korea.
- 4th Phase, 11 – 18 February, when the CPVA attempted to finally eject UNC forces from South Korea. This phase was prematurely terminated due to lack of air superiority over front and heavy interdiction of its supply lines.
176 Weathersby, p.48.
177 Futrell, p.246; Morozov *et al*, p.31; McLaren, *Mustangs*, p, 21; Thompson, *F-51*, p.32 & Williams, pp.4, 7.
178 Futrell, pp.273, 281 & Williams, pp.7, 10. See also CIADB, 5 January 1951; 9 January 1951; 13 January 1951 & 15 January 1951.
179 On 9 November, two MiG-15s (72nd GvIAP) shot up RB-29A 44-61813, (31st SRS) so badly that it crashed on approach for landing at Johnson AB, Japan, killing five crewmen. The next day six MiG-15s attacked B-29A 45-21814, (307th BW/371st BS) over Uiju resulting in it crashing seven miles southwest of Kusong with three dead, one MIA, and eight POWs. Futrell, pp.226, 228; Krylov *et al*, p.16 & Naboka, pp.34, 36.
180 To train the two PLAAF ADs the 151st GvIAD was reorganized into two fighter divisions. The 151st GvIAD trained the 3rd AD at Shenyang, while the new 28th IAD was to train the 4th AD at Liaoyang. See Halliday, p.151; Krylov *et al*, p.13-18; Naboka, pp.32-36, 42-43; Seidov, pp.46, 49, 61, 64 & Zhang, pp.88-89, 215.
181 Futrell, pp.228, 245; Krylov *et al*, pp.18-22; Naboka, pp.41-43, 45, 58, 59, 61-65; Seidov, pp.64-85 & Zhang, pp.88, 89, 249. The Sabre lost was F-86A (49-1176 from the 335th FIS); Capt Lawrence V. Bach ejected to become a POW. The 50th IAD also shot down an NAA RB-45C Tornado jet reconnaissance aircraft (48-015 from 84th BS/Recon Det A; two POW, two MIA) on 4 December. In addition to the losses to F-86s, the 50th IAD lost one MiG-15bis to B-29 gunners and two others that broke up in flight during hard manoeuvring; the pilots were KIA. All told, the 50th IAD lost seven MiG-15bis with five pilots KIA and one WIA during its December-January deployment to Andong. Krylov *et al*, pp.19-20 & Naboka, pp.45-49,62-64, 74, 82.
182 Zhang, pp.101-103, 251n15.
183 These were Namsi and Taechon with others at Namyong-ni (also called Kangdong), Sunch'ŏn (also called Pyong-ni), Sunan, and Yongyu. Additionally, the KPAF constructed a well-camouflaged grass airfield at Sariwon, 35 miles (56km) south of P'yongyang, to be used by light aircraft such as the Po-2s. The original KPAF airfields to be 'rehabilitated' included Heijo, Yonpo, Wonsan, Ongjin, Anak, Sinanju, and Sinmak. Sinuiju airfield was maintained and improved by the KPAF. Futrell, p.293 & Zhang, pp.109-113.
184 *Ibid*. & Demin, p.19.
185 These were the 3rd and 4th ADs with MiG-15s, the 2nd AD with one MiG-15 and one La-11 regiments, the 5th AD with Il-10s, and 8th AD with Tu-2s. Zhang, pp.109, 119, 215, 217.
186 Seidov, pp.126-127 & Zhang, pp.100, 103.
187 Halliday, pp.152-153 & Seidov, pp.45, 46, 49.
188 AIIR, p.49; Harden, p.94, 97; Krylov *et al*, p.24 & Seidov, p.62.
189 Halliday, p.151 & Krylov *et al*, pp.23-24.
190 Having begun its existence as the 55th CAD in 1950, this unit was reportedly re-designated the 1st CAD while it was rebuilding at Yanji during October-December 1950. Info via Tom Cooper, 8 July 2014.
191 Futrell, pp.286, 293, 302, 308. FEAF Intel reported the Lavochkins as 'La-5s', but now they are known to have been La-9s.
192 Futrell, pp.302 & Weathersby, p.48.
193 Futrell, p.281.
194 *Ibid*., p.288.
195 *Ibid*.; Naboka, pp.80-84; Thompson, Jet Aces, pp.4-5 & Thompson, *F-84*, pp.21-22.
196 Futrell, pp.287-288.
197 Thompson, *F-84*, p.25.
198 McLaren, *Mustangs*, p, 105. For a different version of this encounter, see Thompson, *F-51*, pp.46-47.
199 Futrell, pp.293. President Truman peremptorily relieved the obstreperous 70-year-old MacArthur of all his commands on 11 April 1951.
200 CIADB, 20 March 1951.
201 *Ibid*., & CIADB, 24 February 1951 & 18 March 1951.
202 CIADB, 31 May 1951, 6 & 24 July 1951, 5.
203 Hallion, *Naval Air War*, p.156 & Thompson, Jet Aces, p.11
204 Thompson, *F4U*, p.58
205 *Ibid*.; Hallion, *Naval Air War*, p.156 & Thompson, Jet Aces, p.11.
206 Hallion, *Naval Air War*, p.156 & Thompson, *F4U*, p.59
207 Zhang, p.114.
208 Futrell, pp.302, 305 & Seidov, pp.138-139. Actual KPAF aircraft losses are unknown.
209 Zhang, pp.112, 116.
210 Futrell, pp.309; Jackson, p.96 & Williams, pp.7, 10.
211 *Ibid*. & CIADB, 21 May 1951.
212 Futrell, pp.309; Jackson, p.96; Williams, pp.7, 10 & Davis, pp.62-63.
213 Demin, p.36; Futrell, p.310; Naboka, p.177; Seidov, p.153 & Zhang, p.112, 116, p.254n96.
214 McLaren, *Mustangs*, p.111 & Thompson, *F-51*, p.47-48. For reasons unknown, none of these victories were accredited by the USAF, despite of the gun camera images from Saltsman's Mustang, which clearly showed an Il-10 with flames erupting from the rear cockpit and smoke emanating from beneath the lower engine cowling. The USAF photo caption reads: 'The death blow to a Communist fighter, an IL-2 [*sic*], was administered by an F-51 'Mustang' of the Fifth Air Force's 18th Fighter Bomber Wing, this is how it looked to Lt Col Ralph D. [*sic*] Saltsman, Jr., the pilot'.
215 Thompson, *Mustang Units, p.47.*
216 Futrell, pp.310; Krylov *et al*, p.33 & Naboka, pp.177-178.
217 These were the 334th FIS F-86A (49-1281) 17 June (not written off as DBR until June 25), 334th FIS F-86A (49-1307, Capt William D. Crone, KIA) the next day, 336th FIS F-86A (49-1298, 1st Lt Robert H. Laier, KIA) the day after, and 336th FIS F-86A (49-1276, 1st Lt Howard P. Miller, Jr., KIA) on the 22nd.
218 Krylov *et al*, p.33; Weathersby, p.60 & Zhang, pp.118-120.
219 Futrell, pp.309, 310, 423.
220 Thompson, *B-26*, pp.52-53.
221 Dorr *et al*, p.27.
222 Hallion, *Naval Air War*, pp.168-169.
223 No Kum-Sok, pp.45, 48, 64.
224 Harden, pp.68-69.
225 Futrell, pp.192; Morozov *et al*, p.17 & No Kum-Sok, p.62, 68-70.
226 AIIR, pp 2, 52 & No Kum-Sok, pp.72, 76, 77, 81. See also Zhang, p.35, 251n33.
227 No Kum-Sok, p.85.
228 *Ibid*., pp.85-86; AIIR, pp 2, 52 & Harden, p.261n93.
229 AIIR, pp 2, 52; Demin, pp.6, 13; Kramarenko, p.122; Krylov *et al*, p.24 & No Kum-Sok, p.86, 87.
230 Because the 324th IAD was not yet combat-ready, the 151st GvIAD temporarily replaced the 50th IAD at Langtao when the latter unit rotated to 'Mother Russia', on 6 February 1951. This division only lost one MiG-15 directly to combat action with F-80Cs – Guards Capt Gordeyev was shot down (ejected and survived) on 23 February, 1951; no USAF victory being credited that day – but three others were lost in mid-air collisions: two collided with each other while chasing F-80Cs and the third collided with its F-80C target. Despite claiming 24 victories based largely on gun camera films assessment, the only USAF losses to MiG-15s during the 151st GvIAD's tour of duty at Andong was limited to a B-29A (44-69667, 98th BW) on 1 March and the F-80C destroyed (49-1834, 8th FBG/36th FBS) in the mid-air collision. USAF 1st Lt Howard Landry was posthumously awarded credit for a victory in this combat. Against F-86s, on 24 March, the MiG-15 flown by Snr Lt Iu. P. Savinov was lost (pilot KIA), although no 'victory claim' was submitted by any 4th FIW squadrons for this action. See KORWALD, pp.17, 19; Seidov, pp.97, 101; Naboka, p.93 & 'USAF Korean War Victories by Date', pp.2.
231 No Kum-Sok, pp.87, 91.
232 During his intelligence interview/debriefing, defector No Kum-Sok repeatedly referred to his unit as the 'second regiment of

the 1st Air Division', which has become formalized by several historians – and referenced in his own autobiography (written with J. Roger Osterholm) – as the KPAF's 2nd Fighter Regiment. However, the 55-page Fifth AF AIIR resulting from No's extensive debriefing specifically identifies No's unit as the '60th Pursuit Regiment, also known as the 447th Army Unit' (a postal code). AIIR, p.16.

233 Yang's name was also rendered as Yang Tu-Hu and Yang Tuhi in US Intelligence reports, and is probably also the Teng Du-Ho, Teng Doo-Hu, and Teng Du-Hi found in various Russian histories. See CIADB 25 March 1952 & 11 April 1952; Demin, p.47 & Seidov, p.434.

234 No Kum-Sok, pp.78, 96, 105.

235 The 28th IAD was formed in late November 1950 at Liaoyang using the 324th IAD's 139th GvIAP and establishing the 67th IAP, which was created by transferring the aircraft and pilots released by downsizing the division's original three regiments from 40 jets to 32 each to match the size of the PLAAF regiments they were to train. Originally the 28th IAD was scheduled to train the PLAAF 4th AD at Liaoyang, but, due to operational exigencies, the next month the new IAD was transferred to Tianjin (67th IAP) and Qingdao (139th GvIAP) airfields to shield Tianjin, the large port at the mouth of the Hai River (leading to Beijing), and the Shandong Peninsula, respectively, from attack by USN and RN/FAA carrier aircraft. Seidov, pp.85, 439.

236 AIIR, pp.2, 52; No Kum-Sok, pp.88, 89 & Seidov, p.100.

237 Krylov *et al*, pp.23-29 & Naboka, p.151.

238 No Kum-Sok is also rendered as Ro Kum-Suk or No Gim-Sok, which was Anglicized as Kenneth Rowe (Ro/No being the family name in Korean, becoming Rowe in America) after he settled in the USA following his defection from North Korea.

239 No Kum-Sok, p.85.

240 At the time, MiG-15-pilots had no G-suits (USAF fighters from the P-51D on included this system), so their dynamic high-G air combat manoeuvring (ACM) training missions were extremely fatiguing and debilitating, making a period of physical recovery a requirement before engaging, even mentally, in the next training session. Until the arrival of the PPK-1 Anti-G suit system in the later versions of the MiG-15bis, the Soviets attributed the PLAAF and KPAF students' fatigue to their relatively poor, low-calorie diet.

241 No Kum-Sok, pp.92-94.

242 Seidov, p.100.

243 For security reasons, the Soviet records 'coded' the KPAF units using their 'Army Unit numbers'. Similar to V-VS Field Post numbers (or Luftwaffe '*Feldpost Nummer*') the KPAF 'Army Unit code numbers' were used for telegraphic communications, postal correspondence, personnel assignments, supply processes and other administrative procedures. The 1st AD was 'Army Unit 435', the 59th FAR was 'Army Unit 436', and the 60th FAR was 'Army Unit 447'. This has led some Russian histories to report that the 151st IAD trained and transferred its MiG-15s to the KPAF's '435th FAD', etc.

244 *Ibid.*, p.100, 300 & Krylov *et al*, pp.23, 92, 93. Kang's name is also rendered as Kang Tae-Yon; nothing is known about him before his appointment to command the 1st AD.

245 Naboka, pp.94, 108.

246 Morozov *et al*, p.31.

247 From this point on the KPAF's Il-10s were reserved for ground-attack missions only when air superiority was guaranteed.

248 CIADB, 11 October 1951, 6 & 30 November 1951, 5 & Futrell, pp.412.

249 AIIR, 2, 32-35; CIADB, 8 November 1951, 7; Futrell, pp.412 & No Kum-Sok, p.96-98, 105.

250 Info via Tom Cooper, 8 July 2014; CIADB, 5 February 1952 & 2 April 1952.

251 CIADB, 17 January 1952.

252 CIADB, 1 October 1951; 17 October 1951; 26 November 1951; 5 December 1951 & No Kum-Sok, pp.112-113.

253 Maximum number of this type available to the unit (does not include aircraft of this type assigned to other units, lost in accidents or to other causes since arrival from the USSR).

254 Maximum number of this type available to the unit (does not include aircraft of this type assigned to other units, lost in accidents or to other causes since arrival from the USSR).

255 Futrell, pp.426-427.

256 The 68th FAWS was re-designated 68th Fighter-Interceptor Squadron on 25 April 1951.

257 *Ibid.*, pp.428-429. By this time VMF(N)-513 'Flying Nightmares' had lost 26 Corsairs and seven Tigercats to various causes, almost exclusively while flying ground-attack missions by night

258 *Ibid.*, p.431.

259 Hallion, *Naval Air War*, p.169.

260 Werrell, p.107.

261 Demin, p.21 & Zhang, pp.18, 101-103, 109, 118, 119.

262 Zhang, p.149. These were the 3rd and 4th ADs with MiG-15s, the 2nd AD with La-11s and MiG-15s, the 5th AD with Il-10s and 8th AD with Tu-2s. In training on MiG-15s were the 6th (at Anshan), 12th (at Xiaoshan Xian), and 14th (at Beijing) ADs. The combat-ready MiG-9 units were the 7th (at Dongfeng), 16th (at Qingdao), and 17th (at Tangshan) ADs – these would be converted to MiG-15s as soon as Soviet-provided equipment and instructors became available.

263 *Ibid.*, pp.149, 157, 237n62.

264 Daugherty, p.56; Demin, pp.35-36; Seidov, p.242; Werrell, pp.104, 107 & Zhang, p.156. In Chinese, the islands were called the 'Khe-Dao archipelago', named after Ka-do, the largest island in the group. In light of the Communists' preparations for the Pans□ng Islands campaign, Sinmi-do Island, which was considered undefendable, was evacuated on 12 October and was quickly occupied by KPA forces.

265 Zhang, pp.156-157.

266 *Ibid.*; Demin, pp.36-37 & Seidov, p.243.

267 Werrell, p.107 & CIADB, 26 November 1951. This report is from FEAF Intelligence and, consequently, the type mentioned maybe supposition based on knowledge of KPAF AOB at that time. However, given that 14 La-9s, having completed ground-attack training at Fengcheng the month before, were now based at Sinuiju, it is more probable that the heavily armed Lavochkin type, rather than Yak-9P interceptors, were used in the 14 November strafing attacks.

268 *Ibid.*, which says the attack was conducted by 11 bombers. Zhang does not mention this second air attack on Taehwa-do. See also CIADB, 26 November 1951 & 10 December 1951.

269 Demin, p.37 & Seidov, p.268.

270 Demin, pp.37-39; Seidov, pp.268- 269; Werrell, pp.107-110 & Zhang, pp.158-162.

271 Zhang, p.103.

272 *Ibid.*, pp.148, 149, 169, 170, 225. The PLAAF contribution initially consisted of the 3rd and 4th ADs, augmented by the 2nd AD's 6th FAR, totalling 116 MiG-15s. These were reinforced by the arrival of the 6th (at Dadonggou) and 14th ADs (at Dagushan) on 8 and 12 December, respectively.

273 *Ibid.*, pp.145, 148, 150, 168; Futrell, pp.412; Krylov *et al*, p.40; Morozov *et al*, p.31; & Zolotarev, p.70.

274 *Ibid.*, pp.141, 146, 258n67, 259n76; Demin, p.22; & Halliday, p.154.

275 These were located at P'yongyang, Sunch'ŏn, Anju, and Sup'ungdong (near the Suiho Dam), providing a chain of radar sites covering from 60 miles (100km) south of P'yongyang to a 120-mile (200km) wide front along the Yalu.

276 Naboka, pp.71-72, 75, 117; Volkovskiy, pp.392, 405, 407, 409, 410.

277 This capability undoubtedly proved useful in helping Po-2 night raiders return to Namsinuiju during the CVPA's Pansŏng Island campaign.

278 CIADB, 14 December 1951; 19 February 1952 & 6 March 1952.

279 CIADB, 27 November 1951; 30 November 1951 & 6 December 1951.

280 AIIR, p.2. Col Tae Kuk-Sung was assisted by three Soviet advisors (names unknown), headed by a chief who oversaw command and flying operations. The other two were technicians assisting with weapons and ordnance and with the jets' instrumentation.

281 No Kum-Sok, p.99.

282 *Ibid.*, pp.99, 100-102, 110, 112.

283 Davis, p.95; Futrell, pp.415; Harden, p.121 & Werrell, p.210.

284 No Kum-Sok, p.103.

285 *Ibid.*, p.416; Harden, p.123 & Werrell, p.292n71.

286 No Kum-Sok, p.105.

287 KORWALD, p.45 & No-Kum-Sok, p.105.
288 No Kum-Sok, p.107. No maintains that the MiG-15s of the PLAAF's 2nd AD – specifically, the 6th FAR – was stationed at the east end of Langtao airfield, but this is incorrect according to Chinese archive records.
289 Abakumov, pp.133, 136-137.
290 No Kum-Sok, pp.108-109 & Harden, pp.122, 128.
291 CIADB, 11 December 1951 & *USN Chronology, Part 3*, pp.12-13.
292 Futrell, p.431 & *USN Chronology, Part 4*, p.1.
293 CIADB, 26 November 1951; 22 January 1952; 24 January 1952 & 20 February 1952.
294 CIADB 5 February 1952 & 8 April 1952.
295 No Kum-Sok, pp.110, 118.
296 *Ibid*., p.115.
297 Morozov *et al*, p.32 & Futrell, pp.414.
298 *Ibid*., p.421.
299 No Kum-Sok, pp.110, 111.
300 *Ibid*. The victorious USAF pilots were: Maj William Shaefer (51st FIG/16th FIS); Capt Mose Gordon Jr, and 1st Lt Robert Moore (51st FIG/16th FIS); 1st Lt Frank Gately, 1st Lt William Guinther, 1st Lt Anthony Kulengosky Jr, and 1st William Schofner (51st FIG/25th FIS); Capt Robert Latshaw Jr and 1st Lt Conrad Nystrum (4th FIG/335th FIS). The USAF losses were 334th FIS F-86A (49-1191) which crashed due to non-combat engine failure (pilot injured) and 335th FIS F-86A (48-251) due to fuel exhaustion (pilot uninjured). For USAF victory credits, see 'USAF Korean War Victories by Date', p.7; for losses see KORWALD, p.51.
301 *Ibid*., pp.119-120, 125.
302 No Kum-Sok, 117 & CIADB, 25 March 1952.
303 AIIR, p.2.
304 CIADB, 8 February 1952; 18 February 192 & 11 April 1952; Seidov, p.355.
305 CIADB 2 April 1952 & 20 May 1952.
306 CIA Daily Korean Bulletin (CIADKB), 25 April 1952.
307 USAF Historical Study No. 81, pp.16, 20. Considering that the 56th GFAR and its Yak-9Ps were located at Dongfeng at this time, and Sinuiju had only La-9s and Il-10s, the destroyed aircraft were most likely one of these two types. Although Harris and Kincheloe were initially awarded credit for destroying these seven enemy aircraft, these 'kills' – along with all other strafing 'victories' during the Korean War – were deleted from the official tally during the USAF's 1988 review and revision of Korean War Aerial Victory Credits.
308 Demin, p.44; Dorr *et al*, p.27; Futrell, p.422; Seidov, p.370 & 'USAF Korean War Victories by Date', p.11.
309 Demin, p.40.
310 *Ibid*.; Seidov, p.386; Werrell, p.162 & 'USAF Korean War Victories by Date', p.12.
311 Thompson *et al*, *MiG Alley*, p.49 & Werrell, p.162.
312 Earl Brown, 'Memories of Great Fighter Pilots: Frederick C. 'Boots' Blesse,' published on *SabreJet Classics* website, http://sabre-pilots.org/classics/v81boots.htm, p.1; Thompson *et al*, *MiG Alley*, pp 50 & Werrell, pp.163.
313 Seidov, p.386. Capt Hugh P. Farler was not an F-86 pilot but a B-29 crewmember (343rd BS/98th BW) who was killed when his B-29A (S/N 44-86327) was shot down by Soviet MiG-15s on 1 June 1951. See KORWALD Personnel Loss Listing, p.65. According to KORWALD Date of Aircraft Loss Reports, p.64, no F-86s from any unit were lost on 20 June 1952.
314 CIADB, 16 October 1952.
315 Krylov *et al*, pp.61-62. According to Soviet records, in a year of combat the two divisions lost 56 MiG-15s, 49 of them to F-86s, with 32 Russian pilots killed. In this same period 35 Sabres were lost in combat with Soviet MiGs. The two IADs' greatest accomplishment was defeating FEAF's B-29 daylight bombing campaign – shooting down 10 Superfortresses and damaging five more so badly they were scrapped – forcing the Americans to resort to nighttime attacks. In addition, according to US DOD KORWALD data, the Soviets also destroyed 22 other UNC aircraft: 7 F-84Es, 3 F-80Cs, 3 F-51Ds, 1 RF-80C, 1 B-26B, 1 USN F9F, 1 AD Skyraider, and 5 RAAF Meteor F.Mk 8s during the April 1951-January 1952 period. Claiming an exaggerated 468 UNC aircraft destroyed, the two divisions produced 39 aces and 18 HSUs. For details of UNC losses, see: Cull *et al*, p.330 & KORWALD, p.21-52.
316 Demin, p.40; Krylov *et al*, pp.60-62.
317 PVO-Strany was the air defence service of the Soviet Armed Forces, separate from the Soviet Air Force (V-VS) and Air Defence Troops of Ground Forces (PVO Sukhoputnykh Voysk).
318 Demin, p.40; Kramarenko, p.152; Krylov *et al*, p.62-64 & Zhang, p.134, 135. The Sabres lost were: 3 February, 335th FIS F-86A 49-1223 (1Lt Charles R. Spath, MIA), 10 February, 334th FIS F-86E 51-2752 (LtCol George A. Davis, KIA), 11 March, 25th FIS F-86E 50-604 (1Lt James E. Arnold, KIA), 24 March, 334th F-86As 49-1140 (1Lt James D. Carey, KIA) and 335th FIS F-86A 49-1088 (pilot uninjured). The two damaged Sabres (50-628 and 51-2761) were repaired and returned to operations. Thompson, *et al*, *MiG Alley*, pp.53-56.
319 These were the 12th AD at Shanghai, 15th AD at Shenyang, 17th AD at Tangshan, and 18th AD at Guangzhou. Zhang, p.169.
320 Demin, pp.25, 47; Zolotarev, p.70 & Zhang, pp.168-170.
321 Futrell, pp.413, 415 & No Kum-Sok, pp.112, 117.
322 Person, pp.281-282, 285; Demin, p.40; Krylov *et al*, pp.66, 70-71, 88, 89 & Zhang, p.170. For comparison, during this period, the USAF lost nine F-86s (including one due to fuel exhaustion) in combat with MiG-15s, with four pilots being killed, one captured and one MIA. Eleven more F-86s were lost in accidents due to engine and hydraulic failures, weather, fuel starvation and other causes not attributable to enemy action. Thompson *et al*, *MiG Alley*, p.172.
323 No Kum-Sok, p.120.
324 *Ibid*, p.121.
325 *Ibid*, pp.121, 135.
326 *Ibid*, pp.78, 137, 147.
327 *Ibid*, pp.130-131.
328 *Ibid*, pp.130-131; Zhang, p.185. Lobov, Kravoskiy, and Peng were entirely correct in their assessment and concerns. For FEAF contingency plans for attacking 'China's Manchurian air bases if the Red air forces attacked South Korean installations' see Futrell, pp.412-413. These plans had the approval of the US Joint Chiefs of Staff and President Truman's National Security Council as of December 1951.
329 Lansdown, pp.240, 273; Thompson, *Naval Aviation*, p.153. VMF-312 was redesignated a Marine Attack Squadron (VMA) on 25 February 1952.
330 Seidov, p.434 & Zhang, pp.172, 184, 189, 190.
331 Demin, p.47.
332 Thompson, *F4U*, pp.62-63
333 *Ibid*, pp.63-64; Hallion, *Naval Air War*, p.159 & Sambito, p.12. The USMC F4U-4B lost was BuNo 62927.
334 Seidov, p.434.
335 No Kum-Sok, pp.131-132 & Zhang, p.190.
336 CIADB, 6 March 1952; 14 March 1952 & 17 March 1952; CIA Current Intelligence Digest (CIACID), August 1952 & 18 August 1952.
337 No Kum-Sok, p.132; CIADB, 17 March 1952 & CIACID, August 1952, 18 August 1952 & 18 September 1952.
338 'USS Kearsarge Action Report for the Period 14 September 1952 to 20 October 1952', 31 October 1952, pp.3, 24; CIACID, 7 October 1952; Demin, p.47; Hallion, *Naval Air War*, p.160; and No Kum-Sok, p.132. Lt Eugene F. Johnson was flying F4U-4 BuNo 80798, modex '412'. Gan's wingmen were Lts Hwan Su-Song, Chong He-Ham, and Pak Chan-Hung. Gan claimed two 'kills' and a third Corsair damaged, with his wingmen claimed three more shot down and another F4U damaged; Seidov, p.438.
339 'USS Princeton Action Report for the Period 28 September 1952 through 18 October 1952', 1 November 1952, pp.2-3, 11-13. See also CIADKB, 10 October 1952; Hallion, *Naval Air War*, p.160; and Seidov, p.438. Ens John R. Shaughnessy was flying F4U-4 BuNo 96770, modex 'B311'. Gan Gyong-Duk is credited with this victory.
340 McLaren, *Mustangs*, p, 151; Demin, p.47; and CIADKB, 14 October 1952. Lt Trevor R. Fryer was flying F-51 (44-74577/SAAF #392). Gan Gyong-Duk is credited with this victory.
341 No Kum-Sok, p.132; and CIADKB, 21 October 1952.
342 CIADKB, 21 October 1952 and 24 October 1952.
343 AIIR, p.2; CIACID, 16 October 1952, 3; & Zhang, p.190.

344 No Kum-Sok, p.128, 132.
345 *Ibid,* p.133.
346 These were: 22 October: 19th BW/30th BS 44-61656 (crew rescued; one WIA); 23 October: 307th BW/371st BS 42-94045 and 44-70151 (3 KIA, 16 MIA, and 3 POW), and 372nd BS 44-27347 (DBR; one WIA), 44-61940 (3 KIA, 3 MIA, and 7 POW), and 44-86295 (DBR; 1 KIA, 2 WIA); October 24: 98th BW/343rd BS 44-61932 (4 KIA) and 44-86346 (DBR); and 27 October: 19th BW/30th BS 44-62971 (DBR; 7 WIA). KORWALD Date of Aircraft Loss Reports, 41, 42.
347 Hallion, *Naval Air War,* p.170; Krylov *et al,* p.40, 46; Person, p.233; Volkovskiy, p.401; & Zhang, p.136. The 351st OIAP had been in the PRC since February 1950, and after training the PLAAF's 11th FAR, in June 1951, they were transferred to Lüda airfield on the Liaoyang Peninsula, becoming the 83rd OIAK's (PVO) night fighter unit. The regiment was subsequently transferred to Anshan on 9 September 1951. By the end of the year, of the unit's 20 La-11s, four were non-operational due to expired engine life.
348 Dorr, B-29, p.62; Krylov *et al,* p.66, 68-70, 87; Person, p.358; Seidov, p.384; Volkovskiy, p.402; Zhang, p.137. The B-29s shot down were 44-62183 (28th BS; 14 MIA) and 44-61967 (30th BS; 1 POW/12 MIA). On 3/4 July, the 351st OIAP also shot down RB-29A 44-61727 (91st SRS; one KIA, one MIA, eleven POWs). KORWALD, p.63.
349 The RB-26C was 44-35668 (12th TRS) shot down on 15/16 May (three crewmen were listed as MIA). The B-26C was 44-35760 [13th BS(L)/3rd BG(L)] shot down 9 miles southeast of Sinmi-do Island on 5/6 June (three crewmen MIA). KORWALD pp.61-62.
350 Krylov *et al,* pp.66, 68. Two La-11s were written off in non-fatal accidents; Seidov, p.488.
351 CIADB, 8 February 1952 & 18 February 1952; CIACID, 29 April 1952 & 15 April 1952.
352 Futrell, pp.325-326; and Hallion, *Naval Air War,* pp.165-167.
353 *Ibid,* p.169; Seidov, p.387.
354 Morozov *et al,* p.31.
355 CIACID, 21 July 1952, p.4.
356 CIADB, 20 February 1952, 5; & CIACID. 12 August 1952, p.2.
357 CIACID, 29 October 1952, p.4.
358 Futrell, pp.423, 427-428, 659. Ch'o-do island was located about 110 miles south of Andong, 40 miles north of the 38th Parallel, and 125 northwest of the front lines.
359 *Ibid,* p.514 & Werrell, p.104.
360 Futrell, p.429; Hallion, 'T-33 and F-94', pp.17, 18; & Thompson, Year of MiGs, p.111.
361 Hallion, *Naval Air War,* p.173-177; Thompson, Year of MiGs, p.111.
362 CIADB, 5 February 1952, 7; CIACID, 1 April 1952, 3, and 27 August 1952; & CIADKB, 18 April 1952 & 23 April 1952.
363 CIACID, 21 July 1952, 4.
364 CIADKB, 15 October 1952; Futrell, pp.662, 663; *USN Chronology, Part 6,* p.7; & Werrell, p.110.
365 Futrell, pp.663.
366 *Ibid,* p.663; *USN Chronology, Part 6,* p.11; & Werrell, p.110.
367 CIADKB, 6 December 1952 & *USN Chronology, Part 6,* p.12.
368 CIADKB, 11 December 1952; Hallion, *Naval Air War,* p.180; Thompson, Year of MiGs, p.112; and Werrell, p.111.
369 Williams, pp.4, 7.
370 CIA Current Intelligence Bulletin (CIACIB), 5 February 1953.
371 At this time, these included the 351st OIAP's two squadrons, 2nd Eskada of the 147th GvIAP (133rd IAD), and the 1st Eskada of the 535th IAP, 3rd Eskada of the 913th IAP (both components of 32rd IAD); Seidov, p.465, 474.
372 CIADKB, 7 January 1953 and 12 January 1953; Futrell, pp.613 & Krylov *et al,* p.77 & Seidov, pp.465, 474. The B-29s lost to Soviet MiG-15 night fighters at this time were, on 30/31 December 1952: 19th BW/28th BS 44-62011 (tail numbers of two B-29s DBR are unknown); on 10/11 January 1953: 307th BW/372nd BS 44-61802; on 12/13 January: 92nd SRS RB-29A 44-62217; on 28/29 January 1952: 19th BW/28th BS 42-65357; and 30/31 January: B-29 DBR, 307th BW, squadron and serial number unknown. KORWALD Aircraft Type Report, pp.14-16.
373 Although VMF(N)-513 claimed MiG-15 kills on 12, 28 and 31 January, there is no record of corresponding losses in any Russian history of the Korean War.
374 Futrell, pp.615; Hallion, *Naval Air War,* pp.181-182 & Hallion, 'T-33 and F-94', p.18.
375 Captain Ben L. Fithian, 319th FIS, as described to author Warren Thompson.
376 Hallion, *Naval Air War,* p.23.
377 Futrell, pp.505-506.
378 Futrell, pp.515-517; Hallion, *Naval Air War,* p.135; Harden, p.137.
379 Weathersby, p.77; Harden, pp.136-138; and Zhang, pp.188, 263n45-47. Interestingly, this message shows the very first instance of Kim requesting Stalin to consider a cease fire to end the suffering of the Korean people. Evidently the UNC bombing campaign was having the desired effect, at least on the people on the receiving end of the bombardment.
380 Weathersby, pp.77-79; Harden, pp.138, 140; and Zhang, pp.188, 263n45-47.
381 Futrell, pp.522, 525 & Harden, p.139.
382 Person, pp.293-294, 300.
383 CIACID, 25 August 1952; 25 September 1952 & 5 February 1953; No Kum-Sok, pp.72, 132, 157.
384 No Kum-Sok, pp.78, 133, 135. While flying Yak-9Ps Colonel Tae was credited with destroying three 'F-80s' during the first four weeks of the war. For achieving 'ace status' Tae was awarded the 'Hero's Medal' (HDPRK) by Kim Il-Sung in a ceremony in P'yongyang before taking his position in the 2nd AD.
385 *Ibid,* p.134 & Seidov, p.452.
386 Seidov, pp.462, 475.
387 CIACID, 19 November 1952; 13 January 1953 & 14 March 1953.
388 CIACID, 14 December 1952; 21 December 1952; 29 January 1953; 5 February 1953 & 15 March 1953.
389 Futrell, p.610.
390 *Ibid.*; 'Kinsey Shoots Down Communist TU-2 Bomber', *Lubbock Avalanche-Journal,* February 8, 1953, p.57 & Seidov, p.474.
391 Zhang, p.189.
392 Futrell, p.607.
393 CIADB 17 December 1951.
394 Futrell, pp.184, 487 & CIACID, 14 August 1952.
395 CIACIB, 5 February 1953; No Kum-Sok, p.136; Seidov, p.562. No RF-80s were lost during February or March 1953. See KORWALD Aircraft Type Report, p.80.
396 Futrell, pp.611 & No Kum-Sok, p.136.
397 No Kum-Sok, p.136.
398 *Ibid.*
399 Seidov, p.562 & Zhang, p.192. During March 1953, the USAF lost two Sabres in combat with MiG-15s: F-86E-10 51-2827 flown by 1Lt Richard M. Cowden (51st FIW/16th FIS), who was KIA, and F-86E-6 52-2879 flown by Sqn Ldr Graham S. Hulse (RAF exchange pilot flying with 4th FIW/336th FIS), who ejected to become a POW but died in captivity. Four other F-86s were lost due to pilot vertigo, engine failure, mechanical failure, and an excessively hard landing. See Thompson *et al, MiG Alley* & KORWALD Personnel Loss Listing, pp.45, 102.
400 Demin, p.53-54; & Seidov, pp.485, 497, 499, 512, 562.
401 Demin, p.53; Lansdown, p.351; and Seidov, p.485.
402 Demin, p.53 & Seidov, p.497.
403 Davis, p.173. No USAF aircraft were damaged or lost on 28 March 1953. See also 'USAF Korean War Victories by Date', p.21 & KORWALD Date of Aircraft Loss Reports, p.81.
404 No Kum-Sok, p.135 & Seidov, p.499.
405 CIACIB, 15 March 1953. These figures evidently reflect KPAF aircraft based within the PRC and do not appear to include the 24-30 Po-2s, Yak-18, and La-11s of the 3rd Night Bomber Regiment based within the DPRK.
406 Zhang, p.192.
407 CIACIB, 8 April 1953; Futrell, pp.647-648; Halliday, p.162; Seidov, p.522; Weathersby, pp.80-82 & Zhang, p.196, 197.
408 Krylov *et al,* p.88 & Seidov, p.464.
409 Halliday, p.162; Krylov *et al,* pp.83, 85 & Zhang, p.267n102.
410 Seidov, p.476.
411 During this three-month period the USAF lost 10 Sabres and 5 pilots in combat with MiG-15s. Of these, 6 F-86s are known to have been shot down by MiG-15s, resulting in four pilots becoming POWs; one was lost due to fuel exhaustion from fighting MiGs (pilot injured) & three from unknown causes (probably MiGs) while on combat missions, with one pilot (Capt

Floyd W. Salze) KIA. KORWALD, pp.79-85 & Thompson *et al*, *MiG Alley*, pp.173-174.
412 Demin, p.49; Seidov, pp.510, 521, 537; Zhang, pp.193-194, 199.
413 Demin, p.53.
414 Seidov, pp.512-513.
415 Demin, p.48 & Seidov, pp.510, 521, 537. KPAF MiG units flew 216 sorties in April, 96 sorties (down due to weather) in May, 398 in June, and 226 in July.
416 Demin, pp.49, 56 & Seidov, pp.522, 543.
417 Futrell, pp.683; Seidov, p.543-546 & Zhang, p.195. The F-86s 'kills' were credited to Soviet Maj Semyon A. Fedorets (913th IAP) and PLAAF pilot Shen Hongjiang. The Soviets lost two MiG-15s shot down and one pilot killed (Snr Lt Nikolai P. Gerasimchuk, the last Russian pilot to die in the Korean War) on 19 July; PLAAF lost none. KPAF losses that day are not yet known. Krylov *et al*, p.85; Werrell, p.199; &. 'USAF Korean War Victories by Date', p.26.
418 Seidov, pp.544-546.
419 Futrell, pp.663. See also Peter Grier, 'April 15, 1953', *Air Force Magazine*, June 2011, 54-57. Corporal William R. Walsh and Private First Class Herbert Tucker have the sad distinction of being the last US servicemen to have been killed by enemy air attack; Grier, p.56.
420 Futrell, pp.663-665.
421 VMC-1 had been activated on 15 September, 1952, at Pohang (K-3), South Korea, in support of Marine Air Wing One's Marine Air Control Group 2, conducting airborne early warning and ECM in support of combat operations.
422 Futrell, p.664, & 'Korean Air War,' *Naval Aviation News*, October 1953, Issue 53-6, 6-9.
423 Futrell, pp.663-664.
424 Futrell, pp.664; Hallion, *Naval Air War*, p.18, 23 & 'USAF Korean War Victories by Date', 22. Wilcox and Goldberg's aircraft was F-94B 50-887.
425 *Ibid.*, p.665.
426 *USN Chronology, Part 8*, pp.5-6.
427 This victory is not verified in Soviet records, however, it may have been scored against the PLAAF's *ad hoc* composite La-11/MiG-15 night-fighter squadron formed at Andong earlier in 1953.
428 Futrell, p.665. McHale and Hoster's aircraft was F-94B 51-5505.
429 Zhang, pp.197-198. The offensive gained about two miles of territory along an eight mile front at a cost of 16,300 men killed and 81 captured.
430 Williams, pp.4, 7 & *USN Chronology, Part 8*, pp.7-8.
431 'Korean Air War', *Naval Aviation News*, p.6.
432 Hallion, *Naval Air War*, pp.186-187; Morozov *et al*, p.32 & *USN Chronology, Part 8*, p.4.
433 Futrell, p.665; 'Korean Air War', *Naval Aviation News*, p.6 & *USN Chronology, Part 8*, p.9.
434 The VC-3 detachments were Det B on USS *Valley Forge* (CVA 45) until 25 June 1953, Det D on USS *Princeton* (CVA 37), Det H on USS *Boxer* (CVA 21) and Det M on USS *Philippine Sea* (CVA 47) through the end of the war. Thompson, *Naval Aviation*, pp.147-150.
435 Once the US Navy became a part of Fifth AF's air defence system the 502nd TCG's Tactical Air-Control Center at Seoul was renamed the Joint Operations Center, or JOC.
436 Bordelon, pp.46-47.
437 Futrell, p.665; Thompson, *F-84*, p.85 & *USN Chronology, Part 8*, p.10.
438 Bordelon, p.47.
439 *Ibid.*
440 Thompson, *F-84*, p.86.
441 Futrell, p.665.
442 On 24 April 1953, Lobov completed his 'tour of duty' and returned to the USSR, being replaced by his deputy, HSU Maj Gen Sidor V. Slyusarev, for the duration of the conflict. Although not specified, it is believed that Slyusarev headed the Soviet delegation attending the 27 March UAA 'joint conference'. Krylov *et al*, p.87, 88 & Seidov, pp.464, 509.
443 CIACIB, 29 March 1953; Seidov, p.509; Zhang, p.258n54.
444 Seidov, pp.523, 537. As of 1 June 1953, 64th IAK units had 405 MiG-15bis at the Shenyang and Andong area bases. By this time, because they were rapidly being replaced by the new, much improved, MiG-17, Soviet air forces had large inventories of old, obsolete MiG-15s and many newer, obsolescing MiG-15bis available for export.
445 CIACIB, 9 April 1953, 5, and 7 May 1953, 3.
446 The new airfields along the PRC border were Hoeryong (K-35), Chunggangjin and Hyesanjin (not numbered in the FEAF 'K-Sites' airfield designation system). The airfields under repair were Sinmak (K-20), Haeju (K-19), Mirim (K-24), Hamhung West (K-28), and Namsi and Taechon (not numbered as 'K-Sites' because they never became operational during the war). Futrell, p.680.
447 *Ibid.*
448 Replacing the 351st OIAP, the 298th OIAP began flying night intercept missions at the beginning of March, but were unsuccessful in shooting down any B-29s during their entire 'tour of duty'; Seidov, p.489.
449 Futrell, pp.680- 681; Seidov, p.489- 499; & Zhang, p.198.
450 According to CIA COMINT reports, on 16 July 24 La-9s and 20 Il-10s flew from Yanji to Kungchuling/Gongzhuling, with 21 of the fighters deploying to Sinuiju the next day. Arriving in the Andong area the day prior were 'three to six Il-28 twin-jet bombers and two Tu-2 conventional bombers'. The communications intercepted indicated that the bombers were positioned for 'combat missions' – perhaps night bombing sorties planned to support of the CPVA/KPA's final offensive, which began on 12 July′; CIACID, 16 July 1953 & 19 July 1953.
451 Futrell, p.683; No Kum-Sok, pp.139-140.
452 Futrell, pp.683-684; No Kum-Sok, pp.141-142 & Seidov, p.549.
453 *Ibid.* & Hallion, *Naval Air War*, p.150.
454 No Kum-Sok, p.140.
455 Futrell, pp.657 & Seidov, pp.548-549. There is no record of the first two MiG losses in any Russian, Chinese, or North Korean accounts of the air war in Korea.
456 1Lt Sam P. Young, Jr., 25th FIS, as described to author Warren Thompson.
457 No Kum-Sok, pp.140-141.
458 No Kum-Sok, pp.141-142 & Zhang, p.199.
459 Seidov, p.549.
460 No Kum-Sok, p.142.
461 CIACID, 29 July 1953, 5.
462 CIACIB, 30 July 1953 & Morozov *et al*, p.32.
463 Seidov, pp.512-513.
464 *Ibid,* p.562-563.
465 AIIR, p.52. Kim Gi-Ohk is officially credited with shooting down (destroying) 11 USAF aircraft.
466 *Ibid.*, p.35 & Seidov, pp.562-563. According to USAF Intelligence, between 24-28 July 1953, the KPAF flew into Uiju airfield 40 MiG-15bis, 10 Il-28s, 10 Il-10s, 10 Yak-18s, 5 Yak-11s, 5 Tu-2s, and 9 Po-2s.

ABOUT THE AUTHOR

Douglas C. Dildy retired from the US Air Force (USAF) after 26 years of service, during which he flew McDonnell Douglas F-15 Eagle interceptors, commanded the 32nd Fighter Squadron and was vice-commander of the 33rd Fighter Wing. A graduate of the USAF Academy as a history major, and having a masters degree in Political Science, Dildy has written a dozen of books on aerial warfare. He is a feature writer for Aviation Classics, an associate editor of Logbook and a regular contributor to the *Small Air Forces Observer* magazine. Doug lives in Albuquerque, New Mexico.